NEW
TESTAMENT
MODELS
FOR
MINISTRY

NEW TESTAMENT MODELS FOR MINISTRY

Jesus and Paul

COLIN G. KRUSE

Thomas Nelson Publishers
Nashville • Camden • New York

Published in the United States in Nashville, Tennessee by Thomas Nelson, Inc., Publishers and distributed in Canada by Lawson Falle, Ltd., Cambridge Ontario. First American printing: 1985

Library of Congress Cataloging in Publication Data

Kruse, Colin G.
    New Testament models of ministry, Jesus and Paul.

    Originally published: London: Marshall, Morgan & Scott, 1983.
    Bibliography: pp. 222-25.
    Includes indexes.
    1. Pastoral theology—Biblical teaching. 2. Bible. N.T.—Criticism, interpretation, etc. 3. Jesus Christ—Person and offices. 4. Paul, the Apostle, Saint. I. Title.
BS2545.P45K78   1985   253   84-27188
ISBN 0-8407-5957-6

CONTENTS

PREFACE   xi

ABBREVIATIONS   xiii

1. Introduction   1
    The Scope and Aims of this Study   3

PART ONE: JESUS AND MINISTRY   7

2. The Problem of Authenticity   9

3. Jesus and Apostleship   13
    Jesus, Apostle of God   13
    The 'Apostleship' of Jesus' Disciples   24
    The Jewish Šālîaḥ   29
    Conclusions   32

4. Jesus and Servanthood   34
    Jesus, Servant of God   35
    The Servanthood of Jesus' Disciples   45
    Conclusions   50

5. Jesus and the Spirit   52
    Jesus, Bearer of the Spirit   53
    The Spirit and Jesus' Disciples   58
    Conclusions   63

6. Relevant Sayings of the Risen Jesus   65
    Post-Easter Commission Sayings   66
    Conclusions   69

PART TWO: PAUL AND MINISTRY   71

7. Preliminary Comments   73

8. Galatians   76
    Paul's Apostleship   78
    Servanthood and Suffering   82

Christ and the Spirit 83
Conclusions 85

9. 1, 2 Thessalonians 88
Paul's Apostleship 90
Suffering, the Christian's Lot 93
The Holy Spirit and the Ministry of the
    Christian Community 94
The Risen Christ and the Christian Community 95
Conclusions 98

10. 1, 2 Corinthians 101
Paul's Apostleship 106
Suffering and the Servants of God 111
Christ, the Spirit and the Christian Community 114
Charismata and the Metaphor of the Body 116
Eschatological Validation of Ministry 118
Conclusions 119

11. Romans 123
Paul's Apostleship 126
The Service and Suffering of the People of God 129
Charismata and the Figure of the Body 130
Conclusions 131

12. Philippians 134
Paul's Apostleship 136
The Service and Suffering of the People of God 140
Conclusions 142

13. Colossians and Philemon 144
Paul's Apostleship 145
The Christian Community and the
    Service of Christ 151
Head/Body Metaphor: Christ and the Church 152
Conclusions 156

14. Ephesians 158
Apostleship 160
Christ in Apostolic Proclamation and
    as the Giver of the Spirit 164
Head/Body Metaphor: Christ and the Church 169
The Ministry of the Christian Community 173
Conclusions 174

15. General Conclusions   177
    Summary of Results   177
    Paul's Understanding of Ministry: Evolutionary
        Development or Situational Response?   182
    Paul and the Historical Jesus   184

16. Implications for Ministry Today   186

NOTES   193

SELECT BIBLIOGRAPHY   223

INDEX OF AUTHORS   227

INDEX OF BIBLICAL AND OTHER ANCIENT WRITINGS   231

PREFACE

Although a great deal has been written about ministry in the past, there does appear to be a need for a New Testament based study to explore the relationship between Christian ministry and the ministry of Jesus Christ, and that is the aim of this book. For me, one of the exciting results of this exploration was the discovery of the strength of the New Testament witness to a powerful spiritual dynamic in the ministry of the apostolic community; a spiritual dynamic which came from the active involvement of the exalted Christ. It is my hope that, in some small way, the publication of this book will do something to rekindle in the Church an awareness of this involvement of the exalted Christ in her life and witness, and to promote a renewed experience of that spiritual dynamic in her ministry.

I want to take this opportunity to record my thanks: to Dr Ralph P. Martin, who supervised the research upon which this book is based, for his encouragement, constructive comments and continuous availability for consultation and advice at all stages of the research; to Dr James D. G. Dunn, one of the examiners of this work in its thesis form, for his many acute and constructive criticisms; to Mrs Teresa DeLorenzis, assistant secretary at Ridley College, for typing the greater part of the manuscript; to Rosemary, my wife, for typing the bibliography; to Dr Peter Toon, the general editor of this Theological Library, and to the publishers as well, for including this work in their series.

This book is dedicated to my wife Rosemary in grateful appreciation for her willing acceptance of cramped accommodation and a tight budget during the period of research, and more especially for her love and support, for her constant stimulation and encouragement in the service of Christ which we have shared together in Indonesia, the United States and Australia.

Ridley College   COLIN G. KRUSE
University of Melbourne
August, 1980

ABBREVIATIONS

AB	Anchor Bible
APOT	R. H. Charles, ed., *Apocrypha and Pseudepigrapha of the Old Testament*
AV	Authorized Version
BAG	W. Bauer, W. F. Arndt and F. W. Gingrich, *Greek-English Lexicon of the New Testament*
BFCT	Beiträge zur Förderung christlicher Theologie
BHT	Beiträge zur historischen Theologie
BJRL	*Bulletin of the John Rylands University Library of Manchester*
BZ	*Biblische Zeitschrift*
CBQ	*Catholic Biblical Quarterly*
ErJb	*Eranos Jahrbuch*
ExpTim	*Expository Times*
HUCA	*Hebrew Union College Annual*
IB	*Interpreter's Bible*
ICC	International Critical Commentary
Int	*Interpretation*
JB	*Jerusalem Bible*
JBL	*Journal of Biblical Literature*
NCB	New Century Bible
NEB	*New English Bible*
NovT	*Novum Testamentum*
NTS	*New Testament Studies*
RevExp	*Review and Expositor*
RGG	*Religion in Geschichte und Gegenwart*
RHPR	*Revue d'histoire et de philosophie religieuses*
RSR	*Recherches de science religieuse*
RSV	*Revised Standard Version*
SBL	Society of Biblical Literature
SBT	Studies in Biblical Theology
SE	*Studia Evangelica*
SJT	*Scottish Journal of Theology*

ST   *Studia Theologica*
Str-B   [H. Strack and] P. Billerbeck, *Kommentar zum Neuen Testament*
TDNT   G. Kittel and G. Friedrich, eds., *Theological Dictionary of the New Testament*
TLZ   *Theologische Literaturzeitung*
TZ   *Theologische Zeitschrift*
VSpir   *Vie spirituelle*
ZKT   *Zeitschrift für katholische Theologie*
ZNW   *Zeitschrift für die neutestamentliche Wissenschaft*

CHAPTER ONE

INTRODUCTION

The ministry of Christ is the basis of all Christian ministry. This statement would be endorsed by most men and women involved in and training for the various forms of ministry today. It is an assumption, too, which underlies most of what has been written about ministry in recent years. Yet very often the contrasts between our ministries and his are greater than the similarities. This is, in part, to be expected. Jesus carried out his ministry in first century Palestine, in a particular cultural, historical and political context. We must carry out our ministries in the last quarter of the twentieth century, and in cultural, historical and political situations which are very different from his. This will mean that, seeking to follow the example of his identification with people, we shall have to operate quite differently, simply because the peoples we are called to serve are inextricably bound up in very different milieux. Neverthe less, if our ministries are to be truly Christian they must share something of the clearly defined purpose, the powerful spiritual dynamic, the impressive authority and the servant attitude which are all so evident in the gospel presentation of the ministry of our Lord. Yet so often it is in these very areas that the contrasts between his ministry and ours are painfully obvious.

Jesus' Ministry and Ours

The gospels depict Jesus as one who had a clear idea of what he was about. He had been sent with a definite commission and he steadfastly pursued his task, refusing to be turned aside from it either by enthusiastic response in some quarters or by opposition in others. At the end, according to John 17.4, he said: 'I have glorified thee on earth, having accomplished the work which thou gavest me to do'. In contrast to this, many involved in Christian ministry today are confused about their roles. This lack of a clearly defined purpose makes them fall easy victims to the pressures applied by many conflicting demands upon their time and energies. Role confusion is one of the greatest sources of frustration experienced by Christian ministers today.[1]

The ministry of our Lord as it is presented in the gospels is accompanied by a powerful spiritual dynamic. That Jesus amazed his contemporaries with his ability to drive out unclean spirits by a word of command is recognised widely today as belonging to the bedrock of the Jesus-tradition. But the spiritual dynamic of Jesus' ministry is seen even more clearly in the profound impact he made upon the lives of people to whom he ministered. An encounter with Jesus by a notorious Jewish tax-collector so changed the man that he was prepared to return four-fold all monies he had extorted and to sell off half his possessions to provide relief for the poor. Jesus' words were words of grace and power. In our ministries today many words are spoken, but they are not always words of such grace and power. Much is said—and very often rightly said—about the need for Christian involvement in social welfare and social action. What we do not so often see is the operation of a spiritual dynamic that can actually change men's attitudes and actions for the better.

Another outstanding feature of Jesus' ministry is the fact that he spoke with an authority unknown among the religious leaders of the day. He could confront evil after the fashion of the eighth century prophets. He could cut through the casuistry of the pharisaic party while unerringly drawing out from the Scriptures the great truths of justice, mercy and the love of God. Jesus claimed to speak, not on the authority of experts nor simply on his own authority, but with the authority of the One who had sent him. By what authority do we speak today? Are our ministries modelled on his in this regard?

Although manifesting such clarity of purpose, such spiritual power and such authority, Jesus' ministry was nevertheless one of service. He insisted that he did not come to be served like some earthly potentate; he came to serve, and he laid down the same pattern of ministry for his followers. This has not always been the characteristic mark of our Christian ministries. The contrast at this point has sometimes been shamefully apparent.

The ministry of the Jesus of the gospels (and we know no other Jesus) was marked by clarity of purpose, spiritual power, impressive authority and a servant style. His ministry is widely regarded as the basis of all true Christian ministry. But how is his ministry related to ours? Is the relationship simply that of an example to its imitation? Or may we share something of his spiritual dynamic and authority as well? And what about Jesus himself—did he expect that that same power and authority would be seen in the ministry of his followers? If so, how did he conceive the relationship of their ministry to his? It is the conviction of the present writer that there is a very definite relationship between the ministry of Jesus and that of his followers, and that many of the features of his ministry can and ought to be found in our ministries today. This is both a challenge and an encouragement. A challenge not to settle for something less, and an encouragement as we see that Christian ministry is meant to be essentially a participation with our Lord in what he is doing in the Church and in the world today.

THE SCOPE AND AIMS OF THIS STUDY

A very great deal has been written about Christian ministry over the last fifty years or so, and most writers have assumed that the basis of all Christian ministry is the ministry of Christ. However, little has been done to define satisfactorily just *how* Christian ministry is related to the ministry of our Lord either as the historical Jesus or as the exalted Christ.

Some have traditionally linked Christian ministry to the ministry of Christ by means of a particular understanding of apostolic succession. It is the unbroken succession of episcopal ordinations which is all important. This succession forms the essential link between the ministry of Jesus and the (episcopally ordained) ministry today. In recent years attempts have been made to provide proper theological undergirding for this position by appeals to the Jewish concept of the šālîaḥ (envoy). However, few scholars today remain convinced by this approach. There is a fatal flaw in the very foundation of the argument.[2]

Others have defined the relationship in terms of the Pauline image of the body. The Church *is* Christ's body by which he exercises his ministry in the world. But even this approach is open to question because it is not certain that Paul's use of the image is anything more than a metaphor;[3] a metaphor used either in appeals for unity among variously 'gifted' Christians (1 Cor. 12.14ff; Rom. 12.4ff) or in passages where the headship of Christ over the Church is emphasised (Col. 1.18; Eph. 1.22-23; 4.4-16).

The dramatic growth and widespread influence of the charismatic (neo-pentecostal) movement this century has forced many to re-examine their understanding of the role of the Spirit in the early Christian community.[4] The possibility that the relationship of Christ's ministry to that of his followers can be defined best in terms of the Spirit's work is one which demands close investigation.

The Aims of this Study

This study seeks to understand how ministry in the apostolic community related to the ministry of Jesus Christ—to that of the historical Jesus on the one hand, and that of the exalted Christ on the other. This relationship will be explored by an examination of the relevant synoptic sayings of Jesus and relevant passages in the major Pauline epistles. In the first case it is Jesus' own understanding of ministry that is sought, while in the second it is Paul's view.

In the first part of the book it will be seen that Jesus conceived the relationship in several ways. He used three major ministerial themes to express his understanding of it: apostleship, servanthood and the role of the Spirit. In the second part of the book passages in the epistles of Paul are examined. If the picture of the apostle's mission which emerges from this study is compared with the gospel portrayal of Jesus' ministry one thing becomes apparent: the dynamic operating in the Pauline mission is similar to that operating in the ministry of Jesus. The aim of the second part of the book, then, is to show that the three major themes found in the synoptic sayings of Jesus emerge again in the chief epistles of Paul and bear essentially the same meanings. However, to meet fresh situations not encountered during Jesus' ministry, Paul introduced other ministerial themes which have no counterpart in the synoptic sayings of Jesus. These too will be investigated to see what light they throw upon the subject. It will be argued that Paul understood his ministry to be related in specific ways to the ministry of the historical Jesus, and that he believed there was an essential link between the exalted Christ and both his own ministry and that of the Christian community.

Paul's conversion experience, commissioning and empowering for mission all date from the post-Pentecost period. Therefore, no matter into what special category we may wish to place the apostle, he remains one whose call and ministry fall entirely within the present age of the Spirit. Thus we may expect that a study of the way Paul understood his ministry (and that of his colleagues and the early Christian communities) to be related to that of the historical Jesus and the exalted Christ will throw some light upon the nature of Christian ministry today.

The Scope of this Study

This book is concerned primarily with the essential nature of the ministry of the whole people of God as that is related to the ministry of Jesus Christ. This includes, but is not restricted to, what we speak of today as the ordained ministry.

The scope of this study is subject to certain limitations as far as primary sources are concerned. The investigation of Jesus' understanding of ministry is restricted to the synoptic sayings, but where there are parallels (e.g., in the Pauline epistles and the Gospel of Thomas) these are taken into account. This is not meant to imply that the Johannine discourses are historically worthless, but it does mean that the special character of the Johannine material is recognised and, therefore, the best place to begin is with the synoptic tradition. The work on Paul's epistles is restricted to the chief Paulines, partly in recognition of the widespread, but not universal, conviction among New Testament scholars that the Pastoral Epistles betray a hand other than that of the apostle Paul, and partly to keep the length of the book within desired limits.

In many places this study involves detailed exegesis of relevant material in the synoptic sayings of Jesus and the major Paulines. An effort will be made only to draw conclusions which, in the writer's judgement, are justified by an exposition of the texts in their literary, historical and cultural contexts.

All biblical quotations are from the Revised Standard Version except where indicated otherwise.

PART ONE

JESUS AND MINISTRY

CHAPTER TWO

THE PROBLEM OF AUTHENTICITY

The Problem

In this first part of our study we have set ourselves the task of seeking Jesus' understanding of ministry. In pursuing this objective we have to face some special problems; problems which do not arise in the second part of the book where Paul's view of ministry is investigated. When we are dealing with Paul we have his own first-hand accounts to work with. But Jesus left behind no such documents, so we are dependent upon second-hand accounts of his life and teaching; material selected and arranged to meet various needs which arose in the life and witness of the early church.

In recent years the gospel writers have been recognised not only as recorders of the works and words of Jesus, but as those who selected and arranged the traditional material about Jesus so as to present what they believed was of great importance to those for whom they wrote. That the traditional material has been selectively and creatively used in the gospel of John is made abundantly clear in 20.30-31: 'Now Jesus did many other signs in the presence of the disciples, which are not written in this book; but these are written that you may believe that Jesus is the Christ, the Son of God, and that believing you may have life in his name.' The fourth gospel was written with a definite theological purpose, and this is true of the synoptic gospels as well. The recognition of the creative approach of the synoptic evangelists to their materials has raised questions, not so much concerning their inspiration and authority as the word of God for the Church, but rather whether they were intended to be records of the actual words (albeit in translation) of the historical Jesus.

The problem comes into sharp focus in the exegetical studies which make up the major portion of the first part of this book. Many of the sayings of Jesus relevant to our study occur in more than one form, and some in as many as four different forms. Obviously some effort will have to be made to determine which of these forms is the earliest. But then we must ask whether even that form which we judge to be the earliest represents in fact the actual words of Jesus. Perhaps the evangelists would not even understand this obsession with *ipsissima verba*; they were men captured and enthralled by the Christ, and in the liberty of his Spirit felt free to make explanatory additions and modifications to the traditional material with which they worked so as to bring out the full force and implications of his message. They seem to have been far more concerned with the authentic message and its meaning than with the actual words of Jesus.

This brings us to the real crux of the problem: if the synoptic evangelists felt free to work creatively with the Jesus-tradition handed down to them, how do we know they did not feel free as well to add to it creations of their own or of the early Church? We like to separate the words of the historical Jesus from inspired utterances of Christian prophets speaking in the name of the exalted Christ. But did they think it was necessary or even desirable to distinguish between what Jesus said during his Palestinian ministry and what they believed the exalted Christ was, by the Spirit, saying to them through their apostles, prophets and teachers? Are some of the sayings found in the synoptic gospels not authentic sayings of the historical Jesus, but rather formulations of the early Church or even of the synoptic evangelists themselves? How do we deal with this problem of authenticity?

Evaluating Authenticity: The Criteria

Jeremias made a detailed and penetrating study of the form and characteristics of the sayings of Jesus and reached the following conclusion:

> The linguistic and stylistic evidence shows so much faithfulness and such respect towards the tradition of the sayings of Jesus that we are justified in drawing up the following principle of method: In the synoptic tradition it is the inauthenticity, and not the authenticity, of the sayings of Jesus that must be demonstrated.[1]

Few New Testament scholars today would be prepared to adopt Jeremias' principle of method, nevertheless his conclusion does stand as a caution against over-sceptical attitudes toward the synoptic sayings of Jesus. Faced with the problem of authenticity most scholars today resort to the application of three basic criteria for discerning the authentic words of Jesus. These are the criteria of dissimilarity, coherence and frequency of occurrence in the tradition. The criterion of dissimilarity is applied as follows: if there is no obvious source for the saying in contemporary Judaism, and if it is not the sort of saying the early Church is likely to have formulated, then there is little reason to doubt that it originated with Jesus himself. By the application of this criterion those sayings about whose authenticity there can be little doubt may be isolated. Here we are not sailing in uncharted waters. Others have been this way before, so we have the benefit of their soundings. There is a measure of agreement already concerning those sayings whose authenticity should not be doubted. The criterion of coherence is brought into play to further increase the pool of sayings which should be recognised as authentic. This is done by noting those other sayings which, although they do not fit into the previous category, are consonant with those that do. Finally, the third criterion, frequency of occurrence in the tradition, is employed. This is done by noting in how many different strata of the synoptic tradition (Mark, Q, Matthew, Luke) the saying under investigation occurs. A saying found in many strata of tradition is likely to have been widely recognised by the early churches as an authentic word of Jesus. This last criterion is the least determinative of the three.

The Limitations of the Criteria

The limitations on the use of these criteria are obvious. Applied in a positive way the criteria will indicate for us those sayings whose authenticity should not be doubted. But they can also be applied in a destructive fashion, producing excessively sceptical attitudes towards those sayings which do not happen to fit the categories of the criteria. For example, when faced with a saying which is similar to the teaching of either first century Judaism or the early Church, whose consonance with obviously authentic sayings cannot be demonstrated, and which occurs in only one stratum of the tradition, we might conclude that the saying is not an authentic utterance of Jesus. But that conclusion could be mistaken. Jesus was a man of his own time and culture, so it ought not to surprise us if some of what he said was drawn from his own Jewish thought world. Further, we would expect the teaching of the early Church to be deeply influenced by the words of Jesus whom it acknowledged as Lord. Used positively, then, the criterion of dissimilarity can be very helpful, but used negatively it could lead us astray. Again, when we remember that the synoptic evangelists made selections from a large amount of material to construct their gospels, we can appreciate how it could quite easily happen that an authentic saying of Jesus may finally appear in only one stratum of tradition. Summing up, it must be said that it is quite possible that a saying which does not meet the criterion of dissimilarity or is not consonant with those that do, and which is found only once in the strata of tradition may nevertheless be authentic Jesus-tradition.

In the discussion of the authenticity of the sayings which are taken up in the present study of Jesus and ministry, the critical criteria are used in a positive way remembering the limitations which apply.[2] An effort is made to draw conclusions consistent with the degree of certainty which, in the view of the writer, the evidence for authenticity allows.

The first part of the study focusses upon three major emphases in the relevant sayings of Jesus: apostleship, servanthood, and the role of the Spirit. The Son of Man sayings were also considered for separate treatment, but as most of them are included in the discussion of the three major themes, there seemed little to be gained from treating them separately.

CHAPTER THREE

JESUS AND APOSTLESHIP

The purpose of this chapter is to show that Jesus regarded himself as the apostle of God, sent into the world to proclaim and inaugurate the kingdom of God, and that he appointed the Twelve to be his envoys, understanding their mission to be an extension of his. They were apostles of Jesus, representing him, but they were also envoys of God, representing the One who had sent Jesus. Further, the way in which Jesus spoke of the relationship existing between the Twelve, himself, and the Father, is similar to the way in which the rabbinic writings speak of the relationship between the Jewish *šālîaḥ* (envoy/agent) and his principal. The probability that the rabbinic tradition reflects a custom practised also in the first century strongly suggests that Jesus drew on the *šālîaḥ* concept to express these relationships, thus throwing some light on the nature of 'apostleship'.

The pursuit of this purpose involves two major tasks. First, it will need to be shown that a reasonable case for the authenticity of the relevant sayings of Jesus can be made, and that such sayings do find parallels in the rabbinic traditions concerning the *šālîaḥ*. Second, it will have to be demonstrated that there is cause to believe that the later rabbinic *šālîaḥ* traditions reflect a state of affairs existing also in the time of Jesus. It should, perhaps, be pointed out that we are not concerned with the meaning of the Greek word *apostolos*, a word which is found only once in the synoptic sayings of Jesus, and that in a passage whose interpretation is disputed.[1]

JESUS, APOSTLE OF GOD

The sayings in which Jesus refers to his apostolic consciousness, his awareness of being sent by God, fall naturally into two categories. There are, first, those sayings which speak simply of his being sent with a mission, and second, those which assert that men who receive his disciples (or a child) in his name receive him, and by so doing receive not only him but also the One who sent him (a typical Jewish circumlocutory reference to God).

Mark 1.38/Luke 4.43

Both Mark and Luke record the tradition concerning Jesus' departure from Capernaum. According to Mark 1.35-8, Jesus arose very early and withdrew to a desert place to pray. Simon and those with him sought Jesus, and having found him reported that the townsfolk from Capernaum were looking for him. Jesus replied: 'Let us go on to the next towns, that I may preach there also; for that is why I came out (*eis touto gar exēlthon*).' Luke's rendering of the account (4.42-3) appears to be a combination of Mark 1.35-8 and Q tradition (see Matthew 4.23b). There are some differences in the Lucan account. No mention is made of Simon and those with him, instead the crowds are the subject of the search for Jesus. More important for our study is the different form of Jesus' response: 'I must preach the good news of the kingdom of God to the other cities also; for I was sent for this purpose (*hoti epi touto apestalēn*).'

The words 'for that is why I came out' in the Marcan saying are ambiguous. They could simply mean that Jesus left Capernaum because he wanted to preach in other towns as well,[2] or they could be an allusion to his having come out from God. Quite possibly the saying is left intentionally ambiguous by Mark so that, as well as a primary reference to Jesus' departure from Capernaum, it carries also a veiled hint that Jesus came out from God with a specific mission.

Luke's account of the saying has no ambiguity. In place of Mark's 'that is why I came out', he has put 'I was sent for this purpose', which clearly asserts an awareness of 'apostleship' on the part of Jesus, the use of 'I was sent' (*apestalēn*) by Luke being intended to bring out the significance of Mark's 'I came out' (*exēlthon*).[3]

There seems little doubt that Mark's *exēlthon* must be regarded as the earlier tradition, and Luke's *apestalēn* as a later commentary on its significance. Thus the saying in its earlier form contains a hint of apostolic consciousness on the part of

Jesus, but no more. Fortunately we are not confined only to Mark 1.38/Luke 4.43 for there are other attestations of Jesus' apostolic awareness in the synoptic tradition.

Matthew 15.24

The story of the Canaanite/Syrophoenician woman's approach to Jesus on behalf of her demon-possessed child is recorded in Matthew 15.21-8 and Mark 7.24-30. However, only in Matthew are we told that the disciples asked Jesus to send the woman away, and that Jesus himself rebuffed her with the words: 'I was sent (*apestalēn*) only to the lost sheep of the house of Israel' (15.24). These words find a partial parallel in the Matthean account of Jesus' charge to the Twelve prior to the Galilean mission: 'Go nowhere among the Gentiles, and enter no town of the Samaritans, but go rather to the lost sheep of the house of Israel' (10.5-6). Neither of these Matthean sayings of Jesus has any counterpart in either Mark or Luke.

The dominical character of Matthew 15.24. It has been said that this saying is an old tradition that came down to Matthew as an independently circulating logion which he then wove into Mark's dialogue,[4] and that its origin should be sought in the missionary debates of the Palestinian church.[5] The continuity of Matthew 15.21-8 is not disturbed if verses 23-4 are removed, a fact which supports the view that verse 24 was a saying that circulated independently. On the other hand, it is possible that whilst both Matthew and Mark knew of this saying in connection with the Canaanite/Syrophoenician woman's approach to Jesus, Mark deliberately omitted it to avoid offending gentile readers. In that case its retention by Matthew in spite of the embarrassment it might cause in a church already involved in a gentile mission in the pre-Pauline era (see Acts 10.1-48; 11.20-24) would be strong evidence for its dominical character.[6] Further, it has been noted that there are factors indicating an Aramaic original for Matthew 15.24, and this has been adduced as evidence for its authenticity.[7] But a setting in the Palestinian church's missionary debates could equally well account for such an Aramaic original.

The authenticity of Matthew 15.24 has also been questioned because, it is claimed, the word *apestalēn* (I was sent) is typical of the terminology of a later time, evidenced by the use of similar expressions in John (3.19; 8.42; 16.28; 18.37).[8] However, John nowhere uses the passive of *apostellein* or *pempein* to refer to the Father sending Jesus; it is always the active that is used. This suggests that the passive *apestalēn* of Matthew 15.24 is a circumlocutory reference to God which is characteristic of the early tradition.[9]

All in all it appears that the scales tip slightly in favour of the authenticity of Matthew 15.24. There is evidence for an Aramaic original, it is not the sort of saying that a Church already involved in a gentile mission would formulate, and it is retained in a gospel which stresses the universal scope of Jesus' commission (28.19-20). The significance of this conclusion is that we have here explicit reference by Jesus to his consciousness of having been sent by God, and having been sent only to the lost sheep of the house of Israel (though the thrust of the pericope Matthew 15.21-8/Mark 7.24-30 is that the faith of the seeking Gentile will certainly be rewarded).

Mark 12.1-12/Matthew 21.33-46/Luke 20.9-19/
Gospel of Thomas 65
If the parable of the wicked husbandmen can be shown to be reliable Jesus-tradition, and if the owner's son may be regarded as an allegorical self-reference by Jesus, then it will add significantly to the picture of Jesus, 'apostolic' self-consciousness. However, there have been many questions raised about both its authenticity and application.

The authenticity of the parable. The parable of the wicked husbandmen, or, as it has sometimes been called, the parable of the owner's son, is found in all three synoptic gospels and in the apocryphal Gospel of Thomas (logion 65). Each version differs from the others in points of detail. These differences have been summarised succinctly by J. A. T. Robinson.[10] After examining the different versions Robinson concludes: (1) In regard to the context of the parable, the synoptic tradition has strong claims both to originality and reliability. Thomas at this point is worthless. (2) In regard to the form of the parable, the version of Thomas is likely to be the most primitive. (3) Within the synoptic tradition Luke is probably nearer to the original. Matthew's version reveals the highest degree of allegorisation.

However, in the treatment accorded the son, Mark appears to be the most original.[11]

Since Jülicher published his seminal book, *Die Gleichnisreden Jesu*, in 1889, the scholarly world has been aware that, generally speaking, each parable has only one point to make. This has led some to regard the parable of the owner's son (with its multiple points of comparison, e.g., servants = prophets; owner = God; son = Jesus) as an allegory constructed by the early Church. However, the presence of allegory, though unusual in the parables of Jesus, should not be regarded automatically as proof of inauthenticity.[12] And, it has been pointed out, there is nothing in this parable/allegory which contradicts the preaching of Jesus;[13] it could have been allegorical from the beginning.

Apart from the allegorical nature of the parable, the unlikely circumstances reflected in it have also raised doubts about its authenticity. The behaviour of the tenant farmers towards the heir in the naive hope of becoming the owners of the estate has been criticised as most unlikely. On the other hand, the parable becomes more credible in the light of recent understanding of absentee land ownership in first century Palestine.

The problem of the owner's son. Doubts have been expressed also about the latter part of the parable concerning the owner's son. It has been suggested that the original parable contained reference only to the servants, and the section about the son was added later by the Church to make it apply to the Jews' treatment of Jesus as well as their treatment of the prophets. However, most commentators see the episode of the owner's son as an integral part of the original parable. Dodd maintains that 'a climax of iniquity is demanded by the plot of the story' and that 'it is the logic of the story, not any theological motive, that has introduced this figure.' Further, the Marcan 'description of the son betrays no reminiscence of the manner of the death of Jesus', and in Matthew there are signs that the evangelist has tried to remedy this (the son is first taken outside the vineyard and then killed).[14] It may also be noted that the abrupt way in which the story of the son closes—with his murder—makes it difficult to see the parable as an allegory put on the lips of Jesus by the early Church. Had this been the case we would expect some allusion to his resurrection, as it was of such central importance to the early Christian community.[15].

C. E. Carlston, who has made the most recent thorough treatment of the parable, regards it as an 'elaborately artificial construct' used within the Christian community to express opposition to those responsible for Jesus' death. The main reason for his rejection of the parable's authenticity appears to be the fact that it otherwise implies prior knowledge on Jesus' part of his own death.[16] However, there is little cause to doubt that Jesus was conscious that the lives of many faithful servants of God had ended in martyrdom (cf. Matt. 23.29-37/Luke 11.47-51), as was also the case with John the Baptist, and that such must inevitably be his own fate as well.

Another objection to the view that the owner's son is an allegorical reference to Jesus himself is that Judaism is said not to have known the messianic name 'Son of God'. However, evidence from Qumran (4QFlor 10-14) shows that 'Son of God' was in fact used as a messianic title in pre-Christian Judaism. The objection loses much of its force if it is also borne in mind that the parable was not intended to be an unveiling of Jesus' messiahship, but rather to be as clear a warning as possible to Jewish leaders of the heinousness of their plans without betraying the hiddenness of that messiahship.

Jesus' application of the parable. Granted that a reasonable case can be made out for seeing in the owner's son an allusion to Jesus, we must still ask whether Jesus himself intended it to be understood in that way. It must be admitted immediately that there is no explicit identification, owner's son = Jesus, in any version of the parable. However, if, as was suggested above, the parable was meant to be a warning to Jewish leaders, it is quite likely that Jesus did intend the figure of the owner's son to represent himself.

The significance of such a conclusion is (1) Jesus is making another reference to his awareness of being sent by God, (2) the sending of Jesus was in one sense comparable with the sending of the prophets; he was sent to call Israel to her senses, and (3) the sending of Jesus was also different from the sending of the prophets because of the status of the one sent. The owner's son represents the Son of God, and in this representation, as Moule says, we have a 'self-reference by Jesus as striking as it is rare in this Gospel.'[17]

Luke 4.16-30

All three synoptic gospels record a visit by Jesus to the synagogue in Nazareth (Mark 6.1-6a; Luke 4.16-30; Matt. 13.53-8), but only in Luke do we find Jesus quoting from Isaiah 61.1; 58.6 and explicitly claiming to fulfil those Isaianic prophecies. If this were authentic tradition it would be of great significance for both our understanding of Jesus' apostolic consciousness and his awareness of the Spirit in his ministry (Luke 4.16-30 will be taken up again in chapter v). Because the Isaianic quotation and Jesus' application of it to himself are found only in Luke, serious doubts have been expressed concerning its authenticity. Why, for instance, was it omitted from Matthew's gospel where the fulfilment of prophecy plays such an important role? Then there is the apparent programmatic use made of Luke 4.16-30 in the framework of the third gospel. Luke places the incident at the beginning of Jesus' ministry (contrast Mark 6.1-6a and Matt. 13.53-8 where the visit to Nazareth comes much later) as if it is intended to introduce the central motifs of Luke-Acts: the gospel is preached by Jesus in his home town and rejected. This rejection at Nazareth foreshadows the rejection of the gospel by the Jews as a nation and the resulting mission to the gentiles.[18] Is Luke 4.16-30, then, no more than a Lucan expansion of Mark 6.1-6a transposed from its original Marcan setting and placed at the beginning of Luke to foreshadow the central motifs of Luke-Acts?

Even if we grant the programmatic use of the passage in Luke and concede the possibility that it is a Lucan expansion of Mark 6.1-6a, there is still good reason to believe that it rests upon reliable Jesus-tradition. The case for the reliability of the tradition is based on a consideration of the other sayings of Jesus where allusions to Isaiah 61 are found. If there is good cause to believe they are authentic, there is good reason to believe that Luke 4.16-30 rests upon reliable tradition also.

J. D. G. Dunn has discussed in detail those sayings which draw on Isaiah 61.1 (Luke 4.18-21; Luke 6.20/Matthew 5.3-6, and Matthew 11.2-6/Luke 7.18-23) and has argued convincingly that the tradition which shows that Jesus understood his ministry in terms of the anointed one of Isaiah 61.1 has all the hallmarks of authenticity. To begin with, the programmatic nature of Luke 4.16-30 is conceded as is the probability that it represents a Lucan expansion of Mark 6.1-6a. Thus if Luke 4.16-30 was the only place where Jesus was reported to have alluded to Isaiah 61, it would be difficult to demonstrate its authenticity.

Luke 6.20/Matthew 5.3-6. When we come to the allusion to the Isaianic prophecy in these passages we are on firmer ground. Despite the presence of some redactional elements, the case for the basic authenticity of the passages is very strong. The close similarity between Luke 6.20-21 and Matthew 5.3-6 indicates that we are dealing directly with Q material. The use of the eschatological 'blessed' (*makarios*), an expression almost as characteristic of Jesus' speech as his use of *Abba* and *amen*, makes it nearly certain that authentic words of Jesus have been preserved for us in this Q passage. The significant feature of Luke 6.20-21/Matthew 5.3-6 is that it preserves authentic beatitudes of Jesus which show clearly the influence of Isaiah 61.1. 'The poor' and 'those who weep/mourn' clearly describe a group identical with those whom the prophet had in mind. Thus it seems clear that Isaiah 61.1 influenced Jesus' thinking. The beatitudes themselves are Jesus' proclamation of good news to the poor, which suggests that he understood himself to be the one in whom the Isaianic prophecies of the anointed one found fulfilment.

Matthew 11.2-6/Luke 7.18-23. This Q passage provides an even more solid foundation for the belief that Jesus was influenced in his conception of ministry by Isaiah 61.1. In this passage Jesus is approached by the disciples of the imprisoned Baptist with the question: 'Are you he who is to come, or shall we look for another?' To this question Jesus replies: 'Go and tell John what you hear and see: the blind receive their sight and the lame walk, lepers are cleansed and the deaf hear, and the dead are raised up, and the poor have good news preached to them. And blessed is he who takes no offence at me.' The allusion to Isaiah 61.1 is clear. Any decision regarding the authenticity of the passage must be preceded by a satisfactory explanation of its life-setting, and, as Dunn asserts, *'no thesis can be regarded as satisfactory which fails to explain the relation of John's question to Jesus' answer.'* The obvious life-setting for the saying is the time when the note of imminence in John's preaching was being sup-planted or supplemented by the note of fulfilment in the preaching of Jesus. At that time the Baptist and his disciples would be sure to ask: 'Are you he who is to come?' To such a question, coming from men who were puzzled because the judgement John had prophesied was evidently not being manifested in the activity of the Nazarene, Jesus' response in Q is entirely appropriate. 'He says in effect, "Despite the absence of judgement, the blessings promised for the end-time prove that it is already here. The day of God's vengeance is not yet; the year of the Lord's favour is now."' Thus both question and answer fit together if we locate them in the ministry of Jesus, but would not do so if either arose in a post-Easter situation.[19]

The evidence for Jesus' use of the Isaiah 61 prophecy in reference to his own ministry is, therefore, quite strong and supports the view that Luke 4.16-30 rests upon reliable tradition. This means we can say with fairly firm assurance that Jesus understood the prophecy of Isaiah 61.1 to have been fulfilled, and that this fulfilment was accomplished in him and through his ministry. He was not only the end-time prophet of Isaiah 61.1, he was also the one through whose ministry the proclamation of the end-time prophet found actualisation.

Matthew 10.40/Luke 10.16; Mark 9.37/Luke 9.48/
Matthew 18.5

We have to deal now with a series of very similar sayings attributed to Jesus in the synoptic gospels.

Matthew 10.40/Luke 10.16. This first saying is set by the evangelists in the context of Jesus' mission charge to his disciples: to the Twelve in Matthew, and to the seventy(-two) in Luke. Matthew's version runs: 'He who receives you receives me, and he who receives me receives him who sent me', whereas Luke has: 'He who hears you hears me, and he who rejects you rejects me, and he who rejects me rejects him who sent me.'

There can be no real doubt concerning the historicity of a limited Galilean mission undertaken by the disciples during the ministry of Jesus. This is especially so in the light of the explicit and independent witness to it in a saying of Jesus (Luke 22.35-8) for which a strong case for authenticity can be made (see the discussion of Luke 22.35-8 below). However, the mission-charge as it is presented by both Matthew and Luke is clearly a collection of various independent traditional sayings of Jesus, only some of which relate to the Galilean mission.

It has been argued that Matthew 10.40/Luke 10.16 was originally a Jewish saying modified by the Church to serve as an oracle of the exalted Christ.[20] The possibility of a Jewish origin for this saying will be discussed later, but at this point it must be noted that not all modern scholars agree with this judgement. For example, Schweizer says 'the hypothetical original form of the saying in Matthew 10.40 could very well go back to Jesus', and Grundmann identifies a characteristic form of expression used by Jesus in the antithetic parallelism of Luke 10.16.[21] Further, what is said in Matthew 10.40/Luke 10.16 is no more than what is implied by Matthew 10.1. If we accept the historicity of a Galilean mission for which Jesus delegated certain authority to his disciples, then it follows that he would look upon the reception accorded to his delegates as an indication of the people's attitude both to him and to the One who sent him. That Jesus thought along these lines is further supported by the second saying, which we must now consider.

Mark 9.37/Luke 9.48/Matthew 18.5. This saying is placed by all three synoptic evangelists in the context of an exchange between Jesus and his disciples. The latter had been discussing which of them should be greatest, and it is reported that Jesus took a child, set him in the midst, and said: 'Whoever receives one such child in my name receives me; and whoever receives me receives not me but him who sent me' (Mark 9.37). Matthew omits the latter part of the saying, probably because he had already used a similar saying in 10.40 where those who are or are not received are the disciples themselves. Luke follows Mark fairly closely but adds, 'for he who is least among you all is the one who is great.'

S. Legasse has made detailed studies of the synoptic tradition concerning children, little ones, and the simple, in which he suggests that the evangelists have set up children as representatives of human weakness and types of the blessing of salvation. He emphasises the early Church's fidelity to the preaching of Jesus in this matter and regards it as probable that this concept is rooted in Jesus' actual attitude to children.[22] Other modern interpreters see in the children/little ones of Mark 9.37 par. a reference to the disciples (because of that element in the saying which speaks of receiving them 'in my name'); or a reference to those insignificant ones who tended to be neglected in the churches of the first century; or even a reference to Jesus himself, reflecting his awareness that he was the younger one who has taken over the venture pioneered by his elder, John the Baptist.[23]

Whatever may have been the significance of this saying for members of the communities in which the synoptic gospels were written, there is reason to believe that the historical context provided in the three Synoptics was the first life-setting of the saying. The concern about greatness which is there attributed to the disciples of Christ has parallels in contemporary Judaism. The Pharisaic love of prestige is reflected in the gospels (Matt. 23.1-12; Mark 12.38-40; Luke 20.45-7) and the importance of rank and precedence in the Qumran community can be seen in its literature (1QS 2.19-23; 6.8-9; CD 14.3-8). Further, a tradition which puts the 'pillars' of the church in such a bad light is not likely to be a church creation. There is, therefore, good reason to believe that we are in touch with reliable Jesus-tradition at this point.

It seems fair to say that the whole cluster of synoptic sayings in which Jesus asserts that those who receive his disciples/a child in his name receive him, and those who receive him receive the One who sent him, rests on reliable tradition with an original life-setting in the ministry of Jesus. There is no point, as far as our present purpose is concerned, in trying to ascertain the earliest form of the saying. It is sufficient to note that there emerges from this group of sayings a clear picture of Jesus' apostolic awareness; he was one sent by God.

As mentioned above, a Jewish origin has been suggested for these sayings. Attention has been drawn to the rabbinic adage, 'A man's envoy (šālîaḥ) is as himself', as the Jewish proverb which possibly underlies the saying.[24] The parallels between the rabbinic šālîaḥ concept and these sayings of Jesus are striking and have long been noted by scholars. If it could be shown that these sayings were in fact drawing upon the šālîaḥ idea, extra light would be thrown upon the nature of Jesus' apostolic awareness and his view of the 'apostolicity' of the Twelve. This possibility will be discussed after the examination of the sayings of Jesus about the mission of the Twelve.

THE 'APOSTLESHIP' OF JESUS' DISCIPLES

It is stated above that there can be no real doubt concerning the historicity of a pre-Easter Galilean mission of the Twelve. Evidence must be brought forward to support this assertion, for it has been questioned by scholars of repute who claim that the idea of the Twelve itself is a post-resurrection phenomenon.[25] However, several considerations support the view that the existence of the Twelve as a group chosen by Jesus and sent by him on a Galilean mission in the pre-Easter period must be accepted as historical. First, in 1 Corinthians 15.5 Paul speaks of the Twelve as a group to whom Christ appeared in the days immediately following the resurrection. This is the only reference to the Twelve in the writings of Paul. It seems clear that he is here using a formula he did not himself make up, and that the idea of a group of twelve special disciples is pre-Pauline, and therefore very early. Second, the traditions in Mark, Luke, and John speak of Judas Iscariot as 'one of the Twelve' and this makes sense only if such a group existed in the time of Jesus' Palestinian ministry. Third, the references to 'the Eleven' in the gospel traditions would likewise make no sense unless the Twelve had been accepted as a special group prior to Jesus' death.[26] Finally, there is an independent and explicit reference to the mission of the Twelve in Luke 22.35.

Luke 22.35

The saying, Luke 22.35-8, is peculiar to the third gospel. It is set in the context of the final meal that Jesus shared with the Twelve before the crucifixion. He reminds the disciples that on their mission in Galilee they were able to rely on those to whom they ministered for sustenance and shelter; they did not need to take purse or wallet. But times have changed. He now counsels them to take their purses and wallets, and if they have no sword, to sell their cloaks to buy one, for the prophecy of Isaiah 53.12 is about to be fulfilled: 'And he was reckoned with the transgressors.'

Luke 22.35 is not without its problems. Jesus' question, 'When I sent you out with no purse or bag or sandals, did you lack anything?' has its counterpart in Luke 10.4. However, Luke 10 records not the sending of the Twelve, which is found in chapter 9, but the sending of the Seventy(-two). It may be that there were two separate missions and that similar charges were given on both occasions, and that the Twelve were numbered among the Seventy(-two). On the other hand, seeing that the mission of the Seventy(-two) and the saying Luke 22.35-8 are found only in Luke, we must face the possibility that both are Lucan productions. H. W. Bartsch has made a tradition-history study of Luke 22.35-8 in which the redactional parallels, the introductory formula (*to gegrammenon* [What is written], instead of *gegraptai* [it is written]) for the quotation from Isaiah 53.12, the Lucan character of verse 37c, and the eschatological *dei* (NEB 'must') in verse 37a are all regarded as evidence of Luke's editing. For the basic tradition three possible literary origins are listed: (1) An old Jesus-traditon from Luke's special source, in which case it is possible to assume that the passage is an original saying of Jesus; (2) a product of the early Church but found in Luke's special material; and (3) a creation of Luke himself. Bartsch asserts that the content of the saying excludes the possibility that it was created by the early Church or Luke. They would not want to put such a saying on the lips of Jesus while, at the same time, trying to keep the remembrance of him free from any association with the Zealots. He concludes that Luke 22.35-8 is a Lucan reworking of *genuine* Jesus-tradition.[27] It may be added that the very difficulty of reconciling the saying (with its advice to take the sword) with other teaching of Jesus (e.g., the Sermon on the Mount) both supports its authenticity and explains its omission from Matthew and Mark, assuming they knew the saying. It seems, therefore, that Luke 22.35-8 does rest upon reliable tradition, despite its limited attestation. This conclusion strengthens the view that the pre-Easter mission of the Twelve is historical.

Mark 6.7-13/Luke 9.1-6; 10.1-16/Matthew 10.5-15, 40

An account of Jesus' commission to his disciples prior to their Galilean mission is found in each of the synoptic gospels. Mark's account is found in 6.7-13. In Luke commission sayings are found in two places: a charge to the Twelve in 9.1-6 (following the Marcan account) and a charge to the Seventy(-two) in 10.1-16. Matthew's version combines what is found in Luke 9-10, supplements it with special material found only in the first gospel, and presents the whole as a long mission discourse. In this form its life-setting is probably to be sought in the instruction of early Christian missionaries and church leaders.

We have already seen that the case for the historicity of the Galilean mission of the Twelve is strong. It remains for us to examine those commission sayings which are relevant to the present enquiry.

Matthew 10.5-6. Only in this passage do we find the command of Jesus to the Twelve: 'Go nowhere among the Gentiles, and enter no town of the Samaritans, but go rather to the lost sheep of the house of Israel' (10.5-6). The latter part of the saying has a parallel in Matthew 15.24, in Jesus' response to the Canaanite woman's plea for help. In the discussion of this parallel saying above it was suggested that the retention of such an exclusive statement by Matthew indicates his faithfulness to the historical tradition of Jesus. The same can be said about Matthew 10.5-6. Such a tradition would not originate in a Church which was early involved in a mission both to Samaritans and Gentiles (Acts 8.4-25; 11.19-26), nor would it be retained in Matthew which stresses the universality of Christ's commission (28.19-20) if the evangelist did not regard it as an authentic saying of Jesus. The importance of the saying for our study is that it illustrates how the Twelve were acting as representatives of Christ; their mission was governed by the limitations which applied to his at that time: 'to the lost sheep of the house of Israel.' As his envoys they could not extend the scope of their mission.

Matthew 10.7-8. The task committed by Jesus to his disciples (which is essentially the same in both the Marcan narrative tradition [Mark 3.14-15; 6.12-13] and Q [Matt. 10.7-8/Luke 10.9]), is expressed in Matthew: 'And preach as you go, saying, "The kingdom of heaven is at hand." Heal the sick, raise the dead, cleanse lepers, cast out demons' (10.7-8). There is no reason to doubt the authenticity of the tradition—the eschatological element in the proclamation and the emphasis on exorcisms and healing indicate a life-setting in the period of Jesus' ministry. It is important to note that here again the mission of the disciples is clearly an extension of Jesus' own ministry. They are commissioned by him, what they proclaim is what he proclaims, and like Jesus they are to let their proclamation be accompanied by a demonstration of the power of the kingdom in healing and exorcisms.

Matthew 10.40. The representative character of the disciples' mission is summed up in the climactic words: 'He who receives you receives me, and he who receives me receives him who sent me' (Matt. 10.40). Arguments for the authenticity of this type of saying were put forward in the treatment of Matthew 10.40/Luke 10.16 above, so need not be repeated here. Modern commentators see in Matthew 10.40 a return to the missionary theme of Matthew 10.1-15, and understand it to be related to the kind of hospitality Jesus' messengers would find.[28] The significance of the saying for our present purposes is that it clearly implies what has already been deduced from the previous sayings: the mission of the Twelve was an extension of the mission of Jesus. When men received Jesus' messengers they received him. As Jeremias observes, the saying indicates that Jesus himself comes in the person of his messengers, and, to go one step further, 'God himself enters houses with Jesus' messengers.'[29]

The limitations, the task and the representative character of the disciples all indicate that the mission of the Twelve was an extension of Jesus' own ministry. The striking parallels between Jesus' saying, 'he who receives you receives me . . .', and the rabbinic adage, 'a man's envoy (*šālîaḥ*) is as himself,' have been noted already. If this rabbinic concept was current among the Jews of the first century, then Jesus' saying is almost certainly a particular application of that concept. The corollary to this is that Jesus thought it appropriately expressed one important aspect of the relationship between his disciples, himself, and the Father. This possibility will be taken up below following the examination of Matthew 10.16/Luke 10.3.

Matthew 10.16/Luke 10.3

The relationship between Matthew's mission-charge to the Twelve (10.1-15) and Luke's charges to the Twelve (9.1-6) and the Seventy(-two) (10.1-16) received comment above. Jesus' saying, 'Behold, I send you out as sheep/lambs in the midst of wolves', is found both in Matthew's charge to the Twelve (10.16) and Luke's charge to the Seventy(-two) (10.3).

The sheep/wolf metaphor is found often in the Old Testament and Apocrypha (e.g., Jer. 5.6; Hab. 1.8; Ezek. 22.27; 2 Esd. 5.18).[30] More important, the same metaphor is found in another Matthean saying of Jesus: 'Beware of false prophets, who come to you in sheep's clothing but inwardly are ravening wolves' (7.15). The warning of Matthew 7.15 would be particularly appropriate for the situation about AD 80 in Syria-Palestine where Jews made life hard for the Matthean church. Matthew 10.16 would be applicable to that situation, but would also be relevant at a time when the early Church was experiencing persecutions as a result of its initial missionary outreach. Bultmann regards the saying as a word from the risen Lord—a missionary command to the Christian community.[31] However, we do not need to look as far ahead as that for the original life-setting of Matthew 10.16. Although the retention of the saying is probably due to its relevance for the Matthean church, its original life-setting is more likely to have been in the period of Jesus' ministry when both he and his disciples were in repeated conflict with the Jews, especially the Pharisees. Further, it would take no great insight or prophetic fore-knowledge (not that we want to deny either of these to Jesus) to foresee that the proclamation of an imminent messianic kingdom in first century Syria-Palestine would invite trouble for both Jesus and those whom he sent with his message. Jewish passions would be aroused and the Roman occupying forces could not ignore such a proclamation. According to the gospel of John it was fear of Roman reprisals that prompted Jewish leaders to bring Jesus' movement to an end (11.45-53). Thus there is no compelling reason to reject the testimony of Matthew and Luke who attribute the saying to Jesus.

The saying suggests that Jesus' commission to his disciples was not only applicable to the halcyon days of their Galilean mission, but was to carry over into a later time when they would face persecution. During the Galilean mission their hearers were 'sheep'; they did not face 'wolves' till the Lord's death. As the conflict with the Pharisaic party sharpened, and when the Jewish leaders began to take notice of Jesus' movement and make plans to terminate it, Jesus became increasingly conscious of the violent end towards which he moved. At such a time he would warn his disciples that they were sent as 'sheep/lambs in the midst of wolves.' Most likely Jesus had in mind sufferings which his disciples may have to endure at the time when he was put to death and immediately thereafter—in the earliest days of the Christian mission.

THE JEWISH ŠĀLÎAH

Šālîah and New Testament Apostleship

J. B. Lightfoot was the first in recent times to draw attention to the Jewish *šālîah* as the possible background for the New Testament concept of apostleship. He says the idea was in existence in the first half of the first century, even though extant documentation for it is from a later period.[32] The same line of thought was taken up by A. Harnack who brought together an impressive amount of information to produce the following picture of the Jewish apostles:

> (1) they were consecrated persons of a very high rank; (2) they were sent out into the Diaspora to collect tribute for headquarters; (3) they brought encyclical letters with them, kept the Diaspora in touch with the centre and informed of the intentions of the latter (or of the patriarch), received orders relative to any dangerous movement, and had to organise resistance to it; (4) they exercised certain powers of surveillance and discipline in the Diaspora; and (5) on returning to their own countries, formed a sort of council which aided the patriarch in supervising the interests of the Law.[33]

The classic presentation of the case for a *šālîah* background to the New Testament apostolate is found in K. Rengstorf's well-known article in *TDNT*. Following an extended discussion of the data, he concludes that by definition the function of the *šālîah* is not religious, but rather legal, and that it only acquires religious overtones if the actual commission given to the *šālîah* is of a religious nature. It was Rengstorf's article that popularised the rabbinic teaching: 'the one sent by a man is as the man himself' (*Berakot* 5.5). This means that the treatment accorded to a man's messenger was regarded as if it had been done to the man himself. So, for example, the abusing of David's messengers by the Ammonites was sufficient cause for war (2 Samuel

10). According to Rengstorf, the fact that a man's *šālîaḥ* is as himself underlies many of the passages of the New Testament including some of the sayings of Jesus.[34]

The ingenious (but somewhat irresponsible) use made of the *šālîaḥ* data by G. Dix in his article in *The Apostolic Ministry*,[35] as well as later work on the gnostic apostles,[36] has caused the work done by Rengstorf (and Lightfoot and Harnack before him) to fall into the background. Nevertheless, what Rengstorf asserts concerning the *šālîaḥ* as the key to our understanding of the New Testament apostolate and, what is more important for the present enquiry, that which best explains the relationship between Jesus and the Twelve, needs to be taken seriously.

References in the Talmud

The Talmud contains many references to the role of the *šālîaḥ*, in both the Mishnah and the Gemara. However, this does not necessarily mean it was well-known among the Jews of the first century. The dating of the material in the Talmud is notoriously difficult. We do know that the Mishnah was compiled about AD 200, and where the various sections of the Gemara contain ascriptions to individual rabbis, those sections can be dated approximately.

Because of the importance of the rabbinic saying 'a man's envoy is as himself' for our present study, our discussion of the talmudic material will be focussed upon that particular saying. In the Mishnah it is found in *Berakot* 5:5, and later rabbinic citations of this mishnaic adage are found in the Gemara in *Menahot* 93b, *Baba Mesi'a* 96a, *Qiddusin* 41b, *Hagiga* 10b, and *Nazir* 12b. Of these *Nazir* 12b ('R. Jonathan said: In all circumstances do we find that a man's representative [*šālîaḥ*] is equivalent to himself') is the earliest, dating from the second century of the Christian era.[37] Thus it may be said that the *šālîaḥ* concept was well-known in the second century. Further, seeing that the Mishnah was passed on in oral form, it is likely that the idea was current among the Jews long before the close of the first century.

Origins of the Concept

Writing in 1925, H. Vogelstein maintained that the *šālîaḥ* idea can be traced back at least to the late fifth century BC. He cites one of the Elephantine papyri, the Pesach epistle of Darius II, dating from 419 BC. The bearer of this epistle was one Hananiah 'who tarried in Egypt in an authoritative state position, as is confirmed by another papyrus (13494).' He is 'the plenipotentiary (representative) of the king, his šālîaḥ.' In the light of this evidence, it is suggested that the Jews took over the šālîaḥ idea from the Persians. Thus, the appointment of Ezra is to be understood as a commissioning to be a šālîaḥ of the Persian king. Ezra was given a definite task. When it was completed his authority expired and that is probably why we hear nothing about his activities after that. Other examples of similar appointments are cited from the books of Esther, 2 Maccabees, and 2 Chronicles, and it is concluded that 'the Persian state commissaries were the pattern, the model, for the apostles, the commissaries of the religious administrative authorities at Jerusalem.'[38] Rengstorf supports Vogelstein's conclusion and says that the legal institution of the šālîaḥ is old and its existence may be proved from the time after the exile (2 Chr. 17.7-9), but it is probably even older than that.[39]

Thus a good case can be made for the antiquity of the practice among the Jews of appointing šĕlûḥîm, at least from the time immediately following the exile. Evidence from the Talmud makes it clear that in the second century of the Christian era the practice was well established in Judaism. It is reasonable to assume, therefore, that it originated in post-exilic days and was developed among the Jews until, as we see in the Talmud, it became the important institution it was in later Judaism. So there is good reason to believe that it was also well-known among Jews of the first century, and consequently, the underlying concept expressed in the rabbinic adage could have been taken up and given a particular application by Jesus. The close parallel between some of Jesus' sayings and the rabbinic adage strongly confirms this. The concept was appropriate to express one important facet of the relationship existing between the disciples and Jesus, and Jesus and the Father.

CONCLUSIONS

Jesus was indeed aware of being sent by God; sent to proclaim the acceptable year of the Lord to Israel. He believed that the prophecy of Isaiah 61.1 found fulfilment in his ministry; he was the anointed prophet of the end time, sent to proclaim and effect the deliverance of which Isaiah 61.1 speaks. Jesus understood himself to have been sent after the fashion of the prophets of the Old Testament, but also in a way which went beyond the prophetic calling. Like the prophets, Jesus spoke of the day of the Lord's deliverance, but, unlike them, he not only proclaimed it, he also saw it as his mission to bring that deliverance into effect.

The Galilean mission of the Twelve should be regarded not as a post-Easter creation of the Church, but as a historic event. Jesus' commission shows that he regarded their mission as an extension of his: the same limitations applied ('to the lost sheep of the house of Israel'), and the same task was undertaken (to proclaim the kingdom and demonstrate that it had come, proleptically at least, by distributing its blessings). They were Jesus' representatives; when men received them they received him also, and by so doing they received not only him but the One who had sent him.

The close affinity between Jesus' saying concerning the representative character of the Twelve (at least for the duration of the Galilean mission) and the rabbinic sayings concerning the šālîah has been noted. Even though insufficient information is available to show exactly how developed the šālîah idea was in the time of Jesus, this affinity, together with the likelihood that the šālîah idea was well-known in first century Judaism, makes it probable that Jesus drew on this concept to express the relationship between the Twelve, himself, and the Father. This would mean that he regarded the relationship existing between a Jewish šālîah and his principal as an appropriate parallel to the relationship existing between the Twelve, himself, and the Father, or at least to one aspect of it. The significance of all this is that Jesus, in executing the task committed to him, acted as the plenipotentiary of the Father. His authority stood behind what Jesus said and did. Likewise, in so far as the Twelve were carrying out the commission given to them by Jesus, they were acting as his plenipotentiaries. They spoke and acted with his authority, which was backed up by the authority of the Father.

It is impossible to demonstrate from the synoptic sayings of the historical Jesus that the Twelve whom Jesus comissioned for the Galilean mission were also appointed by him to be apostles of the early Church. However, we have seen that Jesus' saying, 'Behold, I send you out as sheep in the midst of wolves', suggests at least that he regarded their comission as applying to the troubled times that came with and immediately followed his death.

An effort has been made not to confuse the commission given by Jesus to the Twelve for the Galilean mission with the apostolic role which is ascribed to them in the book of Acts. However, there are indications outside the book of Acts that suggest that the Twelve were regarded as the first apostles of the Church. The most important of these is Galatians 1.17 where Paul, in defence of his independence as an apostle of Christ, says: 'Nor did I go up to Jerusalem to those who were apostles before me, but I went away into Arabia; and again I returned to Damascus.' Thus, Paul acknowledges the existence of a group of apostles resident in Jerusalem immediately following his own conversion, about AD 31/32.[40] It is difficult to escape the conclusion that he is referring to the Eleven plus Matthias (cf. Acts 1.15-26), possibly already supplemented by James, the brother of the Lord.

CHAPTER FOUR

JESUS AND SERVANTHOOD

One of the striking features of the synoptic presentation of the ministry of Jesus is the consistent avoidance of current Jewish conceptions of messiahship and the repeated characterisation of his ministry as humble service. Our study is restricted to the sayings of Jesus but these should be understood against the wider background of the synoptic tradition concerning the servant character of his life and ministry.

The primitive Christian community soon came to understand and interpret the ministry of Jesus in terms of the suffering servant prophecies of Deutero-Isaiah (cf., e.g., Matt. 3.17; 12.18-21; Luke 22.37; John 12.38; 1 Pet. 2.22, 24-25), but whether or not this interpretation originated with Jesus himself has been the subject of an extended debate. Thirty years ago it had all but come to be regarded as an 'assured result' of scholarship that Jesus understood his ministry, in part at least, in terms of these prophecies. C. R. North could write: 'It is almost universally accepted that Jesus saw his way by the light that Isa. liii shed upon his predestined path', and many others have supported this view.[1] However, it has not gone unchallenged.[2] On the one hand, it has been asserted that 'the tradition of Jesus' sayings reveals no trace of a consciousness on his part of being the Servant of Isaiah 53',[3] and 'the fact that Jesus did suffer preceded the discovery of suitable prophecies.'[4] On the other hand, it has been noted that the *ebed Yahweh* title was no longer commonly used for Jesus in the early Church at the time when the synoptic gospels were written. This makes it 'all the more remarkable that not only Paul but also all three Synoptics in relating the story of the Last Supper recall that Jesus at this decisive moment ascribed to himself the role of *ebed Yahweh*,' thus suggesting that this tradition is of dominical origin.[5]

In the study of the sayings of Jesus which follows, it will be

argued that Jesus believed that the servant-prophecies of
Deutero-Isaiah found a fulfilment in his ministry. He spoke
often of his ministry as one of service and laid down the same
pattern for the ministry of his disciples. There are faint hints
that he regarded them as fellow-servants of God in whose
ministry the servant-prophecies would also find fulfilment, in
part at least.

JESUS, SERVANT OF GOD

The case for saying that Jesus drew on the servant-prophecies
of Deutero-Isaiah to interpret his ministry rests largely upon
conclusions drawn from the examination of the four passages
below. Besides these passages, many others have been suggested as dominical allusions to the servant-prophecies (e.g.,
Mark 2.20/Luke 5.35/Matt. 9.15b; Luke 11.22/Mark 3.27/
Matt. 12.29; Mark 14.8/Matt. 26.12; Luke 23.24; Matt. 11.28-
30; Matt. 11.2-6/Luke 7.18-23), but the so-called allusions are
far from obvious, so any consideration of them is omitted here.
However, the passion-predictions as a group do require some
special mention. Few scholars would want to deny that Jesus
spoke of his death, and most of those who reject the more
detailed predictions do accept that Jesus spoke of it in general
terms. Included in the passion-predictions there is occasionally
the note of fulfilment. Jesus says his death was in fulfilment of
the Scripture (cf. Mark 9.12b; Luke 22.37). It is difficult to
escape the conclusion that, more than any other Old Testament
passage, it was Isaiah 53 which spoke to Jesus of the inevitabil-
ity and significance of his death. But we have gone a little ahead
of ourselves, for it is just this that needs to be demonstrated by
the exegesis of the relevant passages.

Luke 22.37

The passage Luke 22.35-8 includes Jesus' enigmatic 'sword-
word' (v.36) and his assertion: 'I tell you that this scripture nust
be fulfilled in me, "And he was reckoned with the transgressors"; for what is written about me has its fulfilment' (v. 37).
Verse thirty-seven constitutes the only explicit reference to the
servant-prophecies of Deutero-Isaiah made by Jesus in the

synoptic gospels. It is thus of special importance for our present enquiry.

Lucan addition or authentic tradition? The general authenticity of Luke 22.35-8 has been argued above. Nevertheless, we need to respond to the suggestion that the quotation from Isaiah 53.12 is a later Lucan addition to the earlier Jesus-tradition. Even though there is evidence of Luke's editing in the passage, several considerations militate against this possibility. First, Luke himself never connects the suffering of Jesus with Isaiah 53; that connection is never made in editorial comment by the evangelist, as, for example, is the case in the gospel of Matthew (cf. 12.15-20). Second, the citation is not taken from the Septuagint but recalls the Hebrew text, and Luke shows no knowledge of Hebrew. The semitic nature of the quotation is seen in the use of *meta anomōn* (with transgressors) which is independent of the Septuagint's *en tois anomois* (among the transgressors) and nearer the Hebrew *ʾĕt pōšĕʿîm* (with transgressors). Third, Isaiah 53.12a is not an obvious passage to have been chosen by Luke if he wanted to connect Jesus' passion with the suffering servant of Deutero-Isaiah. There are far more obvious texts which could have been selected. Finally, the quotation itself is quite relevant to the historical context provided. To the disciples who, misunderstanding his preceding statement, had produced two swords, Jesus is saying that armed resistance is out of the question, for the prophecy must be fulfilled: 'He was numbered with the transgressors'.

The significance of the quotation. If we accept the reliability of the tradition in Luke 22.37, does that enable us to say that Jesus thought of his death and passion as a fulfilment of Isaiah 53? Barrett says no; the saying refers to nothing more than Jesus' crucifixion along with two evil-doers.[6] However, his interpretation fails to take sufficient note of the historical context, the eve of the crucifixion, when Jesus would be concerned with the significance of his imminent death. The fact that two criminals would die with him would not loom large in his thinking, if indeed he even knew about that beforehand. Barrett's interpretation would be valid if the quotation from Isaiah 53.12a were an addition to the original saying of Jesus *ex eventu*. However, the evidence against this is considerable.

In seeking to understand the significance of the quotation to

Jesus, we need to remember that the words immediately follow-ing constitute one of the clearest references to the climax of the servant's ministry: 'yet he bore the sin of many, and made intercession for the transgressors.' Knowing how Old Testa-ment themes permeated Jesus' thought, it is difficult to believe that he quoted Isaiah 53.12a without having in mind the climax of the servant's ministry which is so clearly expressed in Isaiah 53.12b.

Mark 9.12b/Matthew 17.12

The pericope Mark 9.11-13 contains the disciples' question, 'Why do the scribes say that first Elijah must come?' and Jesus' reply, 'Elijah does come first to restore all things; and how is it written of the Son of man, that he should suffer many things and be treated with contempt? But I tell you that Elijah has come, and they did to him whatever they pleased, as it is written of him.' This pericope is introduced abruptly after Mark's trans-figuration account (9.2-10) and the whole passage 9.1-13 is clearly a Marcan compilation. It has been suggested that 9.11-13 followed straight on from 9.1 in Mark's source, and that he is responsible for the introduction of the transfiguration account at this point.[7] In any case the connection between 9.2-10 and 9.11-13 is not obvious; they may have been placed together simply because Elijah is mentioned in both. It has also been suggested that 9.12b (which temporarily turns the read-er's attention away from Elijah to the Son of Man) is an interpolation, and that 9.13 is the proper continuation of 9.12a.[8] On the other hand, 9.11-13 can be interpreted to reveal a logical progression of thought in a question/answer sequence of which 9.12b forms an integral part. In response to the question about Elijah in 9.11 Jesus concedes that the contem-porary Jewish belief in the appearance of Elijah as the fore-runner of the messiah is correct (12a). However, he then reminds the disciples that *all* the Scriptures must be fulfilled—not only the prophecy concerning Elijah, but also that concern-ing the Son of Man (12b). Just as 'Elijah' has appeared already and been poorly treated (13), so too the Son of Man must 'suffer many things and be treated with contempt.'

A dominical allusion to the servant-prophecies. For our present purposes the major concern is not whether Mark 9.12b is an interpolation, but whether it can be regarded as dominical and whether it is correct to see in it an allusion to the servant-prophecies, in particular to Isaiah 53.3. Jeremias has argued persuasively that Jesus shared the contemporary Jewish belief which increasingly came to see the prophets as martyrs. Jesus believed that martyrdom in Jerusalem was part of the prophetic office (Luke 13.33), and endorsed the wisdom saying which saw the history of salvation as 'an unbroken chain of martyrdoms' of the righteous—from Abel to Zechariah (Matt. 23.35/Luke 11.50-51). At the end of that chain was John the Baptist with whose fate Jesus was acquainted ('they did to him whatever they pleased' [Mark 9.13]), and after John, came Jesus, who expected a fate no better for himself.[9]

The possible allusion to Isaiah 53.3 in Mark 9.12b has often been noted: Mark's *exoudenēthē* (be treated with contempt) recalls the *nibĕzeh* (he was despised) in Isaiah 53.3. However, if there is an allusion here, it does not rest on the Septuagint (which uses *ekleipon* to translate *nibĕzeh*). On the other hand, *exoudenoō* is the normal translation for *bāzâ* (to despise) and is used thus in the Septuagint at Psalm 22.6, and in the Greek translations of the Old Testament by Aquila, Symmachus and Theodotian at Isaiah 53.3. If there is an allusion here it rests on the Hebrew text. Therefore it could not have originated in the hellenistic church. It may have come from the pre-hellenistic church, but this is improbable because of the vagueness of the text's description of suffering.[10] Thus, if there is an allusion to Isaiah 53.3 in Mark 9.12b, the likelihood is that it is of dominical origin.

Mark 14.24/Matthew 26.28/Luke 22.20/1 Corinthians 11.25

Jesus' cup-saying uttered during the Last Supper is found in the three synoptic gospels and the first epistle of Paul to the Corinthians, the Pauline version being, of course, the earliest literary tradition of them all. The texts of the four versions run as follows:

(a) Mark 14.24   This is my blood of the covenant, which is poured out for many.

(b) Matt. 26.28   This is my blood of the covenant, which is poured out for many for the forgiveness of sins.

(c) Luke 22.20　　This cup which is poured out for you is the new covenant in my blood.

(d) 1 Cor. 11.25　This cup is the new covenant in my blood.

An examination of the four texts reveals close similarities between (a) and (b), and between (c) and (d). This suggests that there were two independent traditions circulating: the Marcan/Matthean tradition, and the Pauline/Lucan tradition. It seems clear that Matthew has taken over Mark's version and made the interpretative addition, 'for the forgiveness of sins'. The Pauline version is an earlier literary text than Luke's and it is debatable whether Luke 22.20 is part of a later insertion (19b-20) added to Luke's original account of the words of institution.[11] Whether it is original to Luke or not, it seems clear that it is dependent upon the Pauline account which it has slightly modified and to which the words 'which is poured out for you' have been added, possibly under the influence of the Marcan version.

The cup-saying: highly reliable Jesus-tradition. When we are dealing with the eucharistic words of Jesus, we are dealing with the best attested of all Jesus' sayings and we are in touch with the very bedrock of tradition. Paul indicates that he delivered this tradition to the Corinthians at the time of their conversion (1 Cor. 11.23) which may be dated about AD 50. But in 1 Corinthians 11.23 Paul says also that what he delivered to them was something which he himself had previously received from the Lord. Paul may mean that he received it as a revelation at the time of his conversion, or later, but his use of *paralambanein* (to receive)—a word used for the receiving of tradition (*paradosis*)—suggests that Paul received it as from the Lord through the church (in Antioch). If this was the case, the tradition as we have it in 1 Corinthians 11.25 could have found its present form in Antioch, where it was possibly in use as a liturgical formula. We can take one further step and say that, in this event, the content of the Antiochene form of the tradition was brought from Jerusalem to Antioch by those who first preached the gospel there at the time of the persecution following Stephen's martyrdom. On this reconstruction of events, the Pauline tradition would owe its form to liturgical use in Antioch and so can be dated about AD 40. However, the tradition itself is earlier, having been brought from Jerusalem. This puts the origin of the Pauline saying back into the thirties.

If we compare the Marcan/Matthean version with the Pauline/Lucan version, it seems clear that, although the latter is the earlier literary text, the former is in fact the older tradition. We say this because the Marcan/Matthean version still retains the words, 'this is my blood,' which in Gentile ears would arouse revulsion, being associated with 'a dark animistic abomination'. These words have been modified in the Pauline version to the less offensive 'this cup is the new covenant in my blood.' If the Pauline version can be traced back in its literary form to AD 40, then most likely we have in Mark a tradition whose form was already determined in the late thirties. There is good reason, therefore, to believe that in Mark 14.24 we have the *ipsissima vox* of Jesus. However, if we do not want to go that far, we must still reckon with the fact that we have two traditions, the nuclei of which are essentially the same, and both of which can be traced back to the thirties. There would seem to be no valid reason for rejecting the dominical character of the substance of the tradition. The case is further strengthened when it is remembered that the drinking of human blood was even more abhorrent to Jews than to Gentiles, being forbidden in the Mosaic law. Therefore, a saying which could be misunderstood to mean just that cannot be attributed to the Jerusalem church itself.

For the purposes of the following discussion it will therefore be assumed that (1) Mark 14.24 is the earliest form of the saying, and (2) it is highly reliable Jesus-tradition, if not *ipsissima vox*.

Allusions to Isaiah 53. There are three main emphases in the saying. First, that the cup of wine symbolises Jesus' blood to be shed, second, that the shedding of his blood is related to the establishing of the (new) covenant, and third, that the shedding of his blood was for many/you.

There seem to be in Mark 14.24 echoes of Exodus 24.1-8, the account of the making of the covenant at Sinai, where Moses says: 'Behold the blood of the covenant which the Lord has made with you . . .' (8). There also appear to be echoes of Jeremiah 31.31-4, the promise of the new covenant which the Lord would make with Israel in the last days. Further, it has been argued that there is an allusion to Isaiah 53 in Mark 14.24.

All four versions of the cup-saying contain ideas both of representation and of covenant, and this suggests a direct link with Isaiah 53 where these are the two main concepts associated with the servant-figure. In addition, the blood 'poured out' in Mark 14.24 recalls Isaiah 53.12: 'He poured out his soul' (*he'ĕrâ . . . napĕšô*).

All these so-called allusions to Isaiah 53 are questioned by Hooker. First, the reference to the 'blood of the covenant', she says, was probably lifted straight out of Exodus 24.8 and, therefore, Mark 14.24 should be regarded as a deliberate contrasting of the old Mosaic covenant with the new covenant to be established in Jesus' blood. Thus the covenant idea in Mark 14.24 owes little, if anything, to Deutero-Isaiah. Second, the word *ekchunō* is used in the Septuagint to translate *šāpak* (to pour out), and neither word has any connection with the idea expressed in Isaiah 53.12. Finally, commenting on *pollōn* (many) she says there is no reason to associate it with the *rabbim* (many) of Isaiah 53.[12]

It has to be conceded that, taken separately, the use of the covenant idea, *ekchunnomenon*, and *pollōn* in Mark 14.24 cannot prove dependence on Isaiah 53. However, the concepts do not stand on their own. They are brought together into one saying and the confluence of the three ideas constitutes strong evidence for an allusion to Isaiah 53 where the same three ideas are found together. It is the cumulative character of the evidence which makes the case for a dominical allusion to Isaiah 53 in Mark 14.24 so strong. It seems fairly clear, therefore, that in Mark 14.24 and its parallels we are in touch with Jesus' own understanding of his ministry, at the heart of which was the belief that his vicarious suffering/death for the many would establish the (new) covenant. To express these things, Jesus drew not only from Exodus 24 and possibly Jeremiah 31, but also from Isaiah 53. The significance of this will be discussed at the end of the next sub-section, and in the conclusions of this chapter.

Mark 10.45/Matthew 20.28/Luke 22.27

The tradition in which Jesus reminds his disciples that he came among them not to be served but to serve is preserved in two forms in the synoptic gospels. The first, Mark 10.45/ Matthew 20.28, forms the climax of Jesus' response to the indignant Ten after the sons of Zebedee sought the places of honour when Jesus should come in his glory. The second, Luke 22.27, is the final thrust of Jesus' rebuke to his disciples when they were discussing which of them should be the greatest. The two forms of the tradition run: Mark 10.45: The Son of Man also came not to be served but to serve, and to give his life as a ransom for many. Luke 22.27: But I am among you as one who serves.

The Lucan form is obviously the simpler of the two and for this reason Mark 10.45 has frequently been regarded as a later expansion of Luke 22.27—'heavily freighted with dogmatic import.' This asumes that there is dependence between them, but they could be independent literary versions derived from the same group of logia (Mark 10.42-5; Luke 22.24-7). Jeremias has shown that both versions derive from Palestinian tradition, and that Luke, more than Mark, shows accommodation to Greek ideas (e.g., *euergetēs* [25], *ho neōteros*, *ho hēgoumenos*, *ho diakonōn* [26]).[13]

The authenticity of Mark 10.45. Apart from the assertion that Mark 10.45 is a later expansion of Luke 22.27, there have been other serious doubts regarding its authenticity, especially concerning 10.45b ('and to give his life as a ransom for many'). Thus it has been asserted: (1) It is coloured by Pauline theology, or at least by the later doctrine of the Church. (2) In none of the other synoptic sayings is the concept of the giving of life for the salvation of others connected with the Son of Man. (3) The idea of serving does not need the supplementary element from Isaiah 53, as Luke 22.27 proves. (4) The notion of ransom is alien to the context; it introduces something which is in tension with the train of thought in Mark 10.43-5a.[14]

In response it may be noted: (1) The Pauline influence is more imagined than real. Paul, for instance, never uses the key word *lutron* (ransom), though the cognate *antilutron* is found once, and *apolutrōsis* (redemption) seven times in the Pauline letters. There is a parallel to Mark 10.45 in 1 Timothy 2.6, but, as we have seen already, this is clearly secondary to the Marcan text. (2) Although the use of the title 'Son of Man' in Mark 10.45 may be secondary, the fact that the giving of life for others is connected with this title only in Mark 10.45 is insufficient proof of inauthenticity. Frequency of occurrence is the weakest of the criteria for authenticity. (3) The objection that Mark 10.45b introduces an alien idea into the context is more serious, but if there is an allusion to Isaiah 53.11–12 then it is quite to be expected that the ideas of service and vicarious suffering may be run together. Even without postulating an allusion to that prophecy, however, good sense can be made of the passage. After teaching his disciples the importance of humble service by referring to the servant character of his ministry, Jesus reinforces the lesson with the concrete example of his ultimate act of self-giving: his own life given as a ransom for many. (4) It should be noted that Mark 10.45 says little more than what is clearly implied by Jesus' cup-saying. Thus, if we accept the latter as authentic, we should not hesitate to accept the authenticity of the substance of the former.

The case for authenticity would be strengthened if it could be shown that there is here an allusion to Isaiah 53 (where the ideas of servanthood and vicarious suffering are brought together), and it is this complex problem which we must now consider.

Allusions to Isaiah 53: objections. The earlier consensus of opinion that Mark 10.45 contains clear allusions to Isaiah 53.11-12 is based on several observations. The statement that the Son of Man came to *serve* recalls the ministry of Deutero-Isaiah's servant. The phrase, *to give his life*, and the metaphor of *ransom* recall the self-surrender and vicarious death of the servant of the Lord. The words *for many* find a counterpart in Isaiah 53.11-12 where the word *many* is found no less than three times.[15]

Serious objections have been raised against this view. Both Hooker and Barrett have examined the so-called verbal parallels and conclude that the evidence is not as unambiguous as previously thought. First, the ideas of *service* found in Mark 10.45 and in Isaiah 53 are different. What is emphasised in Isaiah 53 is service to Yahweh, whereas the emphasis in Mark 10.45 is on lowly service to men. Second, though it cannot be denied that the expression *to give his life* finds a linguistic parallel in Isaiah 53.12, the expression 'to give one's life a ransom' was also current among Jews, being used in reference to the Maccabean martyrs. Third, the connection customarily seen between *lutron* (ransom) in Mark 10.45 and *'āsām* ('sin offering') in Isaiah 53.10 rests on no good evidence. 'The *'āsām*, was never a substitute: it was repayment, together with compensation and guilt-offering.' In the Septuagint the word *lutron* is never used to render *'āsām* or any of its cognates. It is a technical term for purchase money, never a sacrificial term. Further, the cognate *lutroō* (to ransom) is used frequently to translate *gā'al* (to redeem) and *pādâ* (to ransom) in Deutero-Isaiah, but in passages that speak of God as redeemer where the primary thought is of historical acts of deliverance; forgiveness of sins, if found at all, is quite secondary. Fourth, the words 'for many' (*anti pollōn*) will not bear the weight of argument that is sometimes placed upon them. *Anti* is bound up with *lutron* simply because the word *lutron* demands an *anti* to follow, and the fact that the fourth servant-song uses the word *many* several times is not all that significant. The Hebrew *rabbim* (many) and the Greek *polus* (many) are, after all, common words in their respective languages. Finally, the logion says it was the *Son of Man* who came to serve and give his life as a ransom. If Jesus was thinking of the Deutero-Isaianic servant, why did he use the title 'Son of Man'?[16]

Arguments for allusions to Isaiah 53. Several comments can be made in response to these arguments of Barrett and Hooker. First, in his treatment of the words *to give his life* and their possible parallel in Isaiah 53, Barrett discusses Isaiah 53.12 (he poured out his soul) but ignores Isaiah 53.10 (he makes himself an offering for sin) which can be regarded as a parallel to the Marcan expression. Second, there *are* in fact uses of *'āsām* in the Old Testament where a substitutionary connotation seems present (e.g., Lev. 5.17-19), and it is translated as *lutrōsis* by Aquila in several places (e.g., Lev. 5.18, 25; 7.1). Further, the universal character of the ransom saying sets it apart from all similar expressions in later Judaism. On the one hand, the Jews never interpret the servant-songs as referring to their martyrs, and, on the other hand, the giving of the lives of the martyrs as a ransom was always of limited application: to atone for Israel and to maintain the validity of the covenant. Finally, if we consider the various elements 'to serve', 'to give his life', 'ransom' and 'for many' separately, it is impossible to prove direct dependence upon Isaiah 53. However, the cumulative effect of so many suggestive words and phrases all with parallels in Isaiah 53 makes it almost certain that Mark 10.45 alludes to that servant-prophecy. It is the fact that 'Mark x.45 sums up the general thought in Isa liii of vicarious death and sacrifice for sin' which constitutes the real basis for the view that the background of Mark 10.45 is to be sought in Isaiah 53.[17]

Concluding our discussion of Mark 10.45, we may say the arguments for authenticity are at least as weighty as those against it, and, likewise, the arguments in support of an allusion to Isaiah 53 are as strong as, if not stronger than, those to the contrary. What definitely tips the scales in favour of both authenticity and the allusion to Isaiah 53 is the existence of those other texts examined already (Luke 22.37; Mark 9.12b and parallels) which also point in the same direction. It is the cumulative effect of all these texts which strongly suggests that Jesus was aware of the servant character of his ministry, and that he knew and used the servant-prophecies of Deutero-Isaiah. In addition, Mark 10.45 indicates what servanthood meant to Jesus. It meant both lowly service rendered to mankind and a vicarious death on its behalf. Jesus' reference to the vicarious character of his death is tantalising. Mark 10.45, as we have seen above, alludes to Isaiah 53, where substitutionary ideas are clearly present. There the servant bears two things on behalf of others: their sins and the punishment which resulted upon them.[18] Just to what extent these ideas influenced Jesus' understanding of the significance of his death it is impossible to say, though, obviously, if Mark 10.45 does allude to Isaiah 53, some influence must be expected.

THE SERVANTHOOD OF JESUS' DISCIPLES

The sayings of Jesus addressed to his disciples concerning the servant character of their ministry contain no obvious allusions to the servant-passages in Deutero-Isaiah. But there are one or two hints that Jesus may have understood their ministry as well to be a fulfilment of those prophecies. Jesus' sayings, for the most part, speak not of the disciples' status or function as servants. The emphasis falls, on the one hand, upon the servant attitude which should prevail in the disciples' relationships with each other, and on the other hand, upon the fact that, as servants of Jesus, they can expect no better fate than his.

Before we examine the relevant sayings, brief mention needs to be made of the parables of Jesus. Many of these include references to servants and masters. The parables generally teach about the kingdom of God. However, each parable builds in its own way upon the fact that servants are expected to be faithful to their masters and in the execution of their appointed tasks. Men are depicted as either good/faithful or wicked/ unfaithful servants of God. It is to his disciples as those who would be faithful servants of God that Jesus gives his teaching about the servant attitude which must prevail in their mutual relationships and the warning that their fate would be as his.

Matthew 10.24-5/Luke 6.40

The text of Matthew 10.24-5 says: 'A disciple is not above his teacher, nor a servant above his master; it is enough for the disciple to be like his teacher, and the servant like his master. If they have called the master of the house Beelzebul, how much more will they malign those of his household.'

Matthew 10.24a (a disciple is not above his teacher) finds an exact parallel in Luke 6.40a, which has no historical context, but is not found in Mark, thus indicating the use of Q tradition. Matthew 10.24b (nor a servant above his master) is in parallel with Matthew 10.24a, and with it forms a double-sided saying which Matthew probably took over from the Q tradition. (In this case Luke 6.40a would be an abbreviated form of the Q saying—shortened, possibly, to achieve good parallelism with 6.40b.) Matthew 10.24 has parallels in John 13.16 and 15.20, suggesting that the saying circulated widely as an independent unit of tradition. Matthew 10.25a ('it is enough for the disciple to be like his teacher, and the servant like his master') appears to be an adaptation of a Jewish proverb ('it is enough for a slave if he is as his master'),[19] and could have been added later to the saying in verse twenty-four. The latter part of verse twenty-five ('if they have called the master of the house Beelzebul, how much more will they malign those of his household') is found only in Matthew.

It is doubtful whether Matthew 10.24-5 was originally a

single utterance of Jesus; it appears, rather, to be a Matthean compilation of separate units of tradition. Nevertheless, there is little reason to doubt that the pericope rests upon reliable Jesus-tradition. The allusion to the Beelzebul insult in verse twenty-five could have originated only in a Palestinian milieu. While its retention in Matthew probably indicates that healing and exorcisms were continuing phenomena in the Matthean community (which, as a result, was subject to abuse), the original life-setting of the saying is to be sought in the ministry of Jesus. His exorcisms, and the charges brought against him as a result, are absolutely basic to the synoptic tradition and the authenticity of this element of the tradition is almost universally recognised (see discussion in Chapter 5 below). That Jesus should allude to these charges in his instructions to his disciples is to be expected. Further, the whole pericope Matthew 10.24-5 represents such a reversal of Jewish expectations concerning the dignity and destiny of the messiah and his people that the substance of this tradition could have originated only with Jesus himself.

The significance of Matthew 10.24-5 and parallels. The significance of this saying is that it shows that Jesus saw that his followers were related to him as disciples to their teacher/rabbi, but with this difference: their discipleship was not a transitional stage leading on to the time when they themselves became teachers in their own right. Even the proverb, 'It is enough for the disciple to be like his teacher', is used, not to signify 'the promotion of the disciples to the rank of their teacher, but refers to the readiness to bear the same abuse which the teacher and master encountered, and to accept it as a mark of supreme distinction'.[20] In addition, Matthew 10.45 reveals that it was not only the disciple/teacher but also the servant/master model which Jesus regarded as appropriate to express one aspect of his disciples' relationship to him. Most important of all, both these figures and the allusion to the Beelzebul insult are used to emphasise that the ministry and destiny of the disciples would follow the pattern of his own. If he suffered, so would they. Schweizer goes further and says that the metaphor 'of the servant or slave and his lord suggests the Old Testament use of "servants of God" as a term of honor for the prophets, and possibly even the eschatological Servant of God (Isaiah 53).'[21]

The suggestion is attractive, but corroborating evidence would be needed before we could confidently interpret the passage in that way.

Mark 10.42-5/Matthew 20.25-8/Luke 22.25-7

In Mark (and Matthew which follows Mark here) this passage constitutes Jesus' response to the indignation of the Ten after James and John had requested the places of honour when Jesus should come into his glory. In Luke it represents Jesus' rebuke to the Twelve when they were discussing among themselves which of them should be greatest. As we have already seen, Luke shows signs of accommodation to the Greek way of thinking at this point; the Marcan/Matthean tradition is thus to be regarded as the older version. However, the substance of the tradition is the same in both versions and includes Jesus' command that, although the rulers of the nations lorded it over their subjects, it was not to be so among his disciples. Among them, the one wishing to be greatest should be servant of all, for even the Son of Man 'came not to be served but to serve, and give his life as a ransom for many.'

Mark 10.45 and its special problems have been treated above. In contrast to Mark 10.45, the preceding verses 42ff. have rarely been regarded as inauthentic tradition; Bultmann lists the verses as a dominical saying.[22]

Mark 10.42-5 consists of three basic elements: first, the reference to the exercise of power by the rulers of the nations— how they lord it over their subjects—and the warning that this must not be so among Jesus' followers. Second, the positive statement that whoever wishes to be great or first should be the servant of all. Third, this pattern of true greatness is laid upon Jesus' disciples because even the Son of Man came not to be ministered to, like some worldly potentate, but to serve others.

The importance of Mark 10.42-5 and parallels. The significance of this logion is that it shows clearly how Jesus demanded a reversal of contemporary standards, insisting that humble service was to be the hallmark of true greatness among his followers. This pathway to true greatness they must tread because the one they followed trod the same pathway before them.

If, in the discussion of Mark 10.45 above, we were correct in concluding that there is an allusion to Isaiah 53 in this saying, perhaps we should also conclude that, in making his servant ministry the pattern for his disciples, Jesus was suggesting that the servant-prophecies of Deutero-Isaiah would find (limited) fulfilment in their ministries as well. At best this can only be taken as a hint in that direction—again, corroborating evidence is needed before the passage could be interpreted in this way.

Matthew 23.11

In Matthew 23.11 there is preserved in another context the saying: 'He who is greatest among you shall be your servant.' Apparently this saying was a widely circulating and independent unit of tradition. Here it forms part of the climax of Jesus' warning to the disciples not to model their ministries on the ministries of the contemporary Pharisees, who loved to be called rabbi (Matt. 23.7). That this pride of status was an ever present temptation (and failing) among students of the Law is amply illustrated by the repeated warnings in the rabbinic writings.[23]

This admonition is recorded only in Matthew (23.8-10). Nevertheless, its authenticity is rarely questioned. Whether the saying in verse 11 followed historically that of verses 8-10 is debatable. As we have already noted, the saying appears to have circulated as an independent unit of tradition, and its inclusion here may be due to Matthew's redaction. On the other hand, it is quite appropriate in its Matthean setting, and we have to allow for the possibility that the saying was not only oft-repeated in the early Christian communities, but that it was uttered on various occasions in different connections by Jesus himself.

Mark 9.35

Here in Mark 9.35 the saying about true greatness is found once again. Its insertion at this point is somewhat awkward: verse thirty-three indicates that Jesus and his disciples were already talking together in the house, but the saying in verse thirty-five is introduced with the words: 'And he sat down and called the twelve'. There is no textual evidence to suggest that it is a later interpolation. It seems, therefore, to be clearly a case of Marcan redaction. The independent logion is inserted into the dialogue to express the principle underlying the exchange between Jesus and his disciples that Mark is reporting.

The incident itself (in response to the disciples' concern to know which of them should be greatest, Jesus set a child in their midst and reminded them that true greatness means humble service, a readiness to serve the insignificant) is recorded in Mark 9.33-7, Luke 9.46-8, and Matthew 18.1-5. Only in Mark is the saying found in this context, further suggesting that its presence here is due to Marcan redaction. However, as we have already noted, there is little doubt that the saying itself rests on reliable Jesus-tradition.

CONCLUSIONS

Despite serious questions raised by Barrett, Hooker and others, a careful examination of the relevant texts has led to the conclusion that the servant-sayings of Jesus do betray the influence of the Deutero-Isaianic servant-prophecies, and that these prophecies did influence Jesus' understanding of his ministry and death.

If Jesus saw his ministry as the fulfilment of the servant-prophecies, it must be added that for him this did not imply so much a special status as a commitment to self-giving service to others. He served the Lord by serving men. This service was given concrete expression, as Luke shows, in lowly table service rendered to his own disciples, and supremely, as Mark reminds us, in the giving of his own life as a ransom for many.

It seemed justifiable to say that both Jesus' ransom-saying and his words of institution are to be understood against the background of Isaiah 53, where substitutionary ideas are clearly in evidence. It would be wrong to try to build a theory of atonement upon these allusions, but it would be equally wrong to overlook the influence of the leading ideas of Isaiah 53 upon Jesus' understanding of the significance of his death.

Jesus spoke of the disciples as *his* servants; the master/servant relationship adequately expresses one important aspect of the relationship existing between Jesus and his followers. As his servants, Jesus expected them to follow the pattern of ministry which he provided. They must be prepared for lowly service to men/one another. They must be ready also to share his fate. The Jewish proverb applies: 'It is enough for a slave if he is as his master.'

If Jesus made the servant-character of his ministry the pattern for his disciples' ministry, and if he regarded it as inevitable that they also would endure sufferings as he did, we are prompted to ask whether he expected the servant-prophecies of Deutero-Isaiah to find fulfilment in their ministries as well. Although there are clear indications that Jesus believed that the servant-prophecies found fulfilment in his ministry, nowhere are there hints that he understood them to be fulfilled in his ministry alone. There is, therefore, no reason why he should not have expected the prophecies to find fulfilment in the ministry of his disciples as well.[24] This would mean that Jesus viewed the disciples not only as his servants, but also as fellow-servants of God together with him. This is not to suggest Jesus taught that his disciples' sufferings and death would have the same vicarious efficacy as his. There is, of course, no hint in any of the sayings of Jesus that this could be the case. However, although vicarious suffering was the climax of Jesus' servant-hood, it was by no means the full extent of it. In those other aspects of ministry and sufferings, Jesus said, his disciples would share.[25]

CHAPTER FIVE

JESUS AND THE SPIRIT

All four evangelists portray Jesus as a unique man of the Spirit. This may be seen in the way in which they associate the various phases of his life with the Spirit. In the birth narratives, Mary is overshadowed by the Spirit (Luke 1.35), and Jesus himself becomes Emmanuel, God with us, because he is conceived by the Spirit (Matt. 1.20-23). Jesus' baptism by John in the Jordan and the Spirit's descent upon him at that time is recorded in all four gospels. For Mark this is the beginning of the gospel (1.1-11), and in John, the Baptist recognises Jesus as the Spirit-baptizer because it was upon him that the Spirit descended and remained (1.32-3). Following his baptism, the three synoptic gospels record, Jesus was driven by the Spirit into the wilderness to be tempted by the Devil (Mark 1.2; Matt. 4.1; Luke 4.1). After the temptation he returned to Galilee in the power of the Spirit to begin his public ministry (Luke 4.14). Both Luke and Matthew show, by explicit quotations from Isaiah (Luke 4.18-21/Isa. 61.1; Matt. 12.17-21/Isa. 42.1-4), that the ministry of Jesus was carried out in the power of the Spirit. Jesus' exorcisms are presented as proof of his Spirit-empowerment, and to attribute these to the power of Beelzebul is to commit the unforgivable sin of blasphemy against the Holy Spirit (Mark 3.22-30; Matt. 12.22-32; Luke 11.14-23). The promise of the Spirit's help for the disciples in time of trial is attributed to Jesus by all three synoptic evangelists (Mark 13.11; Matt. 10.20; Luke 12.12), and in the long paraclete-sayings in the fourth gospel (14.15-17, 25-6; 15.26; 16.7-15). In Matthew we find a trinitarian baptismal formula on the lips of the risen Jesus (28.19), and in Luke-Acts the resurrected Jesus promises the outpouring of the Spirit upon his disciples (Luke 24.49; Acts 1.5, 8). Finally, Acts describes Jesus' post-resurrection teaching as commandment given 'through the Holy Spirit to the apostles' (1.2).

This abundance of material concerning Jesus and the Spirit in the gospel tradition stands in stark contrast to the paucity of the dominical sayings about the Spirit in the synoptic gospels. Even the few sayings of Jesus that are found in the Synoptics have frequently been regarded as secondary tradition.[1]

Barrett devoted the final chapter in *The Holy Spirit and the Gospel Tradition* to a discussion of possible reasons for the paucity of dominical references to the Spirit in the synoptic gospels. He concludes that Jesus avoided speaking of the Spirit because he wanted to keep his messiahship secret. In the contemporary and popular Jewish mind the messiah was to be the bearer of God's Spirit (cf. 1 Enoch 49.3; Pss. Sol. 17.42; Zadokite Fragments 2.10; T. Levi 18.2-14; T. Jud. 24.2f.). Thus, too clear a claim to be the bearer of the Spirit would nullify Jesus' efforts to keep his messiahship veiled.[2] Barrett's suggestion may well be correct. However, the aim of our study is not to explain why there are few Spirit-utterances, but to examine the few there are to see what can be learnt from them.

It is clear that the examination of the case for the authenticity of the few Spirit-sayings will be vital. Conclusions reached at that point will determine whether there is any justification for speaking about Jesus' understanding of the role of the Spirit in his own ministry and the ministry of his followers.

We turn first to a study of the synoptic sayings of Jesus concerning the role of the Spirit in his own ministry.

JESUS, BEARER OF THE SPIRIT

Mark begins his 'gospel of Jesus Christ, (the Son of God)' with an account of the activities of John the Baptist and Jesus' baptism. For Mark the baptism of Jesus, or rather the phenomena attending it—the heavenly voice and the descent of the Spirit—distinguish Jesus as the long-awaited messiah. The voice from heaven using words drawn from Psalm 2.7 with its messianic overtones, and from Isaiah 42.1, one of the servant-passages of Deutero-Isaiah, acclaims Jesus as the messiah, while the Spirit empowers him for his messianic task.

As we have already noted, all four gospels have an account of the baptism of Jesus and the descent of the Spirit upon him at that time, but the inclusion of such an account in the fourth gospel is particularly significant. That John, despite his high Christology, should include it, is strong evidence for the historical reliability of the tradition.

It is against the background of this strong tradition that the few synoptic Spirit-sayings of Jesus must be examined.

Matthew 12.28/Luke 11.20

In this saying the significance of Jesus' exorcisms is stated: 'If it is by the Spirit of God that I cast out demons, then the kingdom of God has come (*ephthasen*) upon you.' That Jesus' ministry included exorcisms has been recognised, in recent years, as belonging to the very bedrock of the Jesus-tradition. The reliability of that tradition can no longer be doubted.[3] The authenticity of Matthew 12.28 is likewise universally accepted.[4]

In both Matthew and Luke the saying is set in the context of a controversy with Jews concerning the power by which Jesus casts out demons. The Jews' charge is that Jesus exorcises by the power of Beelzebul. Jesus counters by saying that a kingdom divided against itself cannot stand and Satan would not be so foolish as to fight against his own forces. Thus Jesus' hearers have to face up to the only other conclusion: if it is not by Beelzebul, then, as our saying asserts, it is by the power of God, and that means the eschatological age has broken through upon them. The section closes with the strong man saying, by which the significance of Jesus' exorcisms is further explained.

The grouping of these various sayings is probably to be traced back to the Q tradition, to which Luke seems to adhere more closely than Matthew—Matthew appears to conflate Q with Marcan material here. Matthew 12.28/Luke 11.20 is probably a detached saying which was handed down without historical context, and then grouped together in Q with the other sayings now associated with it in Matthew 12.22-30/Luke 11.14-23. Even so, we would need to postulate a life-setting like that provided in Matthew and Luke, for the saying itself presupposes a preceding exorcism.

'Spirit of God' or *'finger of God'?* Despite the close verbal correspondence between the Matthean and Lucan versions of our saying, there is one quite significant difference. Matthew has: 'if it is by the Spirit of God (*en pneumati theou*) that I cast out

demons', whereas Luke has: 'if it is by the finger of God (*en daktulō theou*) that I cast out demons.' It is almost universally held that the Lucan 'finger of God' is the earlier form. The main reasons for this opinion are: (1) Luke, who throughout his writings shows such interest in the role of the Spirit, would not alter an original 'Spirit of God' to 'finger of God' and so remove a valuable dominical reference to the Spirit. (2) An alteration of 'finger of God' to 'Spirit of God' in Matthew can be more readily explained. Matthew wanted to prepare the way for what follows: the saying about blasphemy against the Holy Spirit, the sin which the Jews were in danger of committing because they ascribed Jesus' exorcisms to Beelzebul.

In recent times some doubts have been expressed concerning the priority of the Lucan version. It has been noted that 'by the finger of God' is an authentic Old Testament expression (cf. Exod. 8.19; Deut. 9.10) but this does not necessarily indicate that it represents the original form.[5] Beasley-Murray writes:

> It is obvious that Lk. 11.20 echoes the dictum of the Egyptian magicians recorded in Ex. 8.19; it is therefore at least possible that Luke knew the form of the saying as reproduced in Mt. 12.28, and that he modified the wording so as to recall the Exodus narrative, just as he was to do in his reproduction of the eschatological discourse, 21.15.[6]

Beasley-Murray adheres to the 'usual interpretation of the evidence' using the *lectio difficilior potior* principle as his guide, but adds that the other alternative should not be ignored.

Dunn lists several considerations which, for him, 'tip the scales in favour of "Spirit".' First, the fact that the Matthean version has 'kingdom of God' and not 'kingdom of heaven' suggests that Matthew has not modified his source at this point. Second, Matthew's tendency to emphasise parallels between Jesus and Moses would make it unlikely that he would change an original 'finger of God' to 'Spirit of God' because the former is such a clear allusion to Moses' ministry (Exod. 8.19). Third, it is possible that Luke, despite his obvious interest in the Spirit, could have changed an original 'Spirit of God' to 'finger of God' in the interests of his exodus typology.[7]

C. S. Rodd questions the widely held view that Luke shows a greater interest in the Spirit than Matthew. He points out that, infancy narratives aside, Matthew and Luke have the same number of references to the Spirit. Further, an examination of the way Matthew and Luke treat the six Marcan references to the Spirit shows that Matthew includes all the sayings on the whole in the context of their surrounding material and on one occasion includes both the Marcan and the Q form of the saying. Luke, on the other hand, deletes one mention of the Spirit and on two occasions either conflates with Q, prefers Q, or transfers the saying to another context. An examination of the Q sayings indicates that Luke sometimes adds references to the Spirit (cf., e.g., Luke 11.13/Matt. 7.11; Luke 10.21/Matt. 11.25). All the evidence, then, shows that Matthew stays close to his sources, and in the passages examined *never* adds references to the Spirit. Luke, however, both adds and *deletes* references to the Spirit. We ought to conclude, therefore, that Matthew 12.28 rather than Luke 11.20 probably preserves the original from the Q saying.[8]

The various arguments listed above call for a decision in favour of 'Spirit' as the word used in the original form of the Q saying, but, of course, this does not tell us which of the two words represents that used in the original saying of Jesus. In the final analysis the point may be purely academic, because the sense of both is the same. As Windisch says, even if, in the saying about the kingdom in Matthew 12.28/Luke 11.20, the expression 'by the finger of God' should be original, nevertheless, it must denote an organ of power that belongs to the sphere of the Holy Spirit.[9] This has been put in stronger terms by Beasley-Murray: 'It is high time that ungrudging recognition was given to the fact that Matthew's rendering is a correct translation equivalent, and that it represents what Jesus really had in mind.'[10]

The importance of the saying. The implications of Matthew 12.28 par. for our present enquiry are: (1) Jesus had a clear consciousness of the effective power of the Spirit at work in him. (2) He regarded this power as evidence that the Kingdom of God was making itself felt through his ministry.[11] It is interesting to note that Matthew clearly intended his readers to see the healings and exorcisms of Jesus as the result of his anointing with the Spirit. In the immediately preceding passage, Matthew 12.15-21, he says the promise of the Spirit made to the servant in

Isaiah 42.1-4 found fulfilment in Jesus, his healing ministry being the evidence for this. It is a fact that the primitive Christian community very early understood Jesus' ministry in terms of the Spirit-anointed servant, and such an application of Old Testament scriptures could well have originated with Jesus himself.[12]

Brief comment is required here upon the significance of Jesus' sayings about the strong man and the unforgivable sin. As we have seen, the saying concerning the strong man is grouped together with Matthew 12.28 par. in both Matthew and Luke. The saying about the unforgivable sin is found with the strong man saying in Mark (3.27-9) and Matthew, but in Luke (12.10) it has a different setting: in a cluster of sayings without historical context.

Like Matthew 12.28 par., both the strong man saying and the unforgivable sin sayings are best understood against the background of Jesus' ministry, more especially the controversy which arose because of his exorcisms.[13] The strong man saying indicates that Jesus realised that the final battle had already been joined because the demons were being routed by the powerful Spirit of God which was at work in him. The saying about the unforgivable sin underlines again that Jesus knew his exorcisms were effected by the power of the Spirit, and that this fact was of immeasurable importance. It was one thing to criticise Jesus himself, but to perceive the power of the Spirit at work in him and attribute that to Beelzebul was unforgivable. That this was regarded by Jesus as an unforgivable sin suggests a consciousness on his part of a unique relationship to the Spirit: 'Here we see coming to clear expression Jesus' sense of the awfulness, the numinous quality, the eschatological finality of the power which possessed him.'[14]

Luke 4.16-30

This passage has already been discussed at some length above where the problem of its authenticity was dealt with. It was concluded there that, despite its programmatic function in Luke's gospel, there are still good reasons to believe that it rests upon reliable Jesus-tradition.

The great significance of the passage for this part of our study lies in the quotation from Isaiah 61.1 which it contains. As was noted in the previous discussion of the passage, the Isaiah 61.1 prophecy significantly influenced Jesus' understanding of his ministry. The concepts of that prophecy underlie some of the beatitudes. When Jesus said, 'Blessed are the poor . . . blessed are those who mourn . . .', he clearly had in mind a group of people similar to those mentioned in Isaiah 61.1. An allusion to the same prophecy may be heard in Jesus' response to the Baptist's enquiry through his disciples:

> Go and tell what you hear and see: the blind receive their sight and the lame walk, lepers are cleansed and the deaf hear, and the dead are raised up, and the poor have good news preached to them. And blessed is he who takes no offence at me (Matt. 11.4-6).

The following conclusions can be drawn: (1) Jesus believed that his own anointing with the Spirit was in fulfilment of Isaiah 61.1. (2) He believed that this anointing marked him out as the one who was to proclaim the arrival of end-time blessings as proleptic manifestations of the kingdom of God. (3) Jesus interpreted his anointing as evidence, not only that he was the prophet of the end-time, but that he was also the one through whose ministry its blessings were then becoming available.

THE SPIRIT AND JESUS' DISCIPLES

The synoptic sayings of Jesus concerning the Spirit's relationship to the disciples, like those concerning the role of the Spirit in his own ministry, are few indeed, and have likewise been regarded as secondary tradition. The first of these sayings which we must take up is the promise of help in time of trial.

Mark 13.11/Matthew 10.20/Luke 12.12; 21.15

That Jesus promised his disciples assistance in time of trial and persecution is so widely attested in the gospel tradition that its authenticity can hardly be doubted.[15] Besides the synoptic logia discussed in this sub-section, there are the Johannine sayings promising assistance (14.15-17; 15.18-27; 16.1-11).

The promise is found in four forms in the synoptic gospels. In each case the disciples are told not to be concerned about, or to premeditate how they will answer/defend themselves because it will be given them in that hour what they should say. The four forms are:

Mark 13.11 For it is not you who speak but the Holy Spirit.
Matt. 10.20 For it is not you who speak, but the Spirit of your Father speaking through you.
Luke 12.12 For the Holy Spirit will teach you in that very hour what you ought to say
Luke 21.15 For I will give you a mouth and wisdom, which none of your adversaries will be able to withstand or contradict.

The relationship between the various forms of the saying is difficult to determine. Matthew and Mark are similar, but in place of Mark's more usual 'Holy Spirit' Matthew has the unique expression, 'the Spirit of your Father', which probably indicates that Matthew's version is the earlier of the two. Both Lucan forms of the saying differ significantly from the Matthean/Marcan version, more especially Luke 21.15 which contains no reference to the Spirit, and in which Jesus himself becomes the one who gives the assistance. To assign the various versions of the saying to their sources would be very difficult (if at all possible). What concerns us more is which form of the saying is to be regarded as the earliest.

The earliest form of the saying. It is probably right to regard Matthew 10.20 as earlier than Mark 13.11, but what about Luke 21.15 which has no reference to the Spirit? Barrett says that Luke 21.15 is the earliest form of the saying precisely because it alone lacks reference to the Spirit. He reasons that, as in the case of the 'finger'/'Spirit' issue in Matthew 12.28/Luke 11.20, so here. There it was argued that 'finger of God' must be earlier because Luke, with his special interest in the Spirit, would not alter a dominical reference to the Spirit by substituting the less explicit 'finger of God'. So here, too, we must assume that Luke's 'I will give you a mouth and wisdom', since it lacks any mention of the Spirit, is the earliest.[16]

Taylor acknowledges the cogency of Barrett's case, but says the Luke 21.15 version has 'a distinctly Johannine ring and appears to reflect the doctrine of the exalted Christ.' Thus the Matthean version, 'the Spirit of your Father', is most likely to be the earlier of the two. The other alternative, 'Holy Spirit' (Mark 13.11; Luke 12.12), being 'more reminiscent of the Epistles and Acts', is to be regarded as later. As Matthew has otherwise followed Mark so closely at this point, Matthew's 'Spirit of your Father' can have come only from another source known to Matthew, probably Q.[17] Schweizer also regards the Luke 21.15 version as later, being a change made by Luke whose tendency it was to equate the Spirit with the exalted Christ.[18]

It may be added that the case for the priority of Luke 21.15 rests largely upon the assumption that Luke, with his special interest in the Holy Spirit, would not delete a reference to the Spirit if he found that in his sources. However, in the discussion of Matthew 12.28/Luke 11.20 above, we have already seen that Matthew stays much closer to his sources in this regard than does Luke, who both adds and deletes references to the Spirit from the Marcan and Q material. In the case of Luke 11.20 it was suggested that, in the interests of his exodus typology, he had deleted a Spirit-reference in favour of an allusion to an incident in Moses' career. Could the same be the case in Luke 21.15? There is a parallel between Luke 21.15 and Exodus 4.11-12—the words of God to Moses when the latter made excuse on account of his lack of eloquence: 'Who has made man's mouth? Who makes him dumb, or deaf, or seeing, or blind? Is it not I, the Lord? Now therefore go, and I will be with your mouth and teach you what you shall speak.' Has Luke modified the traditional saying with the intention of providing another point of correspondence between the first and second exoduses? It is possible.[19] Then again it is also possible that Luke 21.15 is independent of the other sayings which promise assistance. It could be simply an independent utterance of Jesus, or it could be preserving for us an oracle of a Christian prophet who, speaking in the name of Christ (as the Old Testament prophets spoke in the name of Yahweh), promised assistance to a Church suffering persecution in the midst of its early missionary endeavours. Such a suggestion can offer an explanation why in Luke 21.15 alone Jesus is the one (rather than the Holy Spirit) who provides assistance. However, there is no way of proving that Luke 21.15 is an oracle of a Christian prophet; the question must remain open.

Summing up, we may say that several good reasons can be advanced for rejecting Luke 21.15 as the earliest form of the saying promising assistance in time of trial; a stronger case can be made for Matthew 10.20. Thus, for the remainder of our discussion, Matthew 10.20 will be regarded as the earliest form of the saying, the substance of which is to be accepted as reliable Jesus-tradition.

Application and significance of the saying. One more question needs to be asked. If Jesus did promise the assistance of the Holy Spirit to his disciples in time of trial, what period of time did he particularly have in mind? Matthew sets the saying in the context of the mission charge to the Twelve (10.1-42), yet as we saw in chapter 3 above, the note of opposition and persecution does not tally with the disciples' experiences during the Galilean mission. Mark includes the saying in his 'Little Apocalypse' (ch. 13) where it is associated with missionary proclamation (cf. 13.10), and Luke does the same with his 21.15 version of the saying (cf. 21.10ff.). No particular historical context is provided for Luke 12.12

It is obvious and right that the early Church would have understood Jesus' promise of the Holy Spirit's assistance in time of trial to apply to its members when they experienced persecution as a result of their missionary endeavours. However, we must ask what Jesus himself had in mind when he made this promise. It seems he was thinking of the sufferings to be endured by his disciples immediately following his death, when they would have to stand, as he had stood, before rulers and governors and bear their testimony. Whether Jesus would have identified these sufferings with the persecutions of the end-time is an open question, the more so, as he himself, according to Mark 13.32, disclaimed any knowledge of the time of the end of all things.

It is difficult to infer from this saying just how Jesus envisaged the disciples' relation to the Spirit. Was it an occasional coming of the Spirit during times of persecution only, similar to some of the Old Testament manifestations? Or did Jesus see it as timely help from the Spirit who was to have been already poured out in order to remain with the disciples? Is the expression found in Matthew's version, 'the Spirit of your Father speaking in you', a hint that this was Jesus' expectation?

Or was Jesus influenced by the prophecy of Joel 2.28-9? Interesting though these questions are, it is impossible to answer them from the text. All we can say is that Jesus did anticipate that the disciples would have some special relationship with the Spirit whereby they would receive help in times of trial and persecution.

Matthew 7.11/Luke 11.13

The text of Luke 11.13 runs: 'If you then, who are evil, know how to give good gifts to your children, how much more will the heavenly Father give the Holy Spirit to those who ask him!' This type of statement which compares man on the one hand, with God on the other hand, was common in Judaism,[20] and our text is possibly a particular application of a common Jewish saying.

If Luke 11.13, with its reference to the gift of the Spirit for the disciples, could be traced back to Jesus, it would be a valuable addition to the data concerning Jesus' teaching on the disciples' relation to the Spirit. However, all the evidence points away from that possibility. It appears that Luke has modified his source material again, and that the original form of the Q saying is to be found in Matthew 7.11 where no mention of the Spirit is made. In place of 'Holy Spirit' Matthew has 'good things.'

There are several compelling reasons why Matthew's 'good things' should be regarded as earlier than Luke's 'Holy Spirit': (1) 'Good things' in the latter part of the saying completes the parallelism with the same expression in the former part. So, if human fathers, being evil, give good things to their children, how much more will the heavenly Father give good things to those who ask him. Luke's 'Holy Spirit' destroys this parallelism. (2) The substitution of 'Holy Spirit' for 'good things' by Luke is in line with his tendency to add (and delete) references to the Spirit where it suits his purpose. (3) In the light of the Church's vivid experience of the Spirit after Pentecost, it would be natural for Luke to interpret the more general 'good things' as the 'Holy Spirit', one of the greatest of God's good gifts to the Church.

However, the more general 'good things' can include the more particular 'Holy Spirit', and Luke's emendation of his source is not so much an alteration of the tradition as an interpretation of it. It has been pointed out, too, that in rabbinical writings the term 'good things' refers sometimes to the blessings of the messianic age.[21] Prominent among the prophesied blessings of the messianic age, of course, was the out-pouring of the Spirit upon God's people.

CONCLUSIONS

We began our study by noting that Jesus is portrayed in the gospel tradition as a unique man of the Spirit; every phase of his life and career is closely associated with the Spirit. In this respect it may be said that he fulfilled the contemporary Jewish expectations regarding the messiah.[22] In the synoptic tradition Jesus himself speaks rarely of the Spirit,[23] and this testifies to the fidelity of the evangelists to their sources, especially when we remember that they wrote for Christian communities in which there were manifold expressions of the Spirit. The few sayings which are preserved in the synoptic gospels are very significant and the examination of them allows us to draw several important conclusions.

Jesus had a clear consciousness of the power of the Spirit which was at work in him. For him this power was evidence that the rule of God had begun, the kingdom had come (proleptically at least) in his ministry, and the final battle with the forces of evil had been joined. Such was the seriousness with which Jesus viewed the working of the Spirit through him that if men witnessed it and then ascribed it to Beelzebul their sin was unforgivable.

Jesus interpreted his anointing with the Holy Spirit in the light of Isaiah 61.1. He believed his Spirit-anointing marked him out as the prophet of the end-time, the one who announced the liberation, and preached the gospel to the poor. Yet (as the beatitudes show) he was more than a prophet, he not only proclaimed the coming of the end-time blessings, he pronounced them; he brought them in.

First century Judaism not only expected the messiah to be the bearer of the Spirit, but also expected that the redeemed of the Lord would receive the Spirit of God in the last days. Our examination of the Spirit-logia in the Synoptics showed that only one saying of Jesus regarding the Spirit's relation to the disciples can be received as reliable Jesus-tradition.[24] However, based on this one saying the following observations can be made: (1) Jesus expected his disciples to experience the assistance of the Holy Spirit in the midst of their trials; even more, he promised that they would. (2) Jesus anticipated that this help would be given to them in the trials they would face in the period immediately following his death, when they would stand, as he had stood, before rulers and governors for a testimony. We may wish to add that this was the period of the early Christian mission, but to say that Jesus had that in mind goes beyond the evidence provided in our saying.

Just what particular relationship Jesus expected would exist between his disciples and the Spirit cannot be deduced from our saying, nor can we determine whether Jesus himself expected to pour out that Spirit upon them. The whole matter is dealt with at length in the Johannine sayings of Jesus, of course, but they lie outside the scope of our present study. Our only recourse is to review the sayings attributed to the *risen* Jesus in the Synoptics and Acts. This subject will be treated briefly in the next chapter.

CHAPTER SIX

RELEVANT SAYINGS OF
THE RISEN JESUS

It was the firm conviction of the early Christian community that Jesus appeared alive after his passion to some of their number. This gave them an unshakable assurance that he was Lord over all. The resurrection of Jesus became the centrepiece of the early Christian message—its centrality in the life and teaching of primitive Christianity cannot be denied. However, if we try to ascertain the nature, location, and number of Jesus' resurrection appearances, we find that the New Testament documents provide a somewhat confusing picture. The clarity and singleness of the resurrection *message* proclaimed by the early Church stands in stark contrast to the ambiguity and historical problems associated with the resurrection *narratives*. It is not our purpose to take up the complex problems of Jesus' resurrection appearances, but we are concerned with the commission sayings attributed to the risen Jesus by the primitive Christian Church, and these, too, are problematical. What is clear is this: the first Christians believed that they had been commissioned by the risen Jesus—Matthew, Mark (but only in the longer ending), Luke, John and Acts all combine a commission saying of Jesus with one of the resurrection appearances.[1] Although it is difficult to say in just what circumstances the post-resurrection commission sayings found their present form, it cannot be denied that these sayings enshrine the strong conviction of the primitive Christian community that it was none other than Jesus, risen from the dead, who entrusted them with their mission and who promised/gave them the necessary spiritual power to carry it out.

Important as these sayings are, they are nevertheless, relevant only in a secondary way to this part of our study, for as Barrett observes: 'As soon as the resurrection is reached each evangelist stands on the same side of the Divine event which upset every eschatological *schema* as Paul and the other NT theologians.'[2] We are no longer dealing with tradition concerning the historical Jesus, but with tradition concerning the risen One. The resurrection moves Jesus out of the realm of history that is accessible to normal historical investigation. Thus it would not be appropriate to put the post-Easter sayings of Jesus alongside the earlier traditional sayings of the historical Jesus to produce a composite picture of his teaching. Nevertheless, a few brief comments about the post-resurrection sayings will serve to round off this first part of our study.

POST-EASTER COMMISSION SAYINGS

Matthew 28.18-20

Leaving aside the problems of authenticity and tradition-history which inevitably surround these verses,[3] we will simply note the way in which the Church's conviction concerning her commission by the risen Jesus is expressed in this saying.

Matthew (and presumably the Christian community from within which he wrote) believed the the risen Jesus' commission was given to the same twelve men (less Judas) whom Jesus sent on the Galilean mission, and with whom he celebrated the Last Supper. Matthew wants us to understand that Jesus chose, taught and trained the Twelve during the time of his earthly ministry so that they would be prepared to be sent as his apostles (whether or not Jesus himself ever used such a term).

Furthermore, Matthew reflects the conviction that the restrictions which had applied to both Jesus' and his disciples' ministry in the pre-Easter period were decisively removed by Jesus when he (re-)commissioned the Eleven after his resurrection. From that time on the gospel was to be taken to the nations.

Finally, the formulation of the Matthew 28.18-20 commission is open to interpretation along lines which suggest that Matthew understood the risen Jesus' commission after the fashion of a charge given by a Jewish man to his šālîaḥ. Explanation is first given by Jesus (as the principal) of his authority, and then, based on that authority, the disciples are sent out (as envoys/agents) to make disciples of the nations and baptise them in his name (in fact the triune name), with the assurance that Jesus himself stands behind them till the mission is completed at the end of the age.

Mark 16.14-18

The Marcan commission saying of Jesus is found in the so-called 'longer ending' (16.9-20). There can be no doubt that this passage is a later addition to Mark's gospel.[4] The longer ending (and, therefore, the commission saying) cannot be dated accurately, but probably originated somewhere in the early part of the second century. Though we cannot use Mark 16.14-18 as source material for the primitive Church's understanding of the risen Jesus' commission, nevertheless, we are not that much disadvantaged for its major themes are found in Matthew 28.18-20 and Luke 24.46-9; Acts 1.5, 8.

Luke 24.46-9; Acts 1.5, 8

The writings of Luke present a different picture of the resurrection appearances of Jesus to that found elsewhere in the New Testament, for they record no appearances in Galilee; all the activity is centred in and around Jerusalem.[5] Further, in Luke's writings the apostle-making appearances (excluding the unusual revelation to Paul on the Damascus road) are confined to a forty-day period following the resurrection and terminating with the ascension. These forty days are followed by a ten-day period which ends with Pentecost and the outpouring of the Spirit. This *schema* is found only in Luke's writings and has raised questions concerning Luke's intentions (theological or historical?), but these need not delay us here.[6]

Another unique feature of Luke's presentation is the way in which the prophecies of John the Baptist are taken up, reinterpreted, and portrayed as fulfilled by Christ. According to Dunn, for example, Luke saw a connection between the Baptist's prophecy (Luke 3.16) and Jesus' post-resurrection promise (Acts 1.5). John told his hearers that the coming one would baptise them with 'the Holy Spirit and with fire' (Luke 3.16). Jesus, according to Acts 1.5, referring back to the Baptist's prophecy, told his disciples that what John had spoken of would soon be fulfilled. There is, however, one significant difference between the Baptist's prophecy, and Jesus' promise: the absence in the latter of any reference to a baptism of fire.

Dunn suggests that Luke 12.49 provides for the evangelist the bridge between the Baptist's prophecy and Jesus' promise, and also the clue for understanding how Jesus fulfilled the role predicted for him by John. Jesus, having entered into a new relationship with the Spirit through his experience at the Jordan, had then to undergo vicarious suffering upon the cross, bearing the messianic fire on behalf of his people. 'It is only after fulfilling this role that he can begin to fulfil the role predicted for him by the Baptist—only after his death and resurrection and ascension that he begins to baptise in the Spirit.' For Luke, the reason why Jesus makes no mention of a baptism of fire along with the baptism in the Holy Spirit is because that baptism of fire had already been borne vicariously by Jesus.

Dunn's suggestion assumes that the saying about the fire (Luke 12.49) and the saying about baptism (Luke 12.50) are to be taken as 'parallel members of the one idea.' Thus he can say that, for Luke, Jesus' endurance of the baptism of suffering was, at the same time, Jesus' allowing the fire of judgement to be kindled upon himself.[7]

Jesus, the Spirit and the Christian mission in Luke-Acts. Conceding, for the purposes of our discussion at this point, that Dunn's presentation of Luke's Spirit-theology is feasible as well as fascinating, what can be said about the Lucan view of the relationship between Jesus, his disciples, and the Spirit? We can say that Luke, consistent with his salvation-history *schema*, saw Jesus passing from one stage to another as far as his relationship with the Spirit was concerned. At his baptism he was anointed with the Spirit to be the end-time prophet/liberator/messiah, but following his death he entered a new relationship with the Spirit whereby he could pour out the same Spirit upon his disciples. It is clearly Luke's view that the Spirit who empowered Jesus during his earthly ministry was the One who empowered the early Christian community for their witness and ministry (Luke 24.49; Acts 1.5, 8).

It remains for us to make some comment upon Luke's version of Jesus' commission to the disciples. It can be shown that in Luke's works the commission is directed to the Eleven. The third gospel does present an ambiguous picture in which Jesus appears to 'the eleven gathered together and them that were with them' (24.33), and in which the Eleven are not singled out when the commission is given. But, if we compare that with Acts 1.15-26; 6.1-4, it becomes clear that Luke understood that the commission was given to the Eleven and applied to the reconstituted Twelve. Those who were called by Jesus and sent on the Galilean mission are the same body of men (less Judas) to whom the post-resurrection charge was given. Thus, like Matthew, Luke is convinced that Jesus who called the Twelve for the Galilean mission, singled these same men out to receive his post-resurrection charge. They were his emissaries, bearers of the gospel of the kingdom, both before and after the resurrection. Further, like Matthew 28.18-20, Luke 24.46-9 can be interpreted in terms of a man and his *šālîaḥ*. Jesus (as principal) tells the disciples (his envoys) that they are witnesses of his death and resurrection, and that they must proclaim *in his name* (i.e., as representatives of their principal and not in their own right) the call to repentance and the offer of forgiveness. To this charge Jesus adds the promise of the Holy Spirit who will clothe them with power for the task. He stands behind his witnesses by pouring out upon them the Spirit who both empowers them and gives to their testimony the ring of truth and authority.

CONCLUSIONS

In brief, we may say that the sayings attributed to the risen Jesus in the Synoptics and Acts are meant to form a bridge between the earthly ministry of Jesus and the post-Easter ministry of his followers. In these sayings the same twelve men (less Judas) whom Jesus commissioned for the Galilean mission to Israel are (re-)commissioned for the wider mission which will include both Jews and Gentiles. These commission sayings, like some of the sayings of Jesus in relation to the Galilean mission, lend themselves to an interpretation along the lines of the rabbinic *šālîaḥ* concept.

Of special interest are the sayings attributed to the risen Jesus in Luke-Acts, for there we find the earthly ministry of Jesus linked with the ministry of his followers in the post-Easter period by a distinctive understanding of Jesus' relation to the Spirit. For the duration of his earthly ministry he was the unique bearer of the Spirit, but following his death he entered into a new relationship; he became the bestower of the Spirit. And in Acts 1.1 it is implied that the disciples' ministry in the post-Easter period is a continuation of what Jesus began to do and to teach.

In the study of the Pauline epistles in Part Two it will be interesting to see whether any attempt is made there to link the ministry of the historical Jesus with that of his followers in the post-Easter period.

PAUL AND MINISTRY

CHAPTER SEVEN

PRELIMINARY COMMENTS

In Part One we sought to build up a picture of ministry as Jesus understood it, based on the tradition preserved in the synoptic gospels. In particular it was with Jesus' conception of how the ministry of his followers was related to his own that we were concerned. In Part Two an attempt will be made to build up another picture of ministry, this time based upon the first-hand reflections of the apostle Paul. We want to discover how this later disciple understood his ministry (and that of the Christian community) to be related to the ministry of Jesus Christ.

The second part of our study differs from the first in two significant ways. First, the ministerial relationship is viewed from the opposite side—the side of the Christian believer, not the side of his Lord. Second, the relationship is no longer primarily that between the historical Jesus and those who followed him in Palestine, but between the exalted Christ who stands outside history as we know it, and those who 'follow' him in the Spirit and by faith. Nevertheless, we will see that the apostle Paul still understood his ministry to be related in specific ways to that of the historical Jesus. Despite significant differences, it will be seen that the main elements in the picture of ministry which emerged from our study of the synoptic gospels emerge again in the writings of Paul. However, in the latter fresh ministerial themes are introduced in response to situations which did not pertain in the time of the historical Jesus, and these new themes throw extra light upon the area of our investigation.

Paul's teaching about the ministry of Christ, his own apostolic ministry and the ministry of the Christian community will be studied. Clearly, we shall have to be rigorous in excluding everything which is not directly related to our present enquiry, for each of these subjects represents a major area within the Pauline corpus, and each has given rise to a literature so vast that no one can hope to master it all. This means, for instance, that in Paul's presentation of the ministry of Christ, we will discuss only those aspects which find parallels in/provide models for Christian ministry, or by which the ministry of Christ can otherwise be seen to be related to Christian ministry. Thus, Paul's teaching about the atoning/reconciling efficacy of Christ's death cannot be taken up here. Similarly, in Paul's presentation of the ministry of the Christian community, we will not concern ourselves with ecclesiastical structures or ministerial offices except where these are directly related to our enquiry.

Obviously, an important part of our study of Paul's letters will be that concerned with the Pauline apostolate. This is another area of New Testament study which now boasts a vast literature.[1] One problem that arises is that of the antecedents for the Pauline notion of apostleship. We cannot confront this issue 'head-on' for the complexity of such a task would be great enough to warrant a book of its own. However, the exegesis of several of the texts/passages which are taken up both demands that some stance be assumed, and throws some light upon the problem as well.

The Pauline epistles are occasional letters in the sense that they were written to deal with specific situations. Thus, depending upon the situation of the addressees, we may expect to find different emphases in the treatment of the same general topic. We may even encounter what appear to be contradictory statements, simply because Paul is seeking to correct one aberration in one church and the opposite aberration in another church. Further, we may even find what appear to be conflicting views in letters addressed to the same church, because opposite tendencies arose at different stages in its growth, both of which the apostle felt he had to correct. It will be necessary, therefore, to bear in mind the various situations addressed, as far as it is possible to do so, as we seek to discover what the relevant passages reveal about Paul's understanding of ministry. For this reason, as each epistle is taken up, some preliminary comments about its life-setting will be made.

In the treatment of Paul's writings which follows, his letters are arranged chronologically,[2] so that at the end of our study we may be able to discern in what ways the apostle's thinking in this area developed, bearing in mind that a significant part of that 'development' will be due simply to different emphases.

CHAPTER EIGHT

GALATIANS

Of all Paul's epistles, that to the Galatians is regarded as most characteristically 'Pauline'. Little doubt has been raised concerning its authenticity, even by the nineteenth century Tübingen School or the recent computer analysis 'attacks' on the Pauline corpus.

However, the epistle is not without its problems. There are four major areas of controversy. First, there is a division of opinion concerning the destination of the letter. Was it sent to North Galatia (the Galatians then being the ethnic group by that name), or to South Galatia (the Galatians being members of the Churches founded by Paul on his first missionary journey, i.e., Galatians only because their cities were included in the Roman province of Galatia)? Second, is the problem of the date of writing. The North Galatian theory requires a later date while the South Galatian theory allows an earlier date, possibly even as early as the eve of the Jerusalem Council, in which case Galatians would be the earliest extant letter of Paul. Third, there is the debate concerning the identity of the opponents whom Paul combats in the epistle. Traditionally they have been identified as Judaizers—Jewish Christians who insisted that, as well as repentance and faith in Christ, the Gentiles needed to submit to circumcision and obey the Law in order to be saved. Lightfoot says Paul's antagonists 'were probably emissaries from the mother Church, Jerusalem, either abusing a commission actually received from the Apostles of the circumcision, or assuming an authority which had never been conferred upon them.'[1] In recent years other suggestions have been made concerning the identity of Paul's opponents. These include: Jewish Christians native to Galatia,[2] the Galatian Gentile Christians themselves, who had misunderstood the implications of Paul's gospel,[3] Jewish Christians from Judea who had succumbed to Jewish zealot pressure and instigated a nomistic campaign among their fellow Christians to avoid persecution,[4] and gnostic Christians who had incorporated some elements of the Torah into their system.[5] The consensus of opinion is against the last-mentioned; most interpreters see in Paul's opponents judaizing Christians of one sort or another.

Associated with these problem areas, and especially with the first two, is the thorny problem of the autobiographical data in Galatians, and how these relate to the Acts account of Paul's career, particularly his visits to Jerusalem. Galatians is a first-hand account and much earlier than Acts. It must therefore be treated as primary evidence in any reconstruction of events.[6]

The diversity of scholarly opinion on these matters only underlines the fact that there is insufficient evidence to command a consensus. Each interpreter will come to his task with a predisposition to favour one set of solutions above others, but will need to hold it loosely. For the purposes of this study in Galatians, the following working hypothesis is adopted: the epistle was addressed by Paul to the churches he had founded in South Galatia on his first missionary journey. These churches, along with the church in Syrian Antioch, had been disturbed by Jewish Christians from Jerusalem. These Jewish Christians insisted that Gentiles should be circumcised and should obey the Law if they were to be truly incorporated into the people of God.[7] This disturbance produced two responses. First, Paul sent off a hurried letter to the Galatian churches refuting the assertions of the judaizing Christians, and second, he and Barnabas went up to Jerusalem to meet the church leaders there to obtain a clear decision on the matter (the Jerusalem council of Acts 15). According to this reconstruction, Galatians was written on the eve of the Jerusalem Council, thus making it the earliest of the extant epistles of Paul.[8]

The agitation of the Judaizers in Galatia not only called into question the standing of the gentile Christians, but also constituted a challenge to Paul's gospel and apostleship. In response Paul asserted the divine origin of both his gospel and his apostleship. It is this matter which we must take up in the section which follows. In subsequent sections we will see how Paul, in dealing with the Galatian emergency, touches upon the servant character of his ministry and the role of the Spirit in the

Christian community, and how the coming of the Spirit is related to the death of Christ. We will also see significant points of contact between Paul's treatment of apostleship, servanthood and the Spirit, and the synoptic presentation of Jesus' teaching on the same.

It is clear that Paul had to defend his gospel and apostleship against the attacks of opponents in Galatia. We want to know what light Paul's defence throws upon the relationship between the apostle's ministry and the activity of his Lord.

Paul's defensive (some would say polemical) stance in Galatians is evident in the very first verse: 'Paul an apostle—not from men nor through men, but through Jesus Christ and God the Father . . .' This prepares the way for his later assertions concerning the divine origin of his apostleship and his independence of the Jerusalem apostles. It should be noticed in passing that Paul says he received his apostleship not only from Christ, but through the Father as well. Paul received his commission by a revelation of Christ, but behind that stood the plan and purpose of God. This is why he can speak interchangably of Christ or of God as the one who commissions, empowers, speaks, and acts through him, as we shall see in our study of the Pauline epistles.

Galatians 1.11-2.10

Paul's defence proper which is found in this passage consists of two major arguments. First, he says he received his gospel and apostolic vocation from God alone. It was not something which he had sought. On the contrary, he had been actively and violently persecuting the Church of God when, he says, God 'was pleased to reveal his Son to me, in order that I might preach him among the Gentiles' (1.16). His commission, like his conversion, was at the initiative of God alone (1.11-17). Second, his gospel and apostleship were recognised on his first contact with the Jerusalem apostles (2.1-10), and even his trip to Jerusalem on that occasion was not on his initiative alone; he went up 'by revelation' (2.2). These two arguments are followed up by an account of the incident at Antioch in which Paul withstood Peter to his face (2.11-21). This further attests Paul's independence of man, his authority being derived from God alone.

The divine origin of Paul's gospel and apostleship. Several elements of Paul's defence have bearing upon the present investigation. The first of these is the claim that his gospel, call and apostolic commission have all come to him directly from Christ; they were not mediated to him through men. As for the gospel he says, 'I did not receive it from man, nor was I taught it, but it came through a revelation of Jesus Christ' (1.12). This has generally been taken as a reference to Paul's conversion experience, and probably refers not only to the climactic vision on the Damascus road, but also to the days of blindness with the opportunity for reflection which they afforded him, and the ministrations of the disciple Ananias from Damascus (cf. Acts 9.6, 10-19). If Paul is defending himself against a charge of dependence upon the apostles of the circumcision, this claim to have received both his gospel and the call to preach it directly from the Lord at the time of his conversion would decisively answer that charge.

Paul and the prophets. The second element in his defence, and vital for an understanding of Paul's view of his apostleship, is the passage 1.15-16: 'But when he who had set me apart before I was born, and had called me through his grace, was pleased to reveal his Son to me, in order that I might preach him among the Gentiles, I did not confer with flesh and blood.' Verse fifteen alludes to Jeremiah 1.5 ('Before I formed you in the womb I knew you, and before you were born I consecrated you; I appointed you a prophet to the nations.') and Isaiah 49.1b, 5 ('The Lord called me from the womb, from the body of my mother he named my name', and 'the Lord . . . who formed me from the womb to be his servant'). By these allusions Paul places himself in the long line of independent messengers who have been called by God, a succession which reaches back to the great prophets of the Old Testament. It has been suggested that Paul implies that he needs no ratification from Jerusalem, no more than the prophets did.[9]

It is noteworthy that both the Old Testament passages to which Paul alludes in 1.15-16 speak of a gentile dimension to the messenger's task. Jeremiah is appointed 'a prophet to the nations' and the servant in Isaiah 49 is given as 'a light to the nations' (49.6). Thus it seems that Paul's allusion to the words of these prophets not only illustrates the independent character of his own apostolic calling, but provides a precedent for its scope as well. Therefore, it comes as no surprise when in 1.16 Paul adds that the One who set him apart before he was born revealed his Son to him that he might preach him among the Gentiles. Further, Paul's allusion to the servant-prophecy of Isaiah 49 suggests that he believed the foreign missionary aspect of that prophecy would find fulfilment in his apostolic endeavours. Perhaps Paul was implying that opposition to his gospel was tantamount to opposition to the very purpose of God—the salvation of the Gentiles.

Does Paul compromise his independence in 2.2? In the first chapter of Galatians Paul seems to have adequately defended the divine origin of both his gospel and his calling to preach it to the Gentiles. But, we may ask, did he not compromise all that by what he wrote in the second chapter? There, referring to his second visit to Jerusalem, he says: 'I laid before them (but privately before those who were of repute) the gospel which I preach among the Gentiles, lest somehow, I should be running or had run in vain' (2.2). Did Paul have some misgivings about the gospel he had been preaching which could only be satisfied by referring to the apostles of the circumcision for ratification? Tertullian took it that way,[10] and that seems to be the *prima facie* meaning of the text. If this were the case, there would be far-reaching implications for our understanding of Paul's ministry. We would have to allow for a secondary element in his relationship as an apostle to Christ—the Jerusalem apostles somehow standing between them. However, Tertullian's interpretation is so out of keeping with the rest of the passage and the drift of Paul's whole argument in the first two chapters that it must be abandoned. Most commentators see Paul's motive in seeking the recognition of the Jerusalem apostles as a pragmatic manoeuvre. His concern was to avoid any open break between the Jewish and gentile missions, for such a schism would impair the progress of the gospel and cast a shadow over the gentile mission.[11] This interpretation is confirmed by Paul's assertion that, when false brethren brought pressure to bear upon him to have Titus circumcised during that second visit to Jerusalem, he 'did not yield submission even for a moment, that the truth of the gospel might be preserved for you [Gentiles]' (2.5). Paul's over-riding concern in Jerusalem was not ratification of his gospel by the apostles of the circumcision to quieten his own misgivings, rather it was to defend and maintain the truth of his gospel for the sake of the gentile mission. It has been suggested that the Judaizers had claimed: the leaders of the Jerusalem church are the guarantors of the true gospel, not some fellow like Paul! It was only to silence their objections that Paul sought the recognition of the Jerusalem leaders, not because he himself felt any misgivings about his gospel.[12]

The dynamic aspect of Paul's apostleship. On a more positive note, Paul's defence focuses attention upon two factors in his ministry which convinced the Jerusalem apostles of the legitimacy of his work among the Gentiles. They saw that he had been 'entrusted with the gospel to the uncircumcised' (2.7)[13] and they perceived the 'grace' that was given to him (2.9). To his gospel they found it necessary to add nothing (2.6), and the grace they perceived at work in him for the Gentiles was the same as that they believed was at work through Peter for the Jews (2.8). We meet here for the first time what we will find recurring throughout Paul's writings: a strong sense that the Lord himself was at work in and through his ministry. He knew he was an apostle by the will of God, but that involved more than delegated authority; he was convinced that the Lord himself was actively at work through his ministry. Just as modern commentators have come to see that justification in Paul is more than a legal matter but involves the dynamic of the Spirit as well, so too we must realise that Paul viewed his apostolate as more than a delegated legal authority; it included the dynamic participation of God through the Spirit as well. And that divine dimension of apostolic ministry did not go unnoticed by the Galatians, for, as he testifies: 'Though my condition was a trial to you, you did not scorn or despise me, but received me as an angel of God, as Christ Jesus' (4.14). It is worthy of note that the word *angelos* which the RSV translates as 'angel' can be rendered equally well as 'messenger' or 'one who is sent'. Thus 4.14b could be translated: 'you received me as a messenger of God, as Christ Jesus.' Is Paul's thought here influenced, not only by the remembrance of the enthusiastic welcome he received when he first preached the gospel in Galatia, but also by a certain conception he had of his relationship as an apostle to Christ? Paul's statement, 'you received me . . . as Christ Jesus', suggests that he could think of this relationship in terms of a Jewish *šālîaḥ* ('a man's *šālîaḥ* is as himself'). Further, the statement that he was received both as a messenger of God and as Jesus Christ is reminiscent, at least, of Jesus' words to the Twelve: 'He who receives you receives me, and he who receives me receives him who sent me' (Matt. 10.40).

SERVANTHOOD AND SUFFERING

Jesus gave his disciples an example of humble service which he charged them to emulate in their mutual relationships. Paul, likewise, emphasises the obligation of mutual service when writing to the Galatians: 'Through love be servants of one another' (5.13). More important for our present enquiry is the fact that Paul speaks of himself as 'a servant of Christ' (1.10), and as one who bears in his body 'the marks of Jesus' (6.17). There are hints also that Paul, like Jesus, understood his ministry, partially at least, in the light of the servant-prophecies of Deutero-Isaiah.

We noted above the possible allusion to Isaiah 49.1, 5-6 in 1.15-16, the ideas of being set apart from the womb and of a commission to bring news of salvation to the Gentiles constituting the parallels between the two passages. J. Blank asserts that Paul indeed thought of himself as the servant of the Lord, but he adds: 'Paul understood himself as a *missionary servant of God for the Gentile nations . . . he did not think of himself as the suffering servant of Isaiah 52-53.*'[14] Two comments can be made. First, we have to avoid saying that Paul ever claimed to be *the* servant of the Deutero-Isaianic prophecies in any connection. The most that can be suggested is that those prophecies found a fulfilment in his ministry. Second, it is arguable that Paul not only applied the foreign missionary elements of those prophecies to his ministry, but also that he believed the parts about suffering found a (limited) fulfilment in his ministry as well. An effort will be made to substantiate both these claims in the course of our study of Paul's letters. This brings us to that unique statement of the apostle's in which he says he bears in his body the marks of Jesus.

Galatians 6.17

The text runs: 'Henceforth, let no man trouble me; for I bear in my body the marks of Jesus (*ta stigmata tou Iēsou*).' Lightfoot reminds us that *ta stigmata* was an expression used for the marks of ownership branded on a slave's body. The *stigmata* were used in the case of (1) domestic slaves, (2) temple slaves (*hierodouloi*) or persons devoted to the service of some deity, (3) captives (but rarely), and (4) soldiers, who sometimes branded themselves with the name of their commander. Lightfoot suggests that the second of these alternatives is the most appropriate background for 6.17, especially since the expression *hieros doulos* is mentioned in a Galatian inscription.[15]

In any case, there can be little doubt that the 'marks' which Paul bore were the scars left by the beatings and other forms of abuse which he suffered in the course of his ministry on behalf of the Gentiles. In Ramsay's words, they were the wounds 'cut deep on Paul's body by the lictor's rods at Pisidian Antioch and the stones at Lystra.'[16] Like Antipater, who stripped off his clothes to expose his many scars as proof of his loyalty to Caesar (a loyalty which needed no words, his body cried it aloud), Paul, too, asserts that his loyalty as an apostle of Christ is clearly seen in the scars of persecution which he bore; the results of his labours for Christ.[17]

This is the first of several references in the letters of Paul where the apostle appeals to his sufferings as a demonstration of the genuineness of his apostleship. We will see other and more explicit references when the later epistles are examined. But here we have the first hint that, as far as Paul is concerned, the genuine apostle and true servant of God is the one who shares in the sufferings of the Christ. It is a hint, too, that Paul thought the sufferings as well as the missionary aspects of the Deutero-Isaianic servant-prophecies found a fulfilment in his ministry.

CHRIST AND THE SPIRIT

The Galatian churches appear to have been what we today would call 'charismatic' communities, for they experienced among themselves many miraculous happenings (*dunameis*).

Galatians 3.4-5

When Galatian Christians capitulated so easily to another gospel which stressed observance of the Law, Paul sought to recall them to the truth of his gospel by an appeal to their charismatic experience: 'Did you experience so many things in vain?—if it really is in vain. Does he who supplies the Spirit to you and works miracles among you do so by works of the law, or by hearing with faith' (3.4-5)?

It has been suggested that the reference here is to mighty works performed by Paul among the Galatians when he first proclaimed the gospel to them,[18] but this is unlikely. Both verbs used, *epichorēgōn* (supplies) and *energōn* (works), are present participial forms suggesting an ongoing phenomenon, rather than a once only occurrence completed when Paul ministered among them. Further, the subject of both verbs is the same, so that he who supplied the Spirit is also the one who worked the miracles. Paul would not say he supplied the Spirit to them!

The close association of the supply of the Spirit and the working of miracles indicates that the latter should be taken as the manifestation of the former. Thus, Paul acknowledges as a fact the exercise of extraordinary spiritual powers by his converts. The word used by Paul to describe the manifestation of spiritual power among the Galatians is *dunamis*. It is found in Galatians only here, but is a common word in Paul's writings (used forty-eight times in all), where it can mean simply power, or more particularly, miracles (such as exorcisms, healings, etc.) which is its meaning here. It is important to note that the evidence of the Spirit's working/presence in the Galatian Christian communities was the same as it was in the case of Jesus—the performance of mighty works (*dunameis*). But the manifestation of the Spirit among them was also evidence that they, without circumcision or observance of the Law, had become recipients of the promised blessings to Abraham, and by stressing this, of course, Paul has undercut the teaching of the Judaizers. This is the gist of the next passage.

Galatians 3.13-14

The text of this passage is: 'Christ redeemed us from the curse of the law, having become a curse for us—for it is written, "Cursed be every one who hangs on a tree"—that in Christ

Jesus the blessing of Abraham might come upon the Gentiles, that we might receive the promise of the Spirit through faith.' It is beyond the scope of our present study to discuss just how Christ redeemed men from the curse of the Law; what concerns us is Paul's identification of the blessing resulting from Christ's redemptive work (in part at least) as the promise of the Spirit. What Paul means, of course, is not that as a result of Christ's work, a promise concerning the Spirit was made, rather that the Spirit promised could now be received. What is significant is that the availability of the Spirit to both Jews and Gentiles was somehow dependent upon Christ's death—he 'redeemed us . . . that (*hina*) we might receive the promise of the Spirit.' The two ideas, Christ's redemptive work and the sending of the Spirit, are found together again in 4.4-6 where Paul says the God who sent forth his Son to redeem those who were under the law so that they could receive adoption as sons, also sent forth the Spirit of his Son into the hearts of those who had thus become his adopted sons. In neither place are we given any hint of how Paul saw Christ's death and the coming of the Spirit to be related. We are left wondering whether the suggested interpretation of Luke's presentation of the matter mentioned above (see ch. 6) is not a development of the hints we find in Galatians.

CONCLUSIONS

First, we saw that the Galatian churches were 'charismatic' communities, being recipients of the Spirit whose presence and activity among them found expression in the miracles (*dunameis*) which continued to be performed by members of these communities. That Christians might receive the Spirit, Paul says, was one of the purposes for which Christ died; he redeemed us from the curse of the Law that we might receive the promise of the Spirit through faith. At two places in the epistle Paul links the death of Christ with the giving of the Spirit, but gives no hint concerning the essential relationship between the two events. We will want to be alert to any possible developments along this line in our study of the later epistles of Paul.

Second, we must say something about Paul's own ministry

and its relationship to Christ. Paul believed that his apostolic calling, like his gospel, was something he received directly from the risen Christ who appeared to him on the Damascus road. His calling, like that of the Old Testament prophets, was unmediated; it was communicated directly to him by the Lord. Although Paul referred to himself as an apostle 'through Jesus Christ' and traced his calling back to his conversion experience when Christ revealed himself to him, nevertheless he says he was also an apostle 'through God the Father, who raised him [Jesus] from the dead.' Thus he can speak interchangeably (and indiscriminately) of God the Father or Christ as the One who called him and whose grace was at work through him in his mission to the Gentiles. It is worth recalling that Jesus' commission of the Twelve for the Galilean mission involved a similar double-sided representation: they were sent as Jesus' envoys, but were, at the same time, representatives of the God who sent Jesus. Thus Jesus could say to them: 'He who receives you receives me, and he who receives me receives him who sent me' (Matt. 10.40).

It has already been argued that in the case of the Galilean mission, the disciples' relationship to Christ can be understood against the background of the Jewish šālîaḥ idea. In Galatians there are hints that Paul likewise believed that his commission involved his representing Christ as the Jewish šālîaḥ represented his principal. His statement that the Galatians received him as a messenger of God, as Christ Jesus, is reminiscent at least of the rabbinic statements about envoys (šĕlûḥîm). However, it is the dynamic character of his apostolate that Paul emphasises. His apostleship is not only an authoritative representation of Christ/God the Father, it involves the dynamic participation of God through the Spirit as well.

Finally we may note that Galatians contains the first mention of Paul's conviction that suffering is the hallmark of the genuine apostle of Christ. Paul's reference to 'the marks of Jesus' which he bore in his body is the first budding of a conviction that an apostle must share the sufferings of Christ; that in an apostle's ministry, as in the ministry of Christ, the element of suffering in the Deutero-Isaianic servant-prophecies will find fulfilment. It must be admitted that the allusion to the aspect of suffering in the servant-prophecies is at best a rather veiled one. However,

Paul's allusion to the foreign missionary aspect of those prophecies is clearer. Paul couches the account of his apostolic calling in terms which are reminiscent not only of Jeremiah's call, but also of the second servant-prophecy of Deutero-Isaiah (Gal. 1.15-16/Isa. 49.1, 5-6). Paul associates his ministry with the ministry of Christ by placing himself alongside his Lord as one in whose ministry the servant-prophecies also find fulfilment.

CHAPTER NINE

1, 2 THESSALONIANS

According to Acts 17-18, Paul, during the course of his second missionary journey arrived in Thessalonica and preached on three successive sabbaths in the Jewish synagogue in that town. As a result some Jews were converted as well as many devout Greeks. Other Jews in Thessalonica were filled with jealousy and stirred up opposition against Paul so that he had to flee first to Beroea and then to Athens. From Athens Paul moved on to Corinth where Timothy and Titus joined him.

It is generally held that 1 Thessalonians was written from Corinth shortly after the arrival of Timothy and Titus, and that 2 Thessalonians followed soon afterwards, also from Corinth.[1] The authenticity of both epistles is widely accepted and need not be argued here.

Paul had wanted to return to Thessalonica (1, 2.17-18), but, hindered from doing so, he sent Timothy both to comfort and strengthen the new Christians there and to obtain news of their faith—whether it was standing up amid the persecutions they were experiencing (1, 3.1-5). 1 Thessalonians was written shortly after Timothy's return with the good news of the Thessalonian Christians' steadfastness of faith and their continued affection for Paul and his colleagues (3.6). Paul expresses his joy at their response to the gospel and progress in the faith (1.2-10; 2.13-16), reminds them of the manner of his ministry among them (2.1-12), urges them to live godly lives (4.1-12), and gives an explanation concerning the lot of those who die before the coming (parousia) of Christ and concerning the nature of that coming itself (4.9-5.11). He gives instructions about the attitude they should have towards the Christian workers who labour among them (5.12-13), some general exhortations (5.14-18), and a reminder not to quench the Spirit or despise prophesying (5.19-20).

The greater part of 2 Thessalonians is given over to further explanation concerning the parousia. In 1.5-12 Paul describes the nature of Christ's coming and its effect upon the believing and the unbelieving, and adds an appeal that his readers walk worthy of their calling. In 2.1-12 he deals with a rumour abroad in Thessalonica to the effect that 'the day of the Lord has come.' This, says Paul, is impossible for certain events which had not yet taken place must occur before that day. In the third chapter Paul instructs his readers to dissociate themselves from any fellow-Christian who lives in idleness (3.6), reminding them of his own example of diligence (3.7-9) and of the command he gave them previously—'if any one will not work, let him not eat' (3.10). All this Paul included in his letter because he had heard that there were those 'living in idleness, mere busybodies, not doing any work' (3.11).

Paul's Defensive Attitude

The problems that Paul took up when he wrote the Thessalonian epistles do not all appear to have been of a pastoral or doctrinal nature. There are strong indications that his own ministry was under attack in Thessalonica. In 1, 2.1-12 he protests: 'Our appeal does not spring from error or uncleanness, nor is it made with guile (3) . . . we never used either words of flattery, as you know, or a cloak for greed, as God is witness, nor did we seek glory from men (5-6) . . . We worked night and day, that we might not burden any of you, while we preached to you the gospel of God. You are witnesses, and God also, how holy and righteous and blameless was our behaviour to you believers' (9-10).

Various explanations have been suggested for the defensive attitude of the apostle. Most commentators believe Paul is defending himself against charges made by some opponents. Some suggest these opponents were heretical pseudo-apostles,[2] while others identify them as Judaizers,[3] Gnostic Christians,[4] spiritual enthusiasts,[5] and Jews.[6] Some commentators maintain that Paul was not responding to charges made against him by any opponents, rather the sense of need to defend his ministry in Thessalonica arose from his own spiritual state at the time,[7] or from his desire to glorify God (who had worked so marvelously among the Thessalonians), and to edify the church (by causing them to reflect upon the way God had worked among them).[8]

The great variety of scholarly opinion concerning what lay behind Paul's defensive attitude only underlines the fact that the evidence is insufficient to command a consensus. If we were forced to make a choice, perhaps it would be best to say it was a slanderous whispering campaign mounted by unbelieving Jews that Paul felt forced to answer—according to Acts 17 the Jews vigorously opposed Paul in both Thessalonica and Beroea. If we accept this solution, Paul's terrible outburst against Jews in 1, 2.14-16 (so unlike his sentiments in Romans 9-11) can more readily be understood. In any case, Paul's defence provides us with important data for our present investigation.

In the study of the Thessalonian epistles which follows we will see a heightened consciousness of both apostolic authority and the dynamic character of the apostolate, together with the first hint that the validation of apostolic ministry is eschatological; it waits on the revelation of Christ at the Last Day. Further, it will be seen that Paul portrays the risen Christ actively participating in the lives and ministry of Christians, as he does the Holy Spirit, who bestows his gifts upon the Christian community. Finally, we shall see Paul teaches that, like Christ, Christians are destined to suffer: a further hint that he believed the suffering servant prophecies find fulfilment, not only in Christ, but in the lives of his people as well.

PAUL'S APOSTLESHIP

We have already noted the defensive stance adopted by Paul in 1, 2.1-12, and although we cannot be sure from what sources the accusations came, the passage still provides valuable insight into the apostle's view of his ministry. Paul insists that he was not like one of the many contemporary charlatans, preying upon the credulous as they peddled some new philosophy or religious teaching with the one aim of personal profit. He and his colleagues did not make heavy demands upon the Thessalonian believers as they might have done 'as apostles of Christ' (1, 2.6). This is the only place in the Thessalonian epistles where Paul uses the term 'apostle', but this does not mean that the concept of apostleship has fallen into the background. In fact, compared with Galatians, the Thessalonian epistles reflect Paul's heightened consciousness of both the authority and dynamic character of his apostolate. As apostles of Christ, Paul and his colleagues were entrusted with an authority which they expected to be acknowledged. Their exhortations and instructions are given as representatives of Jesus Christ (1, 4.1: 'We beseech and exhort you *in/by the Lord Jesus*'; 1, 4.2: 'For you know what instructions we gave you *through the Lord Jesus*'; 1, 4.15: 'For this we declare to you *by the word of the Lord*'; 2, 3.6: 'Now we command you, brethren, *in the name of our Lord Jesus Christ*') and they expect them to be obeyed. So great is the sense of the authority entrusted to them that Paul, having given his instructions 'through the Lord Jesus' (1, 4.2-7), can say: 'Whoever disregards this, disregards not man but God' (1, 4.8). Paul and his colleagues assume the authority of agents/plenipotentiaries of Jesus Christ, the same sort of authority as that given to the Twelve for the Galilean mission.

The Christian Apostolate and Jewish Propheticism

B. Rigaux makes a suggestion regarding Paul's apostolate which, if correct, would have bearing upon the way we should understand Paul's ministry. Commenting on 1, 2.15-16, he says: 'Paul having reproached the Jews for having killed Jesus and the prophets, continues the parallel: "They have persecuted us . . . hindering us from speaking to the Gentiles that they may be saved."' By this parallelism, Rigaux suggests, it is implied that 'the Christian apostolate has taken the place of the Jewish propheticism.'[9] There are hints in other Pauline letters that the apostle understood his call after the fashion of the calling of the Old Testament prophets (Gal. 1.15-16, cf. Jer. 1.5; Isa. 49.1). If we define the prophetic function as the reception and transmission of the word of God, we may say that Paul functioned as a prophet on some occasions at least. This is known from his other epistles (2 Cor. 12.1-7; Gal. 1.12, cf. Eph. 3.3) and seems to be indicated in our epistles at 1, 4.15 which begins: 'For this we declare to you by the word of the Lord . . .' In the discussion of this verse below various suggestions concerning the source of the 'word of the Lord' will be discussed, but it will be argued that this expression is best understood as a revelation made by the exalted Christ to the apostle Paul. If we adopt this view, then 1, 4.15 becomes evidence in the Thessalonian epistles that Paul the apostle did, at least on occasions, function as a prophet. Nevertheless, to say with Rigaux, that for Paul, the Christian apostolate has taken the place of Jewish propheticism is to go beyond the evidence of the Pauline letters. Paul lists prophets alongside apostles in the catalogues of special ministers (1 Cor. 12.28-29, cf. Eph. 4.11), so it is doubtful whether he understood the Christian apostolate to have replaced the prophetic movement as a one to one equivalent. That, of course, is not to deny that an apostle may also exercise the gift of prophecy. Therefore, although there are certain points of contact between the prophetic and apostolic callings, the overall model for apostleship is best located in the idea of a plenipotentiary of Christ rather than a prophet of Christ.

The Dynamic Aspect of the Apostolate

It was suggested above that the Thessalonian epistles reflect a heightened sense of both the authoritative and dynamic aspects of the apostolate. It is now time to illustrate the latter. Paul insists that his message was not of human origin—it was God's word, and it came with power and the Holy Spirit and with full conviction (1, 1.5). In 1, 2.13 Paul boldly asserts that his gospel is nothing less than the word of God: 'When you received the word of God which you heard from us, you accepted it not as the word of man but as what it really is, the word of God, which is at work in you believers.' In 2, 2.13-14 Paul says that it was *God* who called the Thessalonians to salvation through his preaching, and in 1, 1.2-5 that he knows God has chosen the Thessalonian believers because[10] 'our gospel came to you not only in word, but also in power and in the Holy Spirit and with full conviction' (5). This means that Paul was convinced of his readers' election either because of the sense of spiritual power which was with him when he preached in Thessalonica, or because of the powerful impression made upon them by his preaching and the deep conviction produced in them concerning the truth of his message, or possibly both of these.[11] In any case, we may say that the source of the power of Paul's gospel preaching was the Spirit. The result was that through his proclamation God himself called the Thessalonians to salvation, and they in turn recognised that what was proclaimed was God's word to them. This clearly illustrates the dynamic dimension of Paul's apostolate: he was not only the plenipotentiary of Christ speaking on behalf of his Lord, his Lord actually spoke through him when he preached.

Eschatological Validation

This sub-section dealing with Paul's apostolate may be concluded with a brief reference to the notion of eschatological validation of ministry. In the Thessalonian correspondence we catch a glimpse for the first time of Paul's conviction that the validation of Christian ministry (and in this instance his own) is to be revealed at the Last Day. In 1, 2.19-20 he asks: 'For what is[12] our hope or joy or crown of boasting[13] before our Lord Jesus at his coming? Is it not you? For you are our glory and joy.' Paul's hope/confidence, his joy, and his crown of boasting at the coming of the Lord Jesus are/will be those few Thessalonian converts from paganism. Implied in this statement is Paul's realisation that the validation for his ministry waits upon the revealing of Jesus from heaven. His ministry is based upon an appointment by Christ in the past, but its validation lies in the future. This is the first budding of a conviction which comes to full flower in the later epistles (cf., e.g., 1 Cor. 3.10-15).

SUFFERING, THE CHRISTIAN'S LOT

When writing the epistles to the Thessalonians, Paul was very conscious that he addressed a Christian community which was no stranger to suffering and affliction. In 2, 1.4-7 he seeks to comfort those who suffer affliction by turning their attention to the coming Day of the Lord when they shall be granted rest, and their persecutors will be repaid for their evil actions. Also he reminds them that they are not alone in the present difficulties; by suffering affliction they have become 'imitators of the churches of God in Christ Jesus which are in Judea' (1, 2.14), imitators of Paul and his co-workers, and of the Lord himself (1, 1.6).

In 1, 3.1-5 Paul confides that when his anxiety concerning the Thessalonian Christians had become so great that he could 'bear it no longer', he sent Timothy to find out how they were fairing. What concerned Paul was whether his new converts would be able to stand up under the persecution they were experiencing,[14] whether their faith would stand firm (2-3). It is against this background that he reminds them that suffering is the Christian's lot: 'You yourselves know that this is to be our lot (*autoi gar oidate hoti eis touto keimetha*) (3)'. The verb *keimai* usually has the spatial sense, 'to lie', but can also be used figuratively with the meaning 'to be appointed or destined'. It bears this latter sense in Luke 2.34 ('Behold this child is set [*keitai*] for the fall and rising of many in Israel') and this is also its meaning in the present passage. Literally translated, then, our text would read: 'For you yourselves know that we [all] are destined for this [to endure afflictions]'. Thus, according to Paul, afflictions and sufferings were not abnormal for him as an apostle or for his converts—they were destined for this.

Elsewhere Paul refers to his filling up that which is lacking in the afflictions of Christ (see discussion of Col. 1.24 in ch. 13), and 1, 3.3-4 seems to suggest that Paul understood that this privilege was not his alone, but all members of the Christian community were equally destined to share in it. If we ask how Paul arrived at this conclusion, the most ready answer is that it was the result of his reflections upon the suffering-servant passages of Deutero-Isaiah which he boldly applied both to himself and his fellow-believers.

THE HOLY SPIRIT AND THE MINISTRY OF THE CHRISTIAN COMMUNITY

In the previous sub-section we noted the dynamic dimension of Paul's apostleship brought about by the intimate participation of the Holy Spirit in the missionary preaching of the apostle. Here we must note Paul's acknowledgement of the activity of the Spirit among the Christians in the church at Thessalonica as well. In chapter 7 we saw Paul's reference to the Spirit's activity in the Galatian churches (Gal. 3.4-5). We have evidence of a similar phenomenon in the church at Thessalonica.

The passage which demands attention is 1, 5.19-22: 'Do not quench the Spirit, do not despise prophesying, but test everything; hold fast what is good, abstain from every form of evil'. Paul here commands his readers to stop quenching the Spirit.[15]

Most modern commentators interpret this as a command not to refuse opportunity to exercise spiritual gifts, especially prophesyings,[16] and this is what the context suggests.

The content of prophecy in the New Testament is various. It can deal with a new initiative in mission (Acts 13.1-3), exhortation for the upbuilding of believers (1 Cor. 14.3), foretelling of future events (Acts 11.27-28; 21.10-11), a word from the risen Lord (1 Thess. 4.15-17), and eschatological/apocalyptic information (the Revelation to John is called prophecy in 1.3; 10.11; 22.7, 10, 18-19). The chances are that the prophetic revelations (*prophēteia*) which were being despised by some of the Thessalonians were of this last type. The low regard in which some people held prophesyings would be understandable if it was the influence of such prophecies on unstable minds that had led some to give up their normal occupations and become idlers (cf. 1, 4.11; 2, 3.6-13).

In view of the high regard in which prophets were held in the early church,[17] it is unlikely that the Thessalonians would have despised the message of recognised prophets. This suggests that it was the utterances of those who were not regular prophets which were despised. The fact that the prophesyings were despised (*exoutheneō*), not rejected, could indicate that the prophets involved were given to unbridled ecstasy. This, as well as the possible effect of the prophecies upon unstable minds, could have aroused feelings of revulsion.

Though many of the issues raised by 1, 5.19-22 cannot be settled with certainty, one thing is clear: the Holy Spirit was active among the young Christians at Thessalonica. He had given them gifts of ministry, especially of prophesying. This Paul regarded as normal and legitimate and as something which should not be quenched or despised. When we come to our study of the Corinthian epistles we will see that Paul practically identifies the Spirit as the presence of Christ among his people.

THE RISEN CHRIST AND THE
CHRISTIAN COMMUNITY

Several statements in the Thessalonian epistles show that Paul did not conceive of the risen Christ as an 'absentee landlord' as far as his relationship to the Church was concerned. Christ's activity among and on behalf of his people was expected and experienced.

In 1, 3.11-13 we find one of Paul's prayers. He asks that God the Father and the Lord Jesus may direct his path so he may visit his friends in Thessalonica. He prays also that the Lord (Jesus) may cause his readers to increase in love to one another and to all men, and that he may establish their hearts unblamable in holiness. Similarly, in 2, 2.16-17 he prays that 'our Lord Jesus Christ himself and God our Father' may comfort their hearts and establish them in every good work and word. Other prayers found in 2, 3.5 and 2, 3.16 reveal the same expectation, i.e., that Christ will be active among his people.

1 Thessalonians 4.15

Of particular interest here is 1, 4.15: 'For this we declare to you *by the word of the Lord*, that we who are alive, who are left until the coming of the Lord, shall not precede those who have fallen asleep.'

This statement is part of a longer passage (1, 4.13-18) where Paul seeks to allay the fears of his readers concerning the fate of those believers who have already died, and thus have not survived until the parousia. They are not to grieve over those of their company who have died in the way that those outside Christ grieve for their departed (13). Christ's death and resurrection have become the basis of our assurance that God will raise up those who have died (14). Those who have died before the parousia, far from missing out, will actually be raised first and then joined by those who survive. To convince his readers of the reliability of this teaching, Paul claims to have it 'by the word of the Lord' (15).

An unknown saying of Jesus? At first reading the expression 'the word of the Lord' could be taken to refer to one of the sayings of Jesus in the Synoptics (or John). However, there is no saying in any of the gospels which even resembles what we find in this passage. Another explanation must therefore be sought. One suggestion is that the passage is a Pauline adaptation of an otherwise unknown but genuine saying of Jesus intended to prepare his disciples to face the fact that some of them were destined for martyrdom (cf. Mark 8.34-37; 10.39; 13.12-13;

Matt. 10.28; 24.9; John 16.2).[18] The major weakness of the suggestion is that, if Jesus did make such a statement, it would almost certainly have been preserved in our gospel traditions. Such a saying would have been of very great importance to the whole Church scattered abroad and susceptible to persecution in the first century.

A quotation from an unknown apocalypse? Alternatively, it has been suggested that 1, 4.16-17 is a citation from an apocalyptic writing which Paul quotes as a 'word of the Lord', perhaps because it has been ascribed to Jesus, as, it is said, the Little Apocalypse in Mark 13 has been ascribed to him.[19] This is a remote possibility as there are no other known quotations from apocalyptic sources in Paul's letters.[20]

A general reference to Jesus' apocalyptic teaching? A third view, while rejecting the notion that Paul is citing some unknown saying of Jesus or an apocalypse that is no longer extant, maintains that 1, 4.16-17 refers in a general way to apocalyptic teaching of Jesus similar to that found in Mark 13.[21] The suggestion is attractive as it accounts for the use of the rather vague expression 'by the word of the Lord' instead of the more explicit and usual 'as it is written'. The main problem with this view is that we have no evidence whatever that any such apocalyptic teaching of Jesus ever existed.

A word from the exalted Christ? Finally, we may note a view accepted by several modern interpreters,[22] that Paul is referring to a word given to the Church by the exalted Christ through one of the prophets, most likely through Paul himself. At this point a comparison with 1 Corinthians 15.51-52 which deals with the same subject as 1, 4.15-17, is instructive. There are marked similarities between the two passages. For instance, in both the trumpet of God gives the signal for the resurrection of the dead and the transmutation of surviving believers. In 1 Corinthians 15.51 these events constitute the mystery which Paul makes known to his readers. Further, in 1 Corinthians the term 'mystery' is consistently applied to the final glory of believers, and the mystery itself is something revealed to Paul *by the Spirit* (2.7-10). In 1 Thessalonians 4.15 Paul asserts that knowledge of these same events was made known to him *by the word of the Lord*. In light of the intimate relationship between the Lord and the Spirit in the Pauline epistles (cf. 2 Cor. 3.17; Rom.

8.9-11), and the similarities between the events described in 1 Thessalonians 4.16-17 and 1 Corinthians 15.51-52, we ought to conclude that 'the word of the Lord' in 1 Thessalonians 4.15 is nothing other than a revelation made by the exalted Christ through the Spirit to the apostle Paul.

This is then further evidence that Paul believed that Christ continued to be actively involved with his followers even after the ascension: he, through the Spirit, communicated new truth about the last things to his apostle for the comfort of his people.

CONCLUSIONS

What light do the Thessalonian epistles shed upon the relationship between Christ and Christian ministry as Paul understood it? The following conclusions seem to be in order.

First, the risen Christ is portrayed as actively participating in the life and ministry of the Christian community. Paul's prayers indicate that he expected Christ (and God the Father) to establish Christians in holiness, good works, and peace, and he asked that Christ might direct his own paths. Further, Paul spoke of the revelation of new truth about the last things which Christ had revealed to him through the Spirit. In addition, he refers to the One who supplies the Spirit to Christians and works miracles among them—clearly a reference to the activity of Christ/God the Father among his people. Obviously, Paul sees the risen Christ actively involved in the life and ministry of his people, although, it must be added, he appears to see no point in distinguishing between the activity of Christ and that of God the Father in this regard.

Second, where Paul alludes to his own apostolic ministry, we detect a significantly heightened consciousness of the authority accorded to an apostle of Christ. He gave commands to his readers in the name of Christ and expected them to be obeyed. If a man disregarded the command of the apostle, he disregarded not man but God. The sense of being an authoritative representative of Christ, backed up with the authority of God, is again reminiscent of the sort of authority given to the Twelve by Jesus for their Galilean mission. Alongside Paul's heightened sense of apostolic authority, there is a correspondingly greater awareness of the dynamic character of his apostolate. We saw the first hints of this in Galatians where Paul says his apostolate had been recognised by the apostles of the circumcision because they perceived not only the truth of his gospel, but also the grace of God that was at work in him. In the Thessalonian epistles Paul's consciousness of the power of God at work through him is far greater. We saw, for example, that Paul believed that it was *God* who called the Thessalonians to salvation through his preaching, and he was convinced that his missionary proclamation was carried out in the power of the Holy Spirit. In the later epistles we shall see that this activity is attributed to Christ, further evidence that Paul saw no need to distinguish between Christ, the Father, and the Spirit in this respect.

In the Thessalonian epistles (in line with the emphasis upon the parousia of Christ) we see for the first time Paul's belief that the validation of ministry is eschatological. His statement that the few converts in Thessalonica are his hope, his joy and his crown at the coming of Christ is the seed of the more fully developed teaching concerning eschatological validation of ministry which we find in the Corinthian epistles. Paul's ministry is related to the risen Christ in that he knows all he does must come under Christ's scrutiny at the Last Day.

Third, we saw that, like the Galatian churches, the Thessalonian community was a 'charismatic' group. The Holy Spirit was active among them, particularly inspiring men to prophesy. Thus Paul acknowledged that the dynamic dimension which he spoke of in his own mission had its counterpart in the life and ministry of the Christian community. As Christ/the Father is actively involved in the ministry of the apostle, so, too, he is active in the ministry of the Christian community, through the Spirit. We may note also that Paul, who in Galatians alluded to his own share in the sufferings of Christ, here in the Thessalonian epistles taught that *all* Christians have been destined to suffer. It was suggested that Paul came to this understanding by his reflection upon the significance of the servant-prophecies of Deutero-Isaiah. If this and the suggestion made previously about the parallel teaching in Galatians are correct, then what we have in the Thessalonian epistles is a development of the idea found in Galatians. Not only does an apostle stand alongside Christ as one in whose life and ministry the servant-prophecies find fulfilment, but so, too, does the Christian community, which is also destined to suffer. All Christians, then, stand together with Christ as fellow-servants of God. In the study of later epistles we will want to see whether this view finds any support and confirmation.

CHAPTER TEN

1, 2 CORINTHIANS

The church in Corinth, according to Acts 18, was founded by the apostle Paul on his second missionary journey (c.AD 49). He spent about eighteen months there 'teaching the word of God among them' before returning to Syrian Antioch via Ephesus. Paul's converts in Corinth were mainly Gentiles but included some Jews also (Acts 18.8). Many of them were of lowly status, but a few of noble birth also believed (1, 1.26-28).

Paul's Correspondence with the Corinthians

The relationship between Paul and the Corinthians, the letters that passed between them, Paul's personal visits and those of his messengers together constitute one of the most complex problems in Pauline studies. We know of four letters which Paul addressed to the Corinthian Christians. The earliest letter (no longer extant) is mentioned in 1, 5.9: 'I wrote to you in my letter not to associate with immoral men.' This letter apparently caused some confusion, for in his next letter (our 1 Corinthians) he had to explain that he meant they should not 'associate with any one who bears the name of brother if he is guilty of immorality . . .' (5.11). He had also to respond to several specific enquiries which the Corinthians had addressed to him in a letter of their own (cf. 7.1 [marital problems], 8.1 [eating food offered to idols], 12.1 [the place of spiritual gifts]). In addition, he sought to correct certain aberrations in their behaviour and conduct of worship services (cf. 1.10-3.17 [party divisions], 5.1-13; 6.12-20 [sexual aberrations], 6.1-11 [legal disputes between Christians], 11.2-14.40 [problems related to worship services]). In 15.1-58 he dealt with problems associated with the resurrection of believers which were apparently disturbing the Corinthian church. The third letter (probably no longer extant, though some think it is preserved in 2 Corinthians 10-13) is mentioned in 2, 7.8, where it is described as a letter which 'grieved' the Corinthians, but the grief it caused was 'godly grief' for it produced repentance (2, 7.9). The fourth letter is our 2 Corinthians (some would say parts of it). It includes Paul's defence against charges of fickleness (1.12-2.4), his apology for the apostolic office (2.14-7.4), and his instructions/recommendations regarding the collection for the Jerusalem saints (8.1-9.15). There is an abrupt change in tone at 10.1, and the last four chapters (10-13) include sharp warnings and an out-spoken defence of his apostleship and integrity.

Reconstructing the Historical Context of the Correspondence

It is extremely difficult to reconstruct the historical context and sequence of these letters, for historical reconstruction can be carried out only after literary questions are answered, but these can be answered only with some knowledge of the historical context. Thus we are working in a circle without the necessary data to break out of its confines. C. K. Barrett, aware that any reconstruction can only be tentative, suggests the following sequence of events after the writing of 1 Corinthians: Paul hoped that the writing of 1 Corinthians would settle problems which had arisen in the infant church, but the epistle was not wholly successful in this regard. It seems that the difficulties in Corinth had been compounded by the arrival of a group who claimed to be apostles. They rejected the legitimacy of Paul's apostolate and established themselves as 'authorities' in the Corinthian church. These men were already in occupation of the church when Paul paid the visit he had promised in 1, 16.5-7 (cf. 1, 4.19-21), so instead of a happy reunion with his converts, Paul found himself the object of an unpleasant attack lead by one of these 'pseudo-apostles', while his beloved converts apparently stood by without coming to his aid. Paul was forced to withdraw to Ephesus. From Ephesus he wrote the painful letter, which he entrusted to Titus for delivery. Paul met Titus returning from Corinth in Macedonia and learned to his great relief that the painful letter had produced the desired result; the Corinthian Christians had been brought to repentance and were now eager to show their loyalty to Paul. Having received this heartening news, Paul wrote a further letter, his fourth, in which he made arrangements for the completion of the collection for the poor Christians in Jerusalem and urged restraint in the punishment of the one guilty of blatant sexual offences. He also gave extended instructions on the true nature of the apostolate, criteria they could use in the situation in which they found themselves—confronted by conflicting claims to authentic apostleship.[1] However, Paul somehow learned that, either Titus had misjudged the situation, or it had radically altered soon after Titus left Corinth, for the intruding false apostles were once again in control and were freely slandering the absent Paul. They seem to have satisfied the criteria which the Corinthian Christians must have evolved for judging the validity of apostolic claims. Paul responded to this situation by writing another letter (2 Corinthians 10-13) in which he further explained what he understood by apostleship, defended his apostolic status, and mounted a blistering attack upon the false apostles. He promised a third visit to Corinth in which he would not spare the offenders; he would take any necessary action, no matter how painful that might be. It seems this last drastic measure was successful, for, in his letter to the Romans Paul says Achaia had contributed to the collection (15.26), and there is no hint of any tension with the Corinthian church.[2] Barrett's reconstruction may be adopted as a working hypothesis, as long as we remember that, like any other reconstruction, it can be held only tentatively, since the complexity of the literary and historical problems defy all attempts to produce a convincing solution.

Paul's Opponents in Corinth

No matter how we reconstruct the sequence of events/letters, it is patently clear that Paul had opponents in Corinth. 1 Corinthians was written in response to a report from Chloe's people concerning factions that had arisen in Corinth, each group claiming the name of an outstanding Christian leader (Paul, Apollos, or Cephas), and one group using the name of Christ in a partisan way (1, 1.10-12). It is possible that it was from this last group that some of the problems that Paul had to deal with arose. In any case, it appears that the gospel which Paul preached underwent a significant transformation in the minds of some. Paul, for example, viewed the indwelling Spirit as the guarantee (*arrabōn*) of resurrected life in the new age.

However, for some in Corinth the present possession and experience of the Spirit was the be all and end all. 'Let others know the exalted Christ as he was proclaimed to them by Paul or Apollos or Peter; they were in direct touch with him by the Spirit, and had no need of such intermediaries.[3] They were men of the Spirit, and the exaggerated evaluation of the more spectacular spiritual gifts which Paul had to combat in 1 Corinthians 12-14 probably originated with this group. If Paul's stress on Christ crucified (1, 1.23; 2.1-2) was also intended to correct a one-sided emphasis made by these men, we may add that they upheld the importance of the exalted heavenly Christ at the expense of the earthly Jesus. How are we to style these men? They are hardly Gnostics in the classical sense of the word—Paul expects them to acknowledge without qualms the traditional gospel (1, 15.1-11). It is perhaps best to use the term 'incipient Gnostics' to describe them, for they laid great store by wisdom (*sophia*) and knowledge (*gnōsis*), as well as stressing spiritual experience.[4] Paul's 'opponents' in 1 Corinthians, then, appear to be simply his own converts who had wrongly interpreted their Christian experience using hellenistic (incipient gnostic) categories.

If the 'opponents' of 1 Corinthians were merely Paul's own converts, those whom he had to answer in 2 Corinthians were antagonists indeed. They denied that Paul belonged to Christ (2, 10.7), blamed him for not being prepared to accept financial support from the church at Corinth (2, 11.7; 12.16), and criticised the weak impression he made when present in person (2, 10.1, 10). Paul described them as false apostles, deceitful workmen (2, 11.13), and servants of Satan (2, 11.15). They were proud of their Jewish ancestry (2, 11.22), called themselves servants of Christ (2, 11.23), gained entrance to the community with letters of recommendation (2, 10.12, 18, cf. 2, 3.1), and preached another Christ and another gospel (2, 11.4).[5]

Who were these opponents whom Paul so mercilessly castigated? Suggested identifications include: (1) representatives of the radical Jewish-Christian group associated with Peter,[6] (2) a group of Palestinian Jewish-Christians who at least laid claim to the authority of the Jerusalem apostles,[7] (3) a group of Palestinian origin, but not necessarily having the authority of the Jerusalem apostles—they were intruders who joined themselves with Paul's gnostic opponents in Corinth, thus broadening the front on which Paul had to fight,[8] (4) Jewish Gnostics,[9] (5) Jews who had adopted the type of propaganda used by the inspired men of the hellenistic world,[10] and (6) Judaizing Jews from Jerusalem who misrepresented the Jerusalem apostles.[11]

The problem of Paul's opponents in Corinth is crucial to our understanding of the development of early Christianity, and yet here again it must be admitted that the data available are insufficient to resolve the problem satisfactorily. Every opinion cited is but a hypothesis, and must remain so until further evidence is forthcoming. It should be noted, however, that in most of the suggestions cited, the opponents that Paul answers in 2 Corinthians 10-13 are identified as Jewish Christians of one sort or another. The major exception is Schmithals' view that they were Jewish Gnostics, but this view has not been widely received.

A Working Hypothesis

For the purposes of our present study the following is assumed as a working hypothesis: in the Corinthian correspondence Paul has first to correct some erroneous conclusions drawn by his own converts who had interpreted their Christian experience using hellenistic categories. But later on anti-Pauline Jewish Christians from Palestine (Jerusalem?) arrived in Corinth. They accommodated themselves to a certain extent to those converts of Paul who had hellenistic leanings and stirred up opposition against Paul personally so that he had to deal with an attack, not only upon the purity of the gospel as he understood it, but also upon the validity of his own apostleship.

No matter how the opponents of Paul are identified, their attack elicited a response from the apostle which provides us with the most revealing portrait that we have of his ministry. We would be much better able to appreciate this portrayal if we could accurately reconstruct the charges to which Paul responds. Nevertheless, there is still much for us to learn, especially from 2 Corinthians 10-13 which provides much of the data for our study of Paul's apostleship. In the sections which follow we will see that several of the ministerial ideas (some of them only seed thoughts) found in Galatians and the Thessalonian letters come to full flower in the Corinthian correspondence; some new ideas are also introduced.

Our study of Galatians and the Thessalonian letters revealed Paul's consciousness of both the authority of his apostolate and also its dynamic character. This was clear enough in Galatians, but was even more evident in the Thessalonian epistles. In the Corinthian correspondence this double-sided character of his apostolate finds it clearest expression.

In both epistles Paul introduces himself as an apostle of Christ Jesus by the will of God. He is an apostle because he has seen Christ (1, 9.1, cf. 1, 15.8), but he calls himself 'the least of all the apostles' saying he is 'unfit to be called an apostle' because formerly he persecuted the church of God (1, 15.9). However, in another place he asserts that he is 'not at all inferior to these superlative apostles' (2, 12.11)—a reference to his opponents in Corinth.

An Ambassador for Christ

Paul's strong sense of being a commissioned agent of Christ is evident throughout these epistles. He says Christ sent him to preach the gospel (1, 1.17) and this he does, not of his own will, but because he is 'entrusted with a commission' and woe betide him if he does not carry it out (1, 9.16-17, cf. 1, 3.10ff.). In 2, 5.19-20 Paul describes himself and his colleagues as 'ambassadors for Christ' (*huper Christou oun presbeuomen*) whose task it was to beseech men, on behalf of Christ, to be reconciled to God. The essential meaning of the verb *presbeuō* is 'to be older or the eldest', but it was used also in connection with functions for which the wisdom of age was a necessary prerequisite, thus in connection with an ambassador who represents the people who send him.[12] It was also used figuratively in the religious sphere. Philo used it for God's emissaries (angels, Moses in his mediatorial role). In gnostic texts the idea of the ambassador is used in relation to the heavenly redeemer, though the word *presbeuō* is seldom found. The cognate *presbeutēs* is the usual term employed to denote heavenly envoys in the Manichean texts (it is also used there for the Mani himself, and for the Manichean teachers), and in early Christianity *presbeutēs* denoted a messenger of God.[13] Thus when Paul used the expression in 2, 5.20 he was employing a well-established concept.

However, Paul did not think of himself in terms of a divine messenger of Hellenism, for he was not simply a teacher of esoteric knowledge, nor the purveyor of heavenly reason; his ambassadorship was inseparable from the reconciling activity of God in and through the death of Christ. This reconciling activity of God was a double-sided unity—on the one hand, God reconciled men to himself through the death of his Son, and on the other hand, the apostle, on behalf of Christ, besought men (on the basis of that death) to be reconciled to God. The unique character of the ambassadorship of Paul (and his colleagues) is seen in the fact that he, unlike the divine messengers of Hellenism, did not offer esoteric teaching, but rather proclaimed a call for reconciliation based on God's own saving intervention in the history of mankind. Thus, Paul's ambassadorship has closer affinities to the sending of the Twelve as heralds of the kingdom of God, than to the coming of a gnostic redeemer or the Manichean envoys.

Despite the well-known differences between the early Christian apostolate and the rabbinic *šālîaḥ* 'institution',[14] there are, nevertheless, some striking similarities as well, in particular the representative character of both. It is this characteristic that is so clearly expressed in 2, 5.19-20. It would be going beyond the facts of the case to say that the early Christians took over the *šālîaḥ* 'institution', but, on the other hand, passages like 2, 5.19-20 suggest that the early Christians sought and found in this concept a means of expressing their understanding of the apostolate, an understanding which had originated with the experiences of some with the risen Christ and had developed with the progress of the Christian mission.[15] Based on our study of the synoptic sayings of Jesus we would want to say that the precedent for such conceptualisation was dominical.

Authoritative Character of Paul's Apostolate

The authoritative character of Paul's apostolate also finds its clearest expression in the Corinthian letters. In the closing verses of 2 Corinthians Paul said he prayed for improvement in the situation at Corinth, and he wrote his harsh warnings and spirited defence so that when he came he would not have to be severe in his use of the authority given him (13.9-10). He had no doubts about the divine origin of his authority and the binding nature of the commands he gave. After giving instructions for regulating the exercise of spiritual gifts in their worship services, Paul said: 'If any one thinks that he is a prophet, or spiritual, he should acknowledge that what I am writing to you is a command of the Lord' (1, 14.37).[16] Clearly Paul implied that, no matter how 'spiritual' some of the enthusiasts in Corinth might be, they must still submit to the authority of their apostle. Their direct link with the exalted Christ via the Spirit does not exempt them from the need to obey the apostle, on the contrary, it should make them more ready to do so, seeing that the authority of Paul was derived from the same exalted Christ.

No passage more strikingly portrays Paul's convictions concerning his apostolic authority than 1, 5.3-5. In his earliest (now lost) letter to the Corinthians Paul had to deal with a case of immorality, and he commanded that the offender be driven out (1, 5.9-13). When he wrote 1 Corinthians the problem still persisted and we find him saying: 'For though absent in body I am present in Spirit, and as if present, I have already pronounced judgement in the name of the Lord Jesus on the man who has done such a thing. When you are assembled, and my spirit is present, with the power of our Lord Jesus, you are to deliver this man to Satan for the destruction of the flesh, that his spirit may be saved in the day of the Lord Jesus' (1, 5.3-5). The passage presents many problems for the exegete,[17] but as Conzelmann observes, 'what is plain is that Paul is resolved upon a judicial act of a sacral and pneumatic kind against the culprit.'[18] Here we see the blending of legal and spiritual power: Paul's authority and the power of Jesus, the authoritative and dynamic dimension of the apostolate.

The Dynamic Dimension of Paul's Apostolate

In the Corinthian letters, Paul refers to his colleagues and himself as fellow-workers with God (1, 3.9, cf. 2, 6.1), speaks of God as the one who works through him (1, 15.10, cf. 2, 2.14-16), and claims that in his ministry the transcendent power of God is manifest (2, 3.5; 4.7). Of particular interest is the statement:

'Thanks be to God who in Christ always leads us in triumph, and through us spreads the fragrance of the knowledge of him everywhere. For we are the aroma of Christ to God among those who are being saved and among those who are perishing' (2, 2.14-15). Although the majority opinion concerning the background for the figures used here by Paul[19] has been questioned in recent years,[20] the main thrust of the passage remains clear enough: God, through the ministry of his apostles, spreads abroad the knowledge of his Son. In short, here again Paul claims that God himself is at work in and through his ministry.

The Simultaneity of Weakness and Power

Paul claimed to be the agent/instrument through whom God worked. His adversaries in Corinth asserted that his lack of a commanding presence and his unimpressive speech (2, 10.10) were inconsistent with his claims. They denied that Christ spoke through Paul so that he was forced to write: 'I warn them now . . . that if I come again I will not spare them—since you desire proof that Christ is speaking in me', and he added, 'he is not weak in dealing with you, but is powerful in you. For he was crucified in weakness, but lives by the power of God' (2, 13.2-4a). And then, to defend the 'weakness' of his own presence and ministry, while at the same time asserting that divine power was manifested through it, he wrote 'for we are weak in him, but in dealing with you we shall live with him by the power of God' (2, 13.4b). Clearly, we are confronted herewith a paradox. Paul's weakness is not to be replaced by the power of God (as his opponents seem to have expected ought to have been the case), but instead it is to be the ever present accompaniment of it. The apostle implies that he is simultaneously identified with the Christ who was crucified in weakness, and the Christ who now lives by the power of God. The *locus classicus* for this teaching is 2, 12.9-10: 'He [the Lord] said to me, "My grace is sufficient for you, for my power is made perfect in weakness." I will all the more gladly boast of my weaknesses, that the power of Christ may rest upon me. For the sake of Christ, then, I am content with weaknesses, insults, hardships, persecutions, and calamities; for when I am weak, then I am strong.'

Paul's words here indicate the simultaneity of weakness and

power; it is in the very weakness of the apostle that the 'epiphany' of God's power takes place. Accordingly, in 2, 4.7-12, after listing some of his experiences of persecution and suffering, he sums up by saying that he and his colleagues are 'always carrying in the body the death of Jesus, so that the life of Jesus may also be manifested in our bodies. For while we live we are always being given up to death for Jesus' sake, so that the life of Jesus may also be manifested in our mortal flesh. So death is at work in us, but life in you.' Thus, against his opponents, Paul insists that the true apostolic ministry is not only a manifestation of power from the exalted Christ, but also involves 'carrying in the body the dying of Jesus.'

Suffering, the Mark of a True Apostle

When Paul wanted to prove that he was better qualified than his adversaries to be recognised as a genuine apostle, he appealed, not only to his pneumatic experiences and powers (2, 12.1-4, 11-12), but also to his many sufferings: 'Are they servants of Christ? I am a better one—I am talking like a madman—with far greater labours, far more imprisonments, with countless beatings . . .' (2, 11.23). We may say that Paul, far from regarding his weakness as something which disqualifies his claim to apostleship, actually appeals to it as the legitimatising evidence.

In brief, Paul believed and asserted that the exalted Christ was actively at work through him. His 'weakness' was not a denial of this, on the contrary, it was its necessary accompaniment—only as he bore in his body the death of Jesus, could the life of Jesus be manifested through him.[21] The corollary, of course, is that the pseudo-apostles, who claimed to manifest the power of the exalted Christ without weakness or suffering, only show that they are not genuine apostles. Where there is no participation in the dying of Jesus, there is no manifestation of the life and power of the exalted Christ.

Living Letters Inscribed by Paul

Paul's consciousness of the power of Christ at work through him, the dynamic aspect of his ministry, finds further expression in 2 Corinthians 3. There he responds to criticism of his ministry: he came without letters of recommendation. He asks:

'Do we need, as some do, letters of recommendation to you or from you?' He then says: 'You yourselves are our letter of recommendation ... a letter from Christ inscribed by us, written not with ink but with the Spirit of the living God, not on tablets of stone, but on tablets of human hearts' (2, 3.1-3). The word *diakonētheisa* which the RSV renders 'delivered' is here translated as 'inscribed', which more accurately conveys Paul's meaning: Christ is the author of the letter, the apostle and his colleagues served as scribes.[22] Christ himself then is the author of 'living letters' written on the hearts of men; letters produced through the 'scribal' ministry of Paul and his colleagues to whom was entrusted the precious 'ink' of the Spirit of God.

In a later section the relationship between Christ and the Spirit in the Corinthian letters will be discussed, but before coming to that the notion of suffering, especially as it is related to servanthood, needs to be further examined.

SUFFERING AND THE SERVANTS OF GOD

On several occasions (1, 3.5; 4.1; 2, 3.6; 4.5; 6.4; 11.23) Paul refers to his colleagues and himself as servants (*diakonos*, four times; *doulos*, once; and *hupēretēs*, once). In face of the factions which sprang up in Corinth around the names of the outstanding early Christian leaders ('I belong to Paul', 'I belong to Apollos', etc., 1, 1.12; 3.4) Paul asserts that these men are but 'servants through whom you believed, as the Lord assigned to each' (1, 3.5), and says they should be regarded simply as servants of Christ (1, 4.1, cf. 2, 4.5).

The most significant feature of Paul's use of the servant motif in the Corinthians letters is its association with the theme of suffering. Thus, in 2, 4.5 Paul says: 'What we preach is not ourselves, but Jesus Christ as Lord, with ourselves as your servants for Jesus' sake', and adds that God has shone into their hearts to give 'the light of the knowledge of the glory of God in the face of Christ' (2, 4.6). He hastens to add further that those to whom this treasure has been entrusted are only 'earthen vessels', men who are afflicted, perplexed, persecuted, and struck down—those who bear the treasure of the knowledge of the glory of God in Christ, also bear in their bodies the death of Jesus, and only because of that, the life of Jesus is also manifest in their mortal flesh (2, 4.7-12). Thus Paul's concept of servant-hood includes the great privilege of sharing the knowledge of God's glory, the inescapable responsibility of bearing in the body the death of Jesus, and the joyous prospect of seeing the life of Jesus manifested also—'death at work in us, but life in you.'

Sharing the Sufferings of Christ

What does Paul mean when he says that he always carries 'in the body the death of Jesus' (2, 4.10)? First of all it can be said that Paul did not have in mind some merely mystical identification with Christ's passion. The context clearly indicates Paul was thinking about concrete sufferings experienced in the course of his ministry. But why are these experiences *of Paul* spoken of as a carrying of the death (*nekrōsin*) *of Jesus?* The word used here for 'death' gives us a clue. When speaking about death Paul usually employs the word *thanatos* (47 times), but here (and elsewhere only in Rom. 4.19) he uses *nekrōsis*. It is, therefore, quite likely that Paul does not mean simply death, but the process leading to death, or making one dead (*nekros*).[23] So bitter were some of the sufferings and persecutions which Paul experienced (cf., e.g., 2, 1.8-9), it must have often seemed to him that death was imminent (cf. Phil. 2.17). In fact he gives expression to just such an awareness in the verse which immediately follows the one being discussed: 'For while we live we are always being given up to death for Jesus' sake.' Therefore, it seems clear that for Paul the carrying in the body of the death of Jesus meant a willingness to be exposed to and experience persecutions and sufferings which may lead even to death. He could call such sufferings the carrying of the death of Jesus because they were borne in identification with Jesus and his mission, and for his sake.

Closely related to all this is Paul's strange statement in 2, 6.4-5: 'As servants of God we commend ourselves in every way: through great endurance, in afflictions, hardships, calamities, beatings, imprisonments . . .' Once again Paul is on the defensive and trying to convince his readers of the genuineness of his credentials. His opponents in Corinth might support their claims to be true servants of God by letters of recommendation, but Paul and his colleagues commend themselves by an appeal to their manifold afflictions. This, indeed, is a strange way to commend themselves, but what is clearly implied is that *the true servant of God is a suffering servant.*

Another passage along similar lines is found in 2, 1.5: 'For as we share abundantly in Christ's sufferings, so through Christ we share abundantly in comfort too.' Again the context shows that it is through the concrete afflictions which the apostle and his colleagues experienced that they somehow came to share in Christ sufferings. How are we to understand all of this?

Sharing the 'Sufferings of the Messiah'?

One important suggestion is that the sufferings of Christ spoken of here are to be understood as analogous to the Hebrew 'sufferings of the messiah'. In the Hebrew mind the sufferings of the messiah were understood to denote a period of tribulation and woe through which God's people would pass. These messianic woes would usher in the messianic age of eternal bliss. On this view, Paul could say he shared in the sufferings of Christ/the messiah because he shared in the sufferings of that final period before the coming of the messianic age. The weakness of this interpretation is that according to the Hebrew view the sufferings of the messiah *preceded* the coming of the messiah; he had no direct share in them. Paul, on the contrary, was quite sure that the Christ had suffered, and was at pains to show the close affinity between his own sufferings and those of the Christ.

In order to overcome the weakness of this view, while still making use of the Hebrew idea of the messianic woes, Barrett suggests that the early Christians came to believe that Christ himself had endured the messianic sufferings on behalf of the elect. Their own 'uncomfortable' experiences were then understood as some of the messianic sufferings 'which had been allowed to reach, and be endured by, his followers.'[24]

By suggesting a Christian interpretation of the messianic woes, Barrett has really produced a picture similar to that which emerges if we use the suffering servant prophecies of Deutero-Isaiah as the background for understanding Paul's saying about sharing the suffering of Christ. In both cases, the Christ and his people share in the same sort of sufferings (though we would have to add that the vicarious sufferings alluded to in the servant-passages were fulfilled in Christ alone).

As we have no explicit evidence for the existence of a Christian interpretation of the messianic woes, while we do have evidence for Paul's application of the servant-prophecies to his ministry (cf. Acts 13.47), it is better to adopt the latter idea as the clue for interpreting 2, 4.10.

CHRIST, THE SPIRIT AND THE CHRISTIAN COMMUNITY

In the examination of Paul's apostleship above, where the significance of 2, 3.2-3 was discussed, it was suggested that Paul saw himself as the 'scribe' by whose agency Christ produced 'living letters'—this scribal work of Paul's being carried out with the 'ink' of the Spirit. Clearly Paul closely associated the exalted Christ with the Spirit in his presentation of the dynamic character of apostolic ministry. At this point we need to take brief note of other passages in which Christ is associated with the Spirit. In 1, 12.4-6, as preparation for his subsequent treatment of 'gifts' (*charismata*), Paul reminds his readers that 'there are varieties of gifts, but the same Spirit; and there are varieties of service, but the same Lord; and there are varieties of workings, but it is the same God who inspires them all in every one.' Thus Paul closely associates Christ (and God the Father as well) with the Spirit in the service which Christians are to carry out. There is another reference, 1, 15.45, in which Christ is referred to as the Last Adam—a life-giving spirit, but this requires more than a passing comment.[25]

1 Corinthians 15.45

The full text of this verse runs: 'Thus it is written, "The first man Adam became a living being"; the last Adam became a life-giving spirit.' Clearly the text is important for an understanding of Paul's view of Christ's relationship to the Spirit, but the exact meaning of the relevant clause, 'the last Adam became a life-giving spirit' is not easy to determine. To begin with it is probably true to say that the Last Adam is a life-giving Spirit because, unlike the first Adam who only participated in life in a natural manner, he was a supernatural being, the source of all life, in particular of eternal life.[26]

A significant contribution to the understanding of this passage has been made by J. D. G. Dunn. He grounds his interpretation of the expression in the controversy Paul had with the Gnostics in Corinth. They distinguished themselves as spiritual men (*pneumatikoi*) from others who were unspiritual (i.e., *psuchikoi*). They denied any real bodily resurrection while claiming to have already shared in resurrection life through their experience of the Spirit. Paul met the Gnostics on their own ground by accepting their distinction between the spiritual (*pneumatikos*) and the physical/unspiritual (*psuchikos*), but he applied it to two *bodily* states. He spoke of a physical body (*sōma psuchikon*—or present mode of existence) and a spiritual body (*sōma pneumatikon*—the mode of existence after the resurrection). So while agreeing that there are two kinds of existence, in the physical body (like the first Adam) and in the spiritual body (like the second Adam), he asserted that the second state follows the first and can only be experienced after death or at the parousia.

Jesus himself now risen from the dead exists as *sōma pneumatikon*. The evidence for this is the spiritual experience of the Christian community. That experience derives from him who as *sōma pneumatikon* is life-giving spirit (*pneuma zōopoioun*) as well. The really significant feature of all this as far as our present enquiry is concerned is the corollary that Jesus is identified as the source of the Corinthians' experiences of the Spirit. In other words, 'the experience of the life-giving Spirit is experience of the risen Jesus.'[27]

If the cogency of Dunn's argument be granted, we may identify in 1, 15.45 a step forward in Paul's understanding of Jesus' relation to the Spirit. We have seen already that in Galatians Paul associates the sending of the Spirit with the death of Christ (even though just what that association might be is not explained). Here he adds that Jesus, crucified and risen, is the source of Christians' experiences of the life-giving Spirit. The similarity between this and Luke's presentation of the matter (discussed in ch. 6) is obvious, and as we shall see later, the idea emerges with greater clarity still in Ephesians.

At various points throughout 1 Corinthians Paul responds to questions raised by the Corinthian Christians themselves (identifiable by the formula 'now concerning'/*peri de* which begins the treatment of the queries). In 1 Corinthians 12-14 Paul takes up the question of spiritual gifts.[28] If it is correct to say that the theme of 1 Corinthians 12 is unity in diversity, we would have to say that Paul's emphasis falls upon the unity rather than the diversity. He reminds them that although there may be various gifts and varities of service and working, there is only one Spirit, one Lord, and one God who works all in all.

Several passages in 1 Corinthians 12 suggest that there were disintegrating forces at work in the Christian community at Corinth (e.g., 1, 12.15-16: 'If the foot should say, "Because I am not a hand, I do not belong to the body . . .'''; 1, 12.21: 'The eye cannot say to the hand, "I have no need of you . . ."'). It appears that, on the one hand, there were those who were made to feel inferior because they did not exercise the same spiritual gifts as others and thought they were unworthy to be regarded as members of the church, while, on the other hand, there were those who became so inflated through the exercise of gifts given to them that they felt no need of other members of the church. Paul's argument, especially in chapter 14, implies that there were 'spiritual men' in Corinth who, because of the gift of tongues which they exercised, thought they were superior to others—perhaps regarding themselves alone as true men of the Spirit. In face of these disintegrating forces, Paul emphasised the corporate nature of the experience of the Spirit (he rarely spoke of an individual experience of the Spirit) and the fact that all the gifts are manifestations of the same Spirit and intended for the common good (1, 12.4-11). It is to illustrate and drive home this important truth that Paul introduced the figure of the body.[29]

The Body of Christ

One of the most controversial aspects of the debate relating to chapter 12 is whether the 'body of Christ' is a metaphor pure and simple,[30] or a 'proper' usage—a sort of cosmic reality of prior existence to which believers are joined.[31] It is important to recall that Paul's aim in chapter 12 is not to make an ontological definition of the Church (though that does not mean such a definition may not be assumed or implied by what he says). Rather he is trying to deal with the problem of enthusiastic individualism which threatens to bring about the disintegration of the Christian community at Corinth. The enthusiasts appear to have viewed their experience of the Spirit in an entirely individualistic way. What Paul wants to stress is the corporate character of the Christian experience of the Spirit. He has already sought to do this by emphasising that all spiritual gifts are from the one Spirit. By the use of the figure of the body he says, in effect, that by the bestowal of the Spirit men are not primarily made into spiritual individuals, but are formed into one charismatic body—the body of Christ.[32] The members of this body are 'gifted' Christians, and it is more accurate to say they exercise gifts rather than to say they possess gifts. Each gift is a new act of grace at each time of its operation, so the unity of which Paul speaks here is not a static affair. It is *an ongoing creative event, constantly dependent on the Spirit manifesting his manifold interacting charismata*', and, it may be added, 'in Paul's view there is no body and no unity apart from *charismata*. (The Spirit of) Christ manifesting himself through different members of the community in dynamic mutual inter-dependence *is* the body (12.12)'.[33]

To sum up, in opposition to the individualistic approach of the enthusiasts, Paul emphasised that the Christian experience of the Spirit is body-forming (continuously so), and orientated towards the common good of the body so formed (12.7). If this interpretation of 1 Corinthians 12 is admitted, it follows that the reality for which the figure of the body of Christ stands is the unity of Christians in the Spirit. It is called the body of Christ (rather than the body of the Spirit) because it is *Christ's* Spirit that binds them together. This conclusion is important for the present enquiry because it enables us to say that, for Paul, ministry in the Christian community is dependent upon (the Spirit of) Christ who bestows the ministrial gifts and (at the same time, and by so doing) creates a unity of interrelated and mutually dependent spiritually gifted people, which may be called the body of Christ.

118

In our study of the Thessalonian epistles we noted how Paul viewed his converts as his crown of boasting before the Lord at his coming (1 Thess. 2.19); the same idea underlies 2 Corinthians 1.14 where he says: 'I hope you will understand fully, . . . that you can be proud of us as we can be of you, on the day of the Lord Jesus.' However, it is in 1 Corinthians that this idea of eschatological validation finds its clearest expression.

In 1, 4.1 Paul, having tried to set the ministry of Apollos and his own ministry in a proper light, says his readers ought to regard both himself and Apollos simply as stewards of Christ. This leads him to reflect upon the accountability of stewards—they must be found faithful (1, 4.2)—but he quickly adds that he is accountable not to his Corinthian readers, but to his Lord. Paul has indeed made himself their servant, but he acknowledges no master but Christ. So he says: 'with me it is a very small thing that I should be judged by you or any human court,' and continues, 'I do not even judge myself' (1, 4.3). It is not fitting for men to pronounce judgement on fellow-servants of God 'before the time, before the Lord comes.' He will bring all things to light then, and according to his righteous judgement every man will receive his commendation (1, 4.5). Plainly, for Paul, the validation of his own ministry was eschatological—'when the Lord comes'.

1 Corinthians 3.10-15

Even clearer teaching upon the eschatological validation of ministry is found in 1, 3.10-15. Like 1, 4.5, this passage is part of Paul's endeavour to set his own ministry and that of Apollos in proper perspective. In 1, 3.5-9 he uses the agricultural figure of planting and watering to describe the relationship between his ministry and Apollos' ministry. Then in 1, 3.9 he introduces the metaphor of the building ('you are . . . God's building') which is further exploited in 1, 3.10-15. He likens himself to a skilled master builder who lays the foundation (10a), and he likens the others who came along later to workmen who raise the superstructure (10b).

Verses 11-15 contain a clear note of warning and a hint of disapproval concerning the workmanship of the superstructure erected upon Paul's 'foundation'. It is unlikely that Paul refers here to Apollos' ministry, for there is no hint of any reticence on Paul's part when he speaks of Apollos' labours in the preceding verses. The allusion here may be to the work of Peter, or perhaps his supporters (the Cephas party), but we cannot be certain about that. In any case, verse 12a makes it plain that what Paul says applies to anyone who takes it upon himself to participate in the erection of a superstructure upon the once-laid foundation.

For our present purposes the important aspect of the passage is that, by use of the building metaphor (with its fabulous as well as mundane building materials), Paul asserts that every man's ministry will be tested at the Last Day (13).[34] It is possible that the results of a man's ministry will not survive the testing, but even so he himself will be saved (15). On the other hand, if it does survive the testing, then the man will receive a reward (14). Thus we may say that the principle of eschatological validation which Paul has hitherto applied to his own ministry, he now extends to cover the ministry of any one who takes it upon himself to build upon the foundation he has laid.

CONCLUSIONS

First, the exalted Christ is regarded by Paul as actively involved in his own ministry and that of his colleagues. He speaks of Christ as the author of a 'letter' (the Corinthian believers) which was 'put into writing' by his apostolic labours and those of his associates using the 'ink' of the Spirit. Thus Paul makes Christ the initiator of the Christian mission, while he himself is the agent through whom Christ accomplishes his purpose by the Spirit.

Christ is closely related to the Spirit in these epistles and, if the interpretation adopted for 1, 15.45 is correct, we may say that Paul portrays him as the life-giving Spirit. By this he implies that Christ is the source of the Christians' experience of the Spirit. In our study of Galatians we saw that Paul associated the sending of the Spirit with the death of Christ. Here in the Corinthian letters we see a development in Paul's understanding of the relation between Christ and Spirit; Christ is now presented as the source of the Christian experience of the Spirit. This receives some confirmation from 1, 12.4-6 where

Christ (and God the Father) are closely associated with the bestowal of ministerial gifts.

Second, we saw several significant developments as far as the ministry of Paul (and his colleagues) is concerned. Paul's realisation that he is Christ's commissioned agent finds its clearest expression in these epistles. He calls himself an ambassador of Christ. However, he does not think of himself in terms of a divine messenger of Hellenism; Paul's ambassadorship is an integral part of the reconciling activity of God in Christ. God reconciled men to himself through the death of Christ, and the apostle, on behalf of Christ (and on the basis of that death), must beseech men to be reconciled to God. His ambassadorship has closer affinities with the sending of the Twelve than it does with the mission of the gnostic redeemer or the Manichean envoys. It approximates more closely to the rabbinic šālīaḥ concept than it does to the hellenistic idea of a divine messenger. Although the early Christians cannot be said to have taken over the šālīaḥ 'institution', nevertheless they appear to have sought and found in that concept a means of expressing their understanding of apostleship which originated with the post-resurrection appearances of Christ and grew with the progress of their mission.

In our study of the Thessalonian letters we noted Paul's heightened sense (compared with what emerges in Galatians) of the authority of his apostolate and its dynamic character. The Corinthian letters reveal an even greater sense of this double-sided character of the Pauline apostolate. However, in the Corinthian epistles Paul was forced to explain how his claims that the exalted Christ was dynamically involved in his ministry could be reconciled with his own unimpressive personal presence and the sufferings which were so much a part of his career. In so doing Paul took another step forward in his understanding of the dynamic character of apostleship: the power of Christ does not replace the weakness of the apostle, rather weakness is the ever-present accompaniment of power. Christ's power is made perfect in weakness.

Closely associated with Paul's teaching on the inter-relationship between weakness and power, is the conviction that the true servant of Christ is a suffering servant. In Galatians 6.17 Paul suggested that his suffering was evidence for the genuineness of his apostleship. This thought is taken up again and developed in the Corinthian letters where Paul uses it forcefully to contrast his own (genuine) apostolate with that of his opponents. The vessel which bears the knowledge of the glory of God in the face of Christ is an earthen vessel, a vessel/body which bears the dying of Jesus so that the life of Jesus may be made manifest. These sufferings were, for Paul, the legitimatising evidence of his apostolate, for they were a sharing in the sufferings of Christ. It was argued that the background to Paul's conviction that the true servant of Christ is a suffering servant is to be found in the servant-prophecies of Deutero-Isaiah, and that Paul increasingly came to view himself as a servant of God in whose ministry those prophecies found fulfilment. He stood alongside Christ as a fellow-servant of God.

Although Paul regarded himself as a servant of men, he owned no master but Christ. As in the Thessalonian epistles, so too in the Corinthian letters, we see Paul's conviction that the validation of his ministry will come from Christ alone, and that at the Last Day. However, this idea of eschatological validation is developed further in the Corinthians letters, for here Paul extends it to cover, not only apostolic labours, but also the work of any man who takes it upon himself to build the Church of God. His work, too, will come under the scrutiny of Christ at the Last Day.

Third, the ministry of the Christian community and its relationship to Christ is further defined in the Corinthian letters. It has already been noted that Paul saw Christ as the source of Christian experiences of the Spirit. However, we also saw that Paul, in face of disintegrating forces at work in Corinth, asserted that the true Christian experience of the Spirit is body-forming. By the bestowal of ministerial gifts (the Spirit of) Christ creates a unity of interrelated, mutually dependent, 'gifted' Christians. Although Paul stresses that the gifts are to be used for the common good of the Christian community, this should not be taken to mean that their use is intended exclusively for the benefit of the existing Church. The first of the gifts, apostleship, clearly has its major orientation towards those who have not yet been incorporated into the body of Christ. Thus we are justified in saying that Christ (through the Spirit) is actively involved in the ministry of the Christian community, both for its internal well-being and in its mission to the world.

CHAPTER ELEVEN

ROMANS

In his letter to the Romans Paul addressed a church which he himself did not found (15.20-22), but which he hoped to visit on his way to Spain (15.24). At that time he wanted to impart some spiritual gift to them (1.10-12), and be helped on his way further westward (15.24). Romans was written by the apostle on the eve of his departure from Corinth to take the Gentile contribution to the poor believers in Jerusalem (15.30-31). Thus we may date the letter towards the close of Paul's third missionary journey (c.AD 55).

The letter contains the most systematised presentation of Paul's theological beliefs found in any of his epistles. It establishes all men's accountability to, and guilt before, God, explains the righteousness of God revealed in the gospel, deals with the proper attitude to sin and the Law, and expounds life in the Spirit. Three chapters are devoted to the problem of Israel's unbelief and her part in salvation-history. The closing chapters take up such matters as spiritual gifts and their use in the Christian community, Christian attitudes to the state, the need for 'weak' and 'strong' brethren to respect one another, and Paul's apostolate and future plans. The final chapter consists mainly of greetings but contains a somewhat surprising reference to some in the church who create dissension and oppose the gospel. (16.17-20).

The Purpose of Romans

A central problem is the question of the origin and purpose of Romans. Is it simply an introductory letter to the Roman church to prepare the way for Paul's intended visit en route to Spain? Is he, then, just introducing himself and his gospel, and mentioning the names of as many mutual acquaintances as possible to prepare the way for his forthcoming visit? Is this explanation sufficient to explain why Paul should write such a theological document?

Most of the Pauline epistles have been subjected to close examination to discover their origin and purpose. However, until relatively recently, with the notable exception of F. C. Baur, scholars have been content to view Paul's epistle to the Romans as a *christianae religionis compendium*. It is only in more recent years that serious attempts have been made to seek a concrete life-setting for this epistle. The enquiry is still in its infancy, and the suggestions concerning the life-setting are many and varied.

One suggestion is that Romans is Paul's manifesto setting forth his deepest convictions on central issues. This manifesto contains the conclusions Paul reached as a result of long controversy, the beginnings of which are reflected in 1 Corinthians and Philippians 3.[1] A second suggestion is that Romans ought to be viewed as Paul's last will and testament. Here again the epistle is seen against the background of Paul's earlier controversies, but unlike his other epistles, Romans lifts the arguments to a new level of generality—'into the sphere of the eternally and universally valid.'[2] A further alternative takes very seriously Paul's 'non-interference' clause in Romans 15.20: 'thus making it my ambition to preach the gospel, not where Christ has already been named, lest I build on another man's foundation.' The suggestion is that Paul has written Romans, which is so much like a theological treatise, because he believed the Roman church to be without apostolic foundation. With this epistle, then, he sought to provide the church with a true presentation of the gospel which he intended to supplement by personal ministry when he himself reached Rome (cf. 1.15; 15.15-29).[3] A fourth proposal takes as its point of departure a conviction that it is futile to seek to understand Romans on the basis of our knowledge of the Roman congregation. Instead, it is argued, Paul wrote the epistle seeking the support and intercession of the Roman Christians to help bring about a favourable reception of the gentile collection when he delivered it to Jerusalem. For in Jerusalem Paul anticipated problems from two sources—unbelieving Jews and the Christian congregation (15.30-33).[4] A fifth suggestion is that the purpose of the epistle is to reunite the factions in the Roman congregation(s)—the 'weak' (Jewish Christians) and the 'strong' (gentile Christians).[5] Finally, mention can be made of the view which notes that positive statements about 'all Israel' appear for the first time in Paul's writings here in Romans. The significance of this is sought against the background of strong anti-Jewish feeling in Rome at the time of Nero and before. By allocating to the people of Israel an important place at the end of salvation-history and by stressing their inalienable heritage, Paul sought to elevate 'the stature of Jewish Christians in the eyes of gentile Christians', while also having in mind that 'majority of the Jewish community which had shut itself off from the Christian mission.'[6]

These are but a sampling of the many suggestions which are being put forward regarding a life-setting for Paul's epistle to the Romans. It is too early, yet, for any consensus of opinion. Once again the very diversity of scholarly opinion should make us cautious, and if we favour one view above others it should be held loosely for the present. It could well be that the only satisfactory solution will be a composite one.

The Textual Problem

In the second and third centuries a shorter form of the epistle which ended with chapter 14 was circulating, especially represented by Marcion's *Apostolikon*. According to Origen, Marcion had expunged chapters 15-16 from the original text. If so, the variations in the text forms can be traced back to Marcion's mutilation of the text, and the various attempts to cope with it and to restore the original.[7] Kümmel concludes that the original text of Romans contained 1.' 16.23; the final doxology (16.25-27) was probably composed and added to the shortened form of the letter to round it off, and later placed at the end of chapter 16, where it stands in our present text.[8]

The epistle to the Romans contains much less material concerning ministry than 1 and 2 Corinthians. Nevertheless, Romans reveals significant developments in the way Paul conceived both his own ministry and the ministry of the Christian community.

PAUL'S APOSTLESHIP

In Romans Paul is able to speak of his apostleship in a dispassionate way, because he did not have to defend it when writing this epistle. Thus we may hope to find a more 'normal' and more balanced expression of his apostolic consciousness. On the other hand, Paul was addressing a church which he had not founded, yet which he regarded as coming under his charge as apostle to the Gentiles. This will to a certain extent colour the way in which his apostleship is presented.

Paul touches upon his apostolic ministry in three places in the epistle. He refers to himself, in passing, as 'an apostle to the Gentiles' in 11.13. The significant statements, however, are found in 1.1-15 and 15.15-21.

Romans 1.1-15

In the opening verse of the epistle Paul introduces himself as 'a servant of Jesus Christ, called to be an apostle, set apart for the gospel of God.' It is worthy of note that, for Paul, apostleship was not only a charismatic endowment like the other gifts of the Spirit, but rested also upon a specific calling.[9] This calling he understood to be analogous to the calling of the prophets of the Old Testament (like Jeremiah he was 'set apart'), a fact which we have already observed in our study of the earlier epistles. It was through Christ that he received his apostleship, the object of which was that he should bring about obedience of faith among all nations (1.5). The representative character of the apostolate is brought out when Paul says that he seeks to promote this obedience of faith 'for the sake of his name[10] among all the nations.'

Of special interest is 1.9 where Paul says: 'For God is my witness, whom I serve (*latreuō*) with my spirit in the gospel of his Son . . .' Here for the first time Paul uses liturgical terminology in relation to his own apostolic ministry. In the Septuagint *latreuō* is always used in reference to service rendered to the God of Israel or heathen gods. It is a word often associated with priestly service in the temple, but is taken over and used by Paul here in relation to service he renders in/with his spirit.[11] That service, as 1.1 indicates, is nothing other than the preaching of the gospel. The idea of apostolic ministry as priestly service is further developed in 15.16 which will be discussed below.

In 1.11-15 Paul says that he longs to see the Romans, for he wishes to impart to them some spiritual gift (11),[12] and 'reap some harvest' among them as he has among the rest of the Gentiles (13), for he is under obligation to preach the gospel to them (14-15). This obligation can be viewed either as something he owes men or, more generally, a duty he has to discharge. In the light of 1 Corinthians 9.16 the latter is to be preferred, for there it is clearly implied that the obligation is one laid upon him by God, even though the discharge of that obligation is effected by the preaching of the gospel to men. Thus we should see here another expression of Paul's realisation that he is a man with a commission from God, and that he is under solemn obligation to carry it out.[13]

Romans 15.15-21

It is in this passage that Paul explicitly characterises his apostolic ministry as priestly service. He is 'a minister (*leitourgos*) of Christ Jesus to the Gentiles in the priestly service (*hierourgounta*)[14] of the gospel, so that the offering (*prosphora*) of the Gentiles may be acceptable (*euprosdektos*), sanctified (*hegiasmenē*) by the Holy Spirit' (16). Paul acts as a priest. He presents an offering consisting of the Gentiles, and he is responsible for the purity of the offering.[15] The Gentiles by nature would be unclean, but, by preaching the gospel to unbelievers and teaching believers, Paul becomes the agent by whom the Holy Spirit sanctifies/purifies the Gentiles so that they become an offering that is holy and acceptable to God. How did Paul come to interpret his ministry in priestly terms? Perhaps it was in response to the criticism of some Jewish Christians in Jerusalem who regarded the Gentiles who were coming into the church as 'unclean'. So Paul characterised himself as a priest who, as the agent of the Holy Spirit, presided over the preparation of the offering of the Gentiles.

The dynamic involvement of Christ. Particularly significant is Paul's statement in 15.18-19: 'For I will not venture to speak of anything except what Christ has wrought through me to win obedience from the Gentiles by word and deed, by the power of signs and wonders, by the power of the Holy Spirit so that from Jerusalem and as far around as Illyricum I have fully preached the gospel of Christ.' In the defence of his apostleship against

charges made by his opponents in Corinth, Paul had appealed
to the 'signs of an apostle' which he had wrought in that city (2
Cor. 12.12). There he simply reminded the Corinthians that
signs and wonders and mighty works had been wrought by him.
The statement in Romans 15.18-19 is more explicit. Here Paul
asserts that it is none other than Christ who works through him
by word and deed, by the power of signs and wonders, and by
the Holy Spirit, to win obedience from the Gentiles. The claim
that the exalted Christ is actively at work through him is
unmistakable. It is noteworthy, too, that the work which the
exalted Christ effects through his apostle, is the same as the
work accomplished by the historical Jesus. The close parallel
suggests that Paul, no more than Jesus, can be written off as just
another wonder-worker (*theios anēr*); his ministry also is the
evidence of the divine presence making itself felt in eschatological acts of power. In addition, we should note again how
closely Paul relates the activity of the exalted Christ to the
Spirit; what Christ effects through Paul is effected through the
Spirit. In the Corinthian letters we saw how Christ was presented as the source of the believer's experience of the Spirit;
here in Romans he is presented as the source of that spiritual
power manifested in the ministry of the apostle.[16]

Paul's use of Isaiah 52.15. Some comment is required concerning Paul's use of the quotation from Isaiah 52.15 in verse 21. As
Jeremias points out, apart from traditional material which Paul
takes over, this is the one explicit christological interpretation
of the servant-passages of Deutero-Isaiah which Paul makes.[17]
Paul explains that his aim is to preach the gospel where Christ
is yet unnamed, and he finds precedent for this ambition in
Isaiah 52.15: 'They shall see who have never been told of him,
and they shall understand who have never heard of him.' Thus
Paul clearly believes that it is right to interpret Isaiah 52.15
christologically, but more than that—and this is really the
thrust of Paul's use of the quotation—his own apostolic ministry can be interpreted as a fulfilment of this part of the fourth
servant-prophecy.[18] He is 'a missionary of the Servant-Messiah
to the world, which, till his *kērygma*, had neither sight nor
hearing of such a one.'[19]

THE SERVICE AND SUFFERING OF THE PEOPLE OF GOD

In the Corinthian epistles we saw developed teaching regarding servanthood and suffering. There is nothing of the same order in Romans. However, there are some echoes of that teaching which call for brief comment here.

Paul introduces himself as a servant of Jesus Christ (1.1), but he regards every Christian as a servant of Christ; each is exhorted to serve the Lord (12.11). Christians ought to be careful about judging one another, for each man stands or falls before his own master, and the Master is able to make him stand (14.4). Christians serve Christ when they seek to preserve harmony in the Church (14.18) and those who sow the seeds of dissension do not serve Christ (16.17-18).

The Priestly Service of All Believers

It is in Romans that Paul introduces for the first time into his presentation of apostolic ministry the concept of priestly service (cf. discussion of 15.15-21 above). However, this is not restricted by Paul to his portrayal of the apostolate; he draws upon the same imagery to depict every Christian's service of God. In 12.1 Paul writes: 'I appeal to you therefore, brethren, by the mercies of God, to present your bodies as a living sacrifice (*thusian zōsan*)[20] holy and acceptable to God, which is your spiritual worship (*logikēn latreian*).'[21] In this case it is not the apostle who must make the offering (of the Gentiles) and ensure its purity, instead each Christian is responsible for the offering of himself to God.

Suffering with Christ

In the Corinthian letters Paul had to lay the suffering servant motif under tribute to defend the genuineness of his own apostolate. Now, in Romans, he brings forward again the idea that all Christians (not just an apostle) are called to suffer afflictions. In Romans 8 Paul lists the privileges of Christians— they are children of God, heirs of God, fellow-heirs with Christ (16-17), but adds that this is the case 'provided we suffer with him in order that we may also be glorified with him' (17).[22] The theme is taken up again in 8.35–7 where Paul asks what can possibly separate the Christian from the love of Christ.

Obviously, no tribulation, persecution or anything else is able to separate us from that love. What is significant in this passage is Paul's citation of Psalm 44.22 ('For thy sake we are being killed all the day long; we are regarded as sheep to be slaughtered') as a precedent for Christian sufferings.[23] Paul, then, sees Christian suffering as both something we share with Christ (17)—as fellow-servants of God (?)—and something we bear for his sake (36).

CHARISMATA AND THE FIGURE OF THE BODY

Paul draws upon the image of the body in Romans 12.3-8 where, as part of his paraenesis, he urges the Roman Christians to be diligent in the exercise of their gifts (*charismata*). The emphasis throughout the passage is on the functionary character of the gifts, and it is in this connection that the figure of the body is introduced. As a body is made up of many members, each having its own function (*praxis*), so, too, Christians (in the local church) form a 'body' whose members serve one another and are mutually dependent upon one another (4-5).

By comparison with the varied and sometimes obscure use made of the image of the body in 1 Corinthians, its usage in Romans is quite straightforward. It is a simile pure and simple: '*as* in one body we have many members . . . *so* we, though many, are one body in Christ' (12.4-5). The expression 'one body *in* Christ' is, of course, quite different from the expression 'the body *of* Christ' which is found in 1 Corinthians 12.27. 'One body *in* Christ' must be interpreted in light of Paul's oft-used phrase, 'in Christ'. In some places this means little more than 'in the Christian community', but in others it is probably best understood against the background of Pauline eschatology, i.e., in Christ—in the New Age. To be in Christ/in the New Age means that one is also the recipient of the Spirit. The possession of the Spirit is the Christian's assurance that he will share in the glory of the New Age at the time of its revealing, and the Christian's foretaste in the present time, of the blessings of that New Age (cf. 8.22-23). Thus it is entirely appropriate that Paul should introduce the concept of one body in Christ when he deals with the exercise of spiritual gifts, for these are from the Spirit of Christ. They are also evidence of the Christian's participation in the New Age, as it is proleptically present in the here and now.

Although Paul does not use the figure of the body here in the same way as he does in 1 Corinthians 12, nevertheless, it depicts the same reality in both places, viz. a spiritual unity made up of 'gifted' Christians.

CONCLUSIONS

The results of our study of Romans in so far as they bear on the relationship between Christ and Christian ministry can now be stated. In several instances what we find in Romans constitutes a significant development in Paul's thinking about ministry when compared with that which emerges in the earlier epistles.

First, Paul, who in the Corinthian correspondence spoke of the 'signs of an apostle' which he wrought amongst his friends in Corinth, here in Romans explicitly affirms that the signs and wonders (which constitute the 'signs of man apostle' in 2 Cor. 12.12) are in fact effected through him by Christ himself, through the agency of the Holy Spirit. Further, those signs which the exalted Christ effects through his apostle are similar to those effected by the power of the Spirit in the ministry of the historical Jesus. This strongly suggests that the ministry which was begun by the historical Jesus is continued by the exalted Christ through his apostle by the Spirit. It is worth noting that it is just this view regarding the continuity between the ministry of Jesus and that of the Christian community that is put forward by Luke (cf. Acts. 1.1-2).

Second, in most respects the presentation of the apostleship of Paul in Romans is as it was in the earlier letters. In Romans, too, his calling to the task is analogous to the calling of the Old Testament servants of God, his function is a representative one, and he is a commissioned agent under obligation to discharge his duty.

The new features which emerge include the more explicit treatment of the 'signs of an apostle' (though that expression is not found in Romans) and, in particular, the presentation of his apostolate in terms of priestly service. Paul speaks of himself as a priest responsible for the offering (consisting) of the Gentiles to God. The Gentiles (in Jewish eyes) were 'unclean', but through the preaching and teaching ministry of the apostle the Holy Spirit sanctified them so that they became an offering acceptable to God. Paul's consciousness of the dynamic dimension to his apostolate is revealed here (the Spirit worked through him to sanctify the Gentiles), as it is also in his statement about Christ effecting signs and wonders through him (by the power of the Spirit) to win obedience from the Gentiles.

Third, all members of the Christian community are regarded as servants of Christ (the service they are urged to render being the preservation of the harmony of the community). Paul took up again the image of the body to portray the unity of the Church. The image is used in a way different from its use in 1 Corinthians 12, but the reality to which it points in both places is the same—the unity of spiritually 'gifted' Christians. In Romans this unity is described with the expression 'one body *in* Christ' (as distinct from 'the body *of* Christ' in 1 Corinthians). This expression probably carries the idea of one body in the New Age, i.e., a body of believers experiencing the blessings/ gifts of the Spirit of Christ. This, in turn, is evidence of the presence now, proleptically at least, of the New Age, the glory of which will only be revealed in the future.

We saw that Paul, who could understand his own apostolic ministry in terms of priestly service, extended this concept to apply to other Christians as well. They are to carry out their spiritual service to the Lord by offering themselves as living sacrifices to him. Paul is the priest presiding over the offering of the Gentiles, but this does not relieve the individual of the obligation to act as priest in the offering of himself to his Lord, for this is his spiritual service.

Finally, the participation of all members of the Christian community in the sufferings of Christ comes to the fore again in Romans. As we have already seen, in Galatians Paul spoke of the results of his own sufferings as the 'marks of Jesus'. In the Thessalonian letters the idea of suffering with Christ was extended to cover all Christians, for to suffer affliction is the Christian's lot. However, in the Corinthian epistles, in response to attacks upon his apostleship, the idea of suffering with Christ as something to be experienced by all Christians receded because Paul needed to use the motif to defend his own apostolate and integrity. But, in calmer times, when the Roman epistle was written, Paul allowed the concept of all Christians sharing the sufferings of Christ to come to the fore once again. To express this idea Paul cited Psalm 44.22, a verse used by the rabbis of Jewish martyrs and the sufferings of the godly in general. The main thrust of Psalm 44.22 has parallels in Isaiah 53 (sheep to be slaughtered), so the suffering servant concept may not have been far from the surface of Paul's mind when he wrote Romans 8.35-36.

Some of the ministerial themes found in Romans are further developed in the later epistles. In particular the theme of priestly service is taken up again in the epistle to the Philippians to which we must now turn.

CHAPTER TWELVE

PHILIPPIANS

The church at Philippi was founded by Paul on his second missionary journey. It was the first church to the planted in Europe. According to the account found in Acts 16, Paul's missionary labours in Philippi involved him in some most unpleasant experiences. He and Silas were dragged before the rulers in the market place and charged with disturbing the city and advocating customs unlawful for Romans to practise. They were severely beaten with rods and thrown into prison (19-24). The miraculous intervention by God through an earthquake, the conversion of their jailor and his family, and the apology of the magistrates did not suffice to erase from Paul's mind the bitterness of his Philippian experience (cf. 1 Thess. 2.2). Nevertheless, the church he planted there continued to be a source of joy to him as can be seen clearly in the letter he wrote to the Philippians.[1]

The Integrity of Philippians

We have referred to Paul's letter (singular) to the Philippians, but some scholars regard the epistle in its present form as a composite production.[2] This suggestion has been made to try to account for the changes in tone (sometimes quite abrupt, cf. 2.19; 3.2; 4.10) which occur in the epistle. One's view concerning the unity or disunity of Philippians rests upon one's ability or inability to understand the various emphases of the epistle against the background of an appropriate set of circumstances in the life of Paul without postulating different periods in his ministry.[3] Also related to the problem of the integrity of the epistle is the christological passage 2.6-11 which is now recognised by most scholars as a pre-Pauline hymn. However, it is generally agreed that if the hymn is pre-Pauline, it was taken over by Paul—with some editing—and included in the epistle for purposes of his own.[4]

Paul's Opponents in Philippians

Despite the basically joyful/thankful tone which pervades the epistle, there are clear indications in Philippians that opponents of Paul and his gospel were present both in the city of his captivity from whence he wrote, and in Philippi itself. In 1.15-18 Paul speaks of those who 'preach Christ from envy and rivalry . . . out of partisanship, not sincerely but thinking to afflict me in my imprisonment.' Elsewhere he charges the Philippians not to be frightened in anything by their opponents (1.28), and with surprising vehemence he warns them to look out for 'the dogs . . . those who mutilate the flesh' (3.2). Finally, in 3.18 he says: 'For many, of whom I have often told you and now tell you even with tears, live as enemies of the cross of Christ.'

The identity of the opponents to whom Paul refers in chapter 3 has been the subject of vigorous debate in recent years.[5] Some of the more important suggestions put forward over the last decade or so include: (1) Jews who offered a perfection based on the Law/circumcision which could be gained on earth,[6] (2) spiritualists with both a judaizing and a libertinistic message,[7] (3) Jewish Christian missionary apostles who preached a perfection (with the possession of the eschatological blessings in full now) attainable through Law-keeping and circumcision,[8] and (4) Jewish Christian Gnostics who claimed circumcision as a badge of membership in their community, who boasted of their knowledge and perfection, and claimed to be recipients of a full divine revelation.[9] Finally, it has been suggested that there were (5) three sets of opponents: first, divine-man missionaries who were operating in the city where Paul was imprisoned (cf. 1.15-18) to be identified with those who 'look after their own interests' (2.21); second, the Judaizing missionaries who were offering perfection via circumcision (3.2-16); and third, libertines who denied the saving efficacy of the cross and even boasted of their immoral behaviour (3.17-19).[10].

The common denominator of the threats to the Philippian congregation posed by the judaizing missionaries on the one hand, and the libertines on the other, is that both groups held out a promise of perfection which removed the cross of Christ from its central position, and offered an easy way out of the pathway of suffering which the Christian is to tread for the sake of Christ. The existence in Philippi of two distinct groups both offering perfection (the one stressing the need to observe the Law and undergo circumcision, the other encouraging libertinism) seems the best explanation for the marked changes in emphases within the apostle's counter-attack in chapter 3.

It is against such a background that we will seek to understand those passages in Philippians which contribute to our understanding of Paul's view of ministry. For the most part, the ministerial ideas which emerge in Philippians only echo those which we have already noted in the earlier epistles. Nevertheless, there are still a couple of areas where those earlier ideas undergo some further development. This is especially so in Paul's statements about the priestly nature of ministry, and the Christian's share in the sufferings of Christ.

PAUL'S APOSTLESHIP

In the opening verse of Philippians Paul introduces himself and his colleague, Timothy, not as apostles,[11] but simply as 'servants of Christ Jesus'. Is this an indication of the close rela·tionship that Paul had with the Philippian church, and that his apostolic authority had never been questioned there? On a casual reading of the epistle this might seem to be the case. On the other hand, if the integrity of the epistle be granted, it would have to be said that chapter 3 shows that Paul felt the need to defend himself, even before the Philippians (cf. espc. 3.4-6). In that case 'servants of Christ Jesus' is perhaps better regarded as a title of honour in which the word 'servant' (*doulos*) has lost its etymological sense and taken on a theologically determined significance—one of the few chosen by God to be entrusted with particular tasks, after the fashion of the special envoys of God in the Old Testament.[12]

The Nature of the Apostolate

Serving the interests of Christ. Philippians 2.19-23 provides a sidelight upon Paul's view of the ministry of a true servant of Christ. In advising the Philippians that he hopes to send Timothy to them soon, he says: 'I have no one like him who will be genuinely anxious for your welfare. They all look after their own interests,[13] not those of Jesus Christ. But Timothy's worth you know, how as a son with a father he has served with me in the gospel' (20-22). The true servants of Christ are those who can put aside their own interests (*ta heautōn*) when necessary, so that they can look after the interests of Jesus Christ (*ta Iēsou Christou*). Or, to put it another way, the servant of Christ is charged with responsibility for the interests of Christ among men.

Apostolic authority. Paul's consciousness of apostolic authority which we have already seen in the earlier epistles, finds expression in Philippians as well, though here it is but a faint echo of that which resounds through the Corinthian epistles. In 4.9 Paul says: 'What you have learned and received and heard and seen in me, do; and the God of peace will be with you.' This is an assertion of the authority of the apostle—his message and his example. These words may be an indication of a defensive stance on the part of the apostle—if it is correct to say his apostolate was under attack. In this case the thrust of Paul's statement would be that his Philippian readers ought to do what they have seen and heard in him, rather than what they see and hear in his opponents. In any case, Paul's sense of apostolic authority is clear.

The dynamism of the apostolate. The dynamic aspect of Paul's apostleship is implied by two statements that he made in particular. In the first of these (1.8) he says: 'For God is my witness, how I yearn for you all with the affection of Christ Jesus.' Paul was convinced that the yearning he felt for the Philippian Christians was nothing other than the affection of Christ expressing itself through him. In the second of these statements (1.19) Paul expresses his assurance that through the prayers of his Philippian friends and the help of the Spirit of Jesus Christ all will turn out for his deliverance. Several commentators note here an allusion to Jesus' promise of the Spirit's assistance in time of trial.[14] Paul's confidence that the Spirit of Jesus will help him would then rest not only upon his belief in the love of God, but also upon a dominical saying (see discussion of Mark 13.11 pars. in ch. 5 above). That Paul can speak of 'the Spirit of Jesus Christ' shows again how closely he associated the work of the Spirit with the exalted Christ. The Spirit's help is none other than the power of Christ made available to his people.[15]

Resurrection Power and the Fellowship of his Sufferings

In our study of the earlier epistles we noted how Paul appealed to his sufferings as evidence for the legitimacy of his apostolate. In 2 Corinthians especially he developed the twin ideas of power in weakness, and suffering as the hallmark of the true servant of God. In each case Paul was responding to some criticism of his own apostleship. In Philippians Paul again takes up the theme of suffering, but this time it seems to be in response to spurious offers of perfection held out to the Philippian church by two very different groups, both of which profess to enable the Christian to attain the goal of perfection without being exposed to suffering.

In Philippians 3 it appears that Paul responds to the challenge of both groups with a single answer; he asserts that perfection is not attainable in this life, but only in a future resurrection (11-16). Moreover, in this life, the apostle (and all Christians with him) experience the power of Christ's resurrection only while they share in Christ's sufferings (10). Hence Paul writes: 'For his sake I have suffered the loss of all things . . . that I may know him and the power of his resurrection, and may share his sufferings, becoming like him in his death' (3.8b-10).[16]

Sharing his sufferings. What does Paul mean by the expression, 'share his sufferings' (*koinōnian pathēmatōn autou*, lit. 'fellowship of/participation in his sufferings')? Several ideas have been put forward. First, it has been suggested that he is speaking of our share in the fellowship created by the sufferings of Christ (taking *pathēmatōn autou* as a subjective genitive).[17] However, in the light of Paul's teaching in earlier letters, and the fact that sharing his sufferings is a parallel idea to knowing the power of his resurrection, this is unlikely. Thus, the majority of interpreters believe that a share in sufferings which in some way belong to Christ, is what Paul means. A second interpretation is that Paul shared in the sufferings of Christ because his old Pharisaic personality was crucified in communion with the judgement signified by God on the cross of Christ.[18] Third, it has been argued that Paul's words imply a 'mystical participation with Christ in his death which was effected in baptism', but where 'the reality of the mystical experience is unfolded and exhibited in the concrete matter-of-fact experience of the outward life.'[19]

A fourth interpretation explains *koinōnia pathēmatōn autou* in the light of the parallel sayings in Romans 8.17 and 2 Corinthians 1.5. It is asserted that it is impossible, in view of these texts, that Philippians 3.10 means Paul's sufferings will simply *conform to* Christ's; they are definitely a *participation in* Christ's sufferings, though in just what way they are so, is not made clear.[20] Finally, it has been suggested that the sufferings of the apostle are a real part of the total suffering which is laid on Christ (cf. Col. 1.24),[21] but again the implications of the view are not made clear.

The best way to approach the interpretation of 3.10 is to bear in mind the influences Paul was seeking to counter. From opposite sides the Philippians were being offered a short-cut to perfection—that state in which they could experience spiritual power (the power of his resurrection) while at the same time being exempt from sufferings. What Paul is saying is that he himself only experiences the power of the resurrection of Christ as he experiences concrete sufferings.[22] But why does Paul refer to a share in *his* sufferings instead of simply a participation in sufferings? At the least we may say that Paul viewed them as sufferings of Christ because he bore them for the sake of Christ. But more than this is involved. The background for this sort of idea is to be sought, as we have already seen (cf. ch. 10), in Paul's reflections upon the servant-prophecies of Deutero-Isaiah. Paul seems to have seen in his own ministry at least a partial fulfilment of the servant-prophecies. And, since he invites his readers to have the same attitude as himself to the matter of perfection and suffering (cf. 3.12-16), he appears to imply that their sufferings are a participation in Christ's sufferings as well. In their lives also the servant-prophecies find a partial fulfilment.

Apostolic Ministry as Priestly Service

In the epistle to the Romans, Paul introduced for the first time the concept of ministry as priestly service. There he referred to himself as a priest charged with the responsibility for the offering of the Gentiles, and he spoke of the priestly ministry of every Christian who must offer his body as a 'living sacrifice' in response to all God's mercies. Priestly/sacrificial terminology is used again in Philippians where, contemplating the distinct possibility of an imminent death, Paul says: 'Even if I am to be poured out as a libation upon the sacrificial offering of your faith, I am glad and rejoice with you all' (2.17). A libation, in both Jewish and pagan religions, was usually a cup of wine poured out to honour deity. The libation was only the accompaniment to the sacrifice, not the sacrifice itself. Paul's death would be the libation, but the sacrifice itself was the offering of the Philippians' faith. (What is meant by the sacrificial offering of the Philippians' faith is discussed below.)

We see here, then, a different application of priestly/sacrificial terminology to the apostle's ministry from that found in his letter to the Romans. There Paul portrays himself as a priest presiding over the offering of the Gentiles to ensure its purity. But here, as he contemplates the possibility of an imminent death, he speaks of his martyrdom as a libation poured out in accompaniment with the sacrificial offering of the Philippians' faith.

Eschatological Validation

In chapter 10 we saw Paul's developed teaching on eschatological validation for ministry as it emerges in the Corinthian letters. It is applied, there, not only to apostolic labours, but to the workmanship of any man who takes it upon hinself to build the Church of God. What we find in Philippians confirms that at the time of writing this epistle Paul still looked toward the future for the validation of his ministry. In 2.14-16 he urges his friends to live blameless lives 'so that in the day of Christ I may be proud that I did not run in vain or labour in vain' (16). Further, in 4.1 he exhorts the Philippian Christians to stand firm in the Lord; they are his 'joy and crown'. Clearly Paul took very seriously the responsibility to give an account of his ministry and he hoped to see it validated on the day of Christ.[23]

THE SERVICE AND SUFFERING OF THE PEOPLE OF GOD

The Priestly Service of the Christian Community

What did Paul mean by the expression: 'the sacrificial offering of your faith' (2.17)? It is more likely to be that sacrifice which the faith of the Philippians impelled them to make, rather than their faith itself. Faith is the impulse for, not the substance of, the sacrifice. The substance of the sacrifice could be their own selves (as in Rom. 12.1), or their substance (cf. 2 Cor. 9.12), but most likely the latter, for in Philippians 4.18, using sacrificial terminology again, Paul refers to the gifts they sent to him with Epaphroditus as 'a sacrifice acceptable and pleasing to God.'

Just as in the letter to the Romans, so also here in Philippians, Paul extends his use of priestly/sacrificial terminology to depict, not only his own apostolic ministry, but that of the Christian community as well. All members of the community offer priestly service in so far as they make acceptable sacrifices to God by giving of their substance to help the needy, in this case their needy apostle (4.18).

Suffering for the Sake of Christ

Paul, who in 3.10 bears witness to his own desire to know Christ, both in the power of his resurrection and in the fellowship of his sufferings, seeks to help the Philippians to understand their sufferings by saying: 'It has been granted to you that for the sake of Christ you should not only believe in him, but also suffer for his sake, engaged in the same conflict which you saw and now hear to be mine' (1.29-30). For Paul suffering is not punishment, but grace—the privilege of suffering for the sake of Christ. He speaks from experience, as the Philippians knew, for they saw him ill-treated in their own city when he brought the gospel to them (1.30a, cf. Acts 16.19-24; 1 Thess. 2.2), and they had heard that he was suffering in prison again for the sake of Christ (30b).

Quite possibly Paul introduced the idea of suffering for Christ's sake as a privilege bestowed by God upon Christians, not only to help the Philippians understand their own bitter experiences, but also with an eye to the false teachers whom he answers more directly in chapter 3.[24] In any case, Paul sought to comfort his readers by assuring them that while they were involved in the same conflict as he was, their sufferings were to be regarded as a gift and a privilege—they were counted worthy to suffer for the sake of his name. It is important to note that Paul did not classify all types of suffering endured for any reason as the gift of God's grace—it is only sufferings that are borne 'in the same conflict', i.e., sufferings endured on account of the gospel, which may be so classified. Paul here plainly associates his readers with himself as those who bear sufferings for the sake of the gospel, or, to put it another way, in pursuance of the servant task of making God's salvation known to the Gentiles. Their engagement in the task included a 'partnership of giving and receiving' with the apostle (4.15-16) as well as their own witness, shining as lights in the world, holding fast/forth[25] the word of life' (2.15-16).

CONCLUSIONS

The results of our study of Philippians can now be summarised. First it seems clear that Paul was confident that the exalted Christ was still actively involved in the ministry of his apostle. It was Christ's compassion which expressed itself in Paul's yearning over the Philippians, and it was help from the Spirit of Jesus Christ that he confidently expected in his time of trial. And so far as this trial is concerned, what Paul expected from the exalted Christ is nothing other than that which was promised by the historical Jesus. Further, the close association of Christ with the Spirit which we saw in our examination of earlier epistles is evident again in Philippians—the Spirit's help is the power of the exalted Christ made available to his people.

Second, the relationship of Paul's apostolic ministry to his Lord is consistent with what we have seen in the earlier epistles. The dual emphasis upon the authoritative and dynamic character of the apostolate is present again. Paul was one of the chosen servants of God, responsible for the interests of Christ among men. This speaks of the representative character of his apostolate and indicates also that the way in which he thought of it was at least compatible, in this respect, with the rabbinic šālîaḥ concept. Paul's understanding of the dynamic aspect of his ministry is revealed in both his confident expectation of the help of the Spirit of Jesus Christ, and in his belief that the yearning he felt for the Philippian church was nothing other than the love of Christ expressing itself through him. In addition, we have seen that Paul was still looking to the future 'day of Christ' as the time of validation for his ministry.

To meet the challenge of spurious offers of perfection, Paul resorted again to his belief that men only share in the power of Christ's resurrection as they share in his suffering. This he applied to himself, but with an eye to those in Philippi who might be tempted by the offers of instant perfection, and easy access to power. This idea of Christian participation in the sufferings of Christ, it was submitted, is still best understood against the background of Pauline reflections on the servant-prophecies of Deutero-Isaiah.

Some movement in Paul's thinking about his ministry may be discerned in his application of priestly/sacrificial terminology in this epistle. In Romans he portrayed himself as a priest responsible for the offering up of the Gentiles and for the purity of that offering. Here in Philippians, as he faced the possibility of an imminent death, he speaks of that death as a libation poured out to accompany the sacrificial offering of the Philippians' faith.

Third, applying the priestly/sacrificial terminology to the Christian community, Paul expressed the view that Christians make an acceptable sacrifice to God when, impelled by their faith, they give of their substance to help those in need, in this case, their own needy apostle. Thus Paul characterised as priestly service, not only apostolic ministry, but also this ministry performed by the Christian community.

In our studies of the earlier epistles we saw how Paul spoke of his own sufferings experienced in pursuance of his apostolic task as the sufferings of Christ. We saw, also, how Paul reminded Christians that they too were destined to suffer. Here in Philippians, for the first time, Paul explicitly associates a Christian congregation with himself as they suffered for the sake of Christ in the struggle to further the gospel. He says they have been privileged to suffer for the sake of Christ in the same conflict in which he himself is engaged. They participate in this because they have entered into a partnership of giving and receiving with their apostle, and because they themselves 'shine as lights in the world'.

CHAPTER THIRTEEN

COLOSSIANS AND PHILEMON

Paul's relationship to the Colossian Church was an indirect one. He did not plant the church in Colossae, yet he was involved in its foundation in a secondary way, for Epaphras, who evangelised the Colossians (1.7; 4.12-13), worked under the direction of the apostle (1.7). Paul himself had never visited the church there, and did not know its members personally (2.1, cf. 1.4, 7-8). He wrote the epistle to the Colossians during one of his imprisonments (4.3, 10, 18), possibly from Ephesus, though the traditional place of writing, Rome, and even Caesarea, must remain as possible alternatives.

The Purpose of Colossians

The purpose of the epistle can only be inferred from its contents. It contains warnings against 'philosophy' (2.8), the observance of food laws, sabbaths and new moon festivals (2.16), self-abasement and the worship of angels (2.18). It emphasises the supremacy of Christ over all created beings (1.15-17) and the Christian's deliverance in him from the powers of darkness (1.12-14). Together these things suggest that the apostle was combating false teaching which threatened to undermine the faith of the Christians at Colossae. It seems that this false teaching included incipient gnostic elements as well as elements drawn from Judaism and the mystery religions.[1]

The Authenticity of Colossians

So far we have assumed the authenticity of Colossians but this has been questioned. Attention has been drawn to the difference in language, style and theology between Colossians and the earlier Paulines, but while the questions are serious, the evidence available from these areas does not constitute a compelling case for non-Pauline authorship.[2] Another objection to Pauline authorship rests on the belief that the 'heresy' combated in the epistle is a form of Gnosticism which can be fitted best into a period after the death of the apostle. However, there is both literary and archaeological evidence to show that the city of Colossae was destroyed in AD 61, and that it was not rebuilt. Paul's letter to the Colossians, therefore, must have been written before that time, i.e., during the apostle's lifetime.[3] This study proceeds, then, upon the assumption that Colossians is an authentic letter of Paul, but at the same time we must be alert to see whether the concepts of ministry presented in the epistle are compatible with what we have seen in the earlier (generally undisputed) epistles of Paul.

The Epistle to Philemon

Paul addressed this epistle to an acquaintance of his, and intended it to be a covering note to ensure that his friend would receive favourably back his runaway slave, Onesimus, whom Paul was returning to his master. Comparison with Colossians suggests that the note was carried by Tychicus together with the letter for the Colossians, and that the slave Onesimus returned to Colossae (and his master) with Tychicus. The letter itself deals with a personal matter, yet it is not so much a private letter from Paul, the man, as an apostolic note concerning a personal matter.[4] It is the apostolic character of Philemon that makes it relevant for our present enquiry.

Colossians and Philemon reveal a picture of the relationship of Christian ministry to Christ which is, for the most part, similar to that which we have seen already in our studies of the earlier epistles. However, in two areas—the idea of sharing Christ's sufferings and the use of the figure of the body—there is significant variation/development.

PAUL'S APOSTLESHIP

The epistle to the Colossians opens with the characteristic words, 'Paul an apostle of Christ Jesus by the will of God', which emphasise Paul's apostolic calling and authority. However the epistle lacks any extended defence of apostleship such as we find, for example in Galatians and the Corinthian correspondence. In fact the title 'apostle' appears only here. On the other hand, the meagre use of the title does not mean that the references to Paul's apostolic ministry in the epistle are correspondingly few, as we shall see.

A Minister of the Gospel and the Church

In chapter 1, having described the supremacy of Christ over all creation and his headship over the Church, and the cosmic reconciliation he achieved, Paul immediately applies this to his readers. He assures them that they too have been reconciled to God and will be presented blameless before him, provided they continue stedfast in the faith and do not move from the hope of the gospel. Of this gospel, Paul says in 1.23b, he became a minister (*diakonos*). It seems that Paul cannot think of the gospel without, at the same time, thinking of his own role as minister of that gospel. Then, in 1.24, he speaks of his sufferings on behalf of the Church. Of that Church he became a minister (*diakonos*) according to the divine office given to him (1.25). Thus, in Colossians we have three ministerial titles which Paul applies to himself: 'apostle' (1.1), 'minister of the gospel' (1.23), and 'minister of the Church' (1.25). The description of his task as a minister of the Church (1.25-9)—basically to proclaim the gospel and lead men to maturity in Christ—shows that it is identical with his task as apostle and as minister of the gospel. In Colossians, therefore, we should regard 'minister of the gospel', 'minister of the church', and 'apostle' as three synonymous titles which Paul uses interchangeably of himself.

Apostolic Authority in Philemon

The authoritative character of Paul's view of the apostolate is clearly expressed in the short letter to Philemon. Paul discusses here a personal matter, yet he does so as one fully aware of his apostolic authority. When he sends Onesimus back to Philemon Paul appeals to the master to receive his slave favourably, yet he reminds Philemon that though he now makes an appeal he could have given a command: 'though I am bold enough in Christ to command you to do what is required, yet for love's sake I prefer to appeal to you—I Paul an ambassador (*presbutēs*) and now a prisoner also for Christ Jesus—I appeal to you . . .' (8-9). Having made his appeal, Paul brings his request to a close with the words: 'Confident of your obedience, I write to you, knowing that you will do even more than I say' (21). That sense of apostolic authority which pervades most of Paul's earlier letters remains undiminished at the time of writing Philemon (and Colossians).

Ambassador in Chains

Paul's use of *presbutēs* in Philemon 9 could be interpreted as either 'ambassador' or 'old man'. It is difficult to know which of these renderings best communicates Paul's intention. The general context is that in which Philemon is reminded of Paul's apostolic authority (8), yet in verse 9 Paul, implying that he waives his right to exercise apostolic authority in this situation, makes his appeal as a *presbutēs* and a prisoner. In this context, it would make good sense to translate *presbutēs* as 'old man'.[5] There is, however, in Ephesians 6.20, a parallel in which the ambassadorship and the imprisonment of the apostle are spoken of together. Perhaps Paul adds poignancy to his appeal by referring to himself, not as an old man in prison, but as an ambassador in chains.[6] If this view is adopted, we would have to see here another expression of Paul's consciousness of the representative character of his apostolate, which, as we have already seen above (ch. 10), bears a closer resemblance to the rabbinic *šālîaḥ* idea than it does to the concept of hellenistic envoys.

'Energised' by Christ

The dynamic character of apostleship as Paul understood it surfaces again in Colossians, in particular in 1.28-9, where Paul sums up the content and manner of his ministry: 'Him we proclaim, warning every man and teaching every man in all wisdom, that we may present every man mature in Christ. For this I toil, striving with all the energy which he mightily inspires within me.' To whom does Paul refer when he says he toils with 'all the energy *he* mightily inspires within me'? Clearly it is a reference to the Christ whom he proclaims and in whom he wishes to present every man mature/perfect. Thus we have here further evidence that Paul did not view his ministry only as a service rendered to his Lord. He also believed that his Lord was actively involved energising him to accomplish that service.

Colossians 1.24

In every epistle of Paul that we have studied so far, the motif of suffering has been present to a lesser or greater extent. In this regard Colossians is no exception. Moreover, in this epistle we find an outstanding statement—Paul claims that he fills up that which is lacking in the sufferings of Christ. The text concerned (1.24) runs: 'Now I rejoice in my sufferings for your sake, and in my flesh I complete what is lacking in Christ's afflictions for the sake of his body, that is the church.'

In all the previous epistles the suffering motif was introduced with a definite purpose. Where it was applied to the Christian community it was usually to provide some explanation for the afflictions which they bore for the sake of Christ. Where it was applied to the apostle himself it was invariably part of Paul's defence of his apostolate and integrity. We have already noted the relatively 'calm' objectivity of Colossians, but that should not be over-emphasised. If Paul was following his usual custom, the introduction of the suffering motif in reference to his own apostleship may well indicate that in Colossae also his apostolate was not completely unquestioned. Perhaps there is implied here a claim that Paul is truly an apostle to the Colossians also, not only because Epaphras was acting on his behalf when their church was founded, but also because Paul's sufferings (in some way) are for their sake as well (1.24a).

To interpret this text two related problems must be solved: first, in what way can it be said that there is something lacking in the afflictions of Christ? Second, how does Paul fill the lack? In relation to the first question it is almost universally agreed that whatever it is that is lacking in Christ's sufferings, that lack is not to be found in their atoning efficacy. It is the consistent teaching of the Pauline corpus, and indeed the New Testament as a whole, that no man can save himself, let alone add anything to the atoning work of Christ for the salvation of others.

Filling a lack in availability/effectiveness. One possible interpretation is that Colossians 1.24 refers to the lack in the availability of the benefits of Christ's death, a lack which was made up by the preaching ministry of Paul. This ministry involved Paul in suffering, so it may be said that Paul's (ministry and) sufferings filled up what was lacking in (the availability of the benefits flowing from) Christ's afflictions.

However, this interpretation does not do justice to the plain meaning of the text which affirms that the lack is in Christ's afflictions and not in the availability of the benefits therefrom. Similarly unsatisfactory is the suggestion that Colossians 1.24 bears the same meaning as 2 Corinthians 4.7, viz. the sufferings of the messenger allow the message itself to become more effective for the edifying of the community.[7] But the plain meaning of the verse is that the lack is in Christ's sufferings, not in the effectiveness of the message based upon them.

Mystical participation in Christ's sufferings. Another interpretation sees the idea of mystical union between Christ and his Church as the background to the passage. It is described as: 'A mystical union with Christ's passion which binds Christ and the community together so that unity with the Lord allows the whole body of Christ to benefit from the sufferings which they experienced.'[8] Proponents of this view refer to Paul's conversion experience as recorded in Acts 9 where the risen Lord asks: 'Saul, Saul, why do you persecute me?' (4). This is taken to indicate that as the Church suffers so does Christ and, therefore, it may be said that the Church fills up what is lacking in Christ's afflictions. This view, however, has been criticised on the ground that its implied mysticism blurs the distinction between the Church and her Lord: a distinction which remains quite clear in the case of Paul who regarded himself 'as an obedient servant who must render service to his Lord.'[9] But the real objection to this view is that any implied lack in Christ or his sufferings which must be filled by the Church or Paul is out of place in Colossians—an epistle in which the apostle is at pains to show that there is *no* lack in Christ.[10]

Sharing in the messianic afflictions. A fourth interpretation draws upon the Jewish apocalyptic teaching about the messianic woes which must be endured before the end time. The messianic woes were the pre-determined number of afflictions through which Israel must pass in the period immediately preceding the advent of the messiah.[11] It is suggested that this Jewish apocalyptic view was modified by Christians. The Jews hoped for the coming of 'an unknown envoy from God' but the Christians looked for the coming of the Christ who was 'already known to the community as the crucified and risen Lord.'[12] The interpretation has found considerable acceptance in recent years, but it is not without its problems. In particular it 'overlooks the fact that in Jewish thought the messianic woes are in no way the sufferings of the Messiah himself,'[13] and there is no evidence for an early Christian modification of the Jewish apocalyptic view.

Corporate personality and the Servant of the Lord. A fifth interpretation draws on the corporate personality concept found in Hebrew thought, or the oscillation between individual and corporate identity. The whole can be represented in the one, and vice versa. Applied to our passage this would mean that the afflictions of the Church (in this case an apostle of the Church) are the afflictions of the Christ. This view can be taken one step further by relating it to the suffering servant passages of Deutero-Isaiah. The servant there is both Israel and an individual who suffers on behalf of Israel (and the Gentiles). Applied to Christ and the Church this would mean that both of them make up the corporate servant, and thus Paul can regard his own sufferings as part of those to be endured by this corporate servant.[14] His sufferings contribute to the filling up of the measure of afflictions to be endured by the servant-Christ and his servant-people.

Reviewing the options. Looking at these various interpretations, we can say that those which speak of a lack in the availability or effectiveness of the message based on Christ's passion are not doing justice to the clear meaning of the passage. The interpretation which draws on the Jewish apocalyptic expectation of the messianic age to be preceded by a definite quota of afflictions is good as far as it goes, but it does not go far enough. In Jewish apocalyptic writings the messianic afflictions are not the afflictions of the messiah himself, but rather those borne by his people prior to his advent. It is possible, as Barrett has suggested, that the Jewish belief in the messianic woes had been subject to a Christian re-interpretation whereby the woes were understood to have been endured by the messiah on behalf of his people, and it is only the 'overflow' which his people are privileged to bear for his sake.[15] If we accept Barrett's suggestion we can make good sense out of 1.24. On the other hand, the text can be understood against the background of the servant-passages of Deutero-Isaiah (even if we do not wish to commit ourselves to the oscillatory corporate personality motif) in a way that is equally satisfying, and essentially the same. These servant-prophecies, containing as they do both individual and corporate aspects, find fulfilment individually in Jesus Christ, and corporately in Christ and his people. While those elements of the prophecies which speak of vicarious suffering find fulfilment in Christ alone, other elements which speak of the servant's mission and the more general sufferings experienced in its pursuance are fulfilled in the ministry of both Christ and his people.

Some support can be found for this view in the Lucan account of the missionary endeavours of Paul and Barnabas in Pisidian Antioch. When their preaching aroused great interest in the city, the Jews were provoked to jealousy and began to contradict Paul and Barnabas. Paul said to them: 'Behold, we turn to the Gentiles. For the Lord has commanded us, saying: "I have set you to be a light for the Gentiles, that you may bring salvation to the uttermost parts of the earth"' (Acts 13.46-7). Here Paul cites from one of the servant-songs in which the servant's task has been expanded to be a ministry, not only to Israel, but also to the Gentiles. Paul takes this charge to the servant to be a command to himself and to Barnabas, and uses it to justify their turning to the Gentiles.

Seeing that we do have Luke's witness at least to Paul's application of the servant-prophecies to his ministry, whereas we have no evidence that the apostle had interpreted the Jewish concept of messianic woes in a Christian fashion, it is best to see in Colossians 1.24 another statement reflecting Paul's belief that the servant-prophecies of Deutero-Isaiah found (partial) fulfilment in his ministry. In other words, he shared the sufferings of the corporate servant/Christ for the sake of the Church, Christ's body.

THE CHRISTIAN COMMUNITY AND
THE SERVICE OF CHRIST

In the *Haustafeln* (household rules) found in the Colossians 3 Paul presents his teaching on the right attitude of Christian slaves to their masters (22-5). They are to be obedient to their masters (22a), they are not to serve in the way of eyeservice as men-pleasers (22b), and they are to work heartily and with a good will (23). All this they must do because in carrying out their duties as slaves of earthly masters, they are, in fact, serving the Lord Christ, and will receive from him their reward for faithful service (24-5). These instructions, together with those addressed to masters (4.1), may have been included with an eye to the expected reconciliation between Philemon and Onesimus, or they may have been for purely general application. Either way the instructions to the slaves have relevance for our present study.

Paul, who was pleased to speak of himself metaphorically as a slave of Christ, could say to those Christian brethren who were slaves belonging to men, that they were nonetheless slaves of Christ. They served not only their earthly masters, but also the Lord Christ (24-5). Their faithful service to earthly masters was regarded as service to Christ, and such service would not go unrewarded. If this applies to slaves whose lives were ordered by the whims of a despotic master, then it is natural to assume that it applies to all other Christians who faithfully carry out their responsibilities.

In Colossians, then, the service of Christ is not restricted to tasks given to special ministers of the Church, or those acts of Christian concern which in Philippians he calls 'a fragrant offering, a sacrifice acceptable and pleasing to God'. The fulfilling of the responsibilities pertaining to the state of life in which each Christian finds himself is also acceptable service to Christ.

HEAD/BODY METAPHOR: CHRIST AND THE CHURCH

Paul made use of the figure of the body in both 1 Corinthians and Romans, as we have seen, to express his understanding of the unity of charismatically endowed Christians. In 1 Corinthians he referred to this unity as the 'body *of* Christ', and in Romans he spoke of it as 'one body *in* Christ'. The images of the body appears again in Colossians, but with a very different intention on Paul's part, and with a very significant change in its application. What Paul emphasises through the use of the image in this epistle is, not the unity of spiritually 'gifted' Christians (in the local church), but the headship of Christ over his body, the (universal) Church. Christians no longer make up the whole body, they constitute the torso and limbs, while Christ himself is portrayed as its head. This concept is introduced first in 1.15-20, a passage with very special characteristics of its own. Before we draw any conclusions about the significance of the new use made of the figure of the body in Colossians, we must seek to establish the apostle's intentions in introducing the figure in 1.15-20.

Colossians 1.15-20

There is agreement among modern commentators that 1.15-20 existed originally as a pre-Pauline hymn.[16] However, opinions vary concerning the form of the original hymn and the extent of Pauline redactional additions.[17] R. P. Martin suggests the following reconstruction of the pre-Pauline hymn:

	Strophe I
Verses 15-16	He is the image of the invisible God
	the firstborn of all creation;
	For in him all things were created
	in heaven and on earth.
	All things were created through him
	and for him.
	Strophe II
Verses 17-18a	He is before all things,
	And in him all things hold together;
	He is the head of the body.
	Strophe III
Verses 18b-20	He is the beginning,
	the firstborn from the dead,
	For in him all the fulness of God
	was pleased to dwell;
	And through him to reconcile to
	himself all things.[18]

In this form the hymn celebrates in turn the cosmic Lord's role in and supremacy over creation (strophe I), his sustaining of the created order (strophe II) and his work of redemption (strophe III). Comparing this reconstructed pre-Pauline hymn with the passage as it stands in the text today, we can see that the following elements are regarded as Pauline additions:

Verse 16   visible and invisible, whether thrones or domin-
             ions or principalities or authorities
Verse 18a   the church
Verse 18b   that in everything he might be pre-eminent
Verse 20b   whether on earth or in heaven, making peace by
             the blood of his cross.

Not all scholars would agree that all of these are redactional additions. However, most commentators do agree that 'the church' in verse 18a is such an addition, and it is this suggested redactional addition which is important for our enquiry.

There is good reason to regard 'the church' as a later Pauline gloss for if the whole were from Paul's hand we might expect him to have expressed the idea as he has done in verse 24 ('his body, that is, the church') instead of using the more awkward expression we find in 18b ('the body, the church').[19] If it is correct to say that Paul added the words 'the church', in verse 18a then it is clear that he was not satisfied with the statement in the original hymn which asserted that Christ was the head of the body, meaning the cosmos.[20] He wanted to alter the meaning of the hymn at this point to assert that, although Christ was indeed head over the cosmos (cf. 2.10), yet the special relationship of head to body pertained not to Christ and the cosmos as a whole, but only to Christ and the Church. By adding 'the church', to the hymn Paul says that real contact with the cosmic Lord is to be experienced only by participation in the Church. Some confirmation for this view is found in 2.19 (see discussion below). Thus Paul's intention in portraying the Church as the body whose head is Christ was to delimit the sphere in which true communion with the cosmic Lord is to be experienced.[21]

Colossians 2.18-19

Paul makes use of the figure of the body again in 1.24 where he speaks of his own sufferings which 'complete what is lacking in Christ's afflictions for the sake of his body, that is the church', and also in 3.15 where he exhorts his readers: 'Let the peace of Christ rule in your hearts, to which you were called in one body.' More significant than these somewhat incidental usages is the statement found in 2.18-19: 'Let no one disqualify you, insisting on self-abasement and worship of angels, taking his stand on visions, puffed up without reason by his sensuous mind, and not holding fast to the Head, from whom the whole body nourished (*chorēgoumenon*) and knit together (*sumbebazomenon*) through its joints (*haphōn*) and ligaments (*sundesmōn*), grows with a growth that is from God.' The thrust of the passage is clearly that the one who is bothering the Colossians shows, by not holding the head (Christ), that he has no share in the body (Church). The whole body draws its growing power from the head, so that those not holding fast to the head have no share either in the growing power experienced in the body.

The meaning of 'joints and ligaments'. In this passage the head/body image is less used to depict Christ's lordship over the Church than it is to portray him as the source of the Church's growth and nourishment. Of special interest for our enquiry into the relationship between Christ and Christian ministry is that here Paul says the nourishment from the head/Christ by which the body/Church grows is mediated in a particular way: 'through its [the body's] joints (*haphōn*) and ligaments (*sundesmōn*)'.[22] However, no hint is given in 2.19 concerning what it is in the church that the *haphai* and *sundesmoi* represent.

The word *haphē* (joint) is found only twice in the Pauline letters; once here in 2.19, and again in Ephesians 4.16 where its meaning is also problematical. *Sundesmos* (ligament) is found three times in the letters of Paul; twice in Colossians (2.19; 3.14) and once in Ephesians (4.3). It is worthy of note that the uses of *sundesmos*, apart from that in Colossians 2.19, are in contexts where Christians are urged to maintain harmony in the Church. In Ephesians 4.3 they are exhorted 'to maintain the unity of the Spirit in the bond of peace (*en tō sundesmō tēs eirēnēs*)', and straightway reminded 'there is one body and one Spirit . . .' (Eph. 4.4). In Colossians 3.14 Christians are urged to 'put on love, which binds everything together in perfect harmony (*ho estin sundesmos tēs teleiotētos*)'. Thus in the one case *sundesmos* is associated with peace and in the other it is identified with love. In both cases this bond binds Christians together in one body. Lacking any other evidence we should probably conclude that the joints (*haphai*) and ligaments (*sundesmoi*) of Colossians 2.19

represent that loving and harmonious interaction between believers through which Christ, the head, nourishes the Church, his body.[23] In such a harmonious situation the Church, relieved of the hindrance of those puffed up without reason by sensuous minds, can grow to maturity in Christ.

CONCLUSIONS

We can now state briefly the conclusions to which our study of Colossians and Philemon has led us. First, Paul still believes that Christ is actively involved in his ministry; it is Christ who energises the apostle for all his toiling and striving on behalf of the Church. However, most significant in this epistle is Paul's use of the metaphor of the body to depict Christ's headship over the Church (and to delimit the sphere in which men may experience real communion with Christ). Christ, as head, is the source of nourishment to enable the Church, his body, to grow, and this nourishment is mediated to the body either through the loving/harmonious interaction of its members, or through the ministry of both special ministers and 'rank and file' members of the Church. If the latter, then we may say that the ministry of all Christians is related to Christ by virtue of the fact that they all are channels through which Christ nourishes his Church. If the former, the result is essentially the same, except that what is emphasised is that it is through the loving/harmonious interaction between these members that Christ nourishes his Church.

Mention ought to be made here of a quite significant change in emphasis found in Colossians compared with the epistles treated earlier. This is the absence of the usual Pauline emphasis on the Holy Spirit. The word *pneuma* is found only twice in the epistle (1.8; 2.5) and only one of these (1.8) is a reference to the Holy Spirit. Christ is the theme of Colossians and he is related directly to his body the Church, and to the ministry of its members.[24]

Second, Paul's consciousness of apostolic authority is undiminished (he may appeal to Philemon as an ambassador in chains, but he could make that appeal a command if he so desired).

Third, the suffering motif which we have seen in all Paul's

previous epistles is to be found also in Colossians. Here he applies it to his own apostolic ministry (possibly to answer criticisms of his apostolate) in a dramatic way—he says he fills up what is lacking in Christ's afflictions for the Church. This is best understood against the background of Paul's reflections upon the servant-prophecies of Deutero-Isaiah. Paul sees his ministry as related to Christ in that he, with him, shares in the sufferings of the servant-messiah for the sake of the Church. The new element in the application of the suffering motif in Colossians is that here for the first time Paul explicitly states that his sharing the sufferings of Christ is not only a privilege given to him, but it constitutes an indispensable (for it fills a lack) part of God's plan of salvation. This also is best understood against the background of the servant-passages of Deutero-Isaiah where the task of the servant, as well as being to make a vicarious sacrifice, is to bring news of salvation to the Gentiles. This Jesus did not do—his ministry was essentially to the lost sheep of the house of Israel—so it is left to his apostle (to the Gentiles) to fill that lack, and in so doing, with all the suffering that it involved, to fill up what is lacking in Christ's afflictions.

Fourth, all members of the Christian community may be said to serve Christ as they carry out their every day responsibilities. This is so in the extreme case of slaves, so its extension to cover the more normal situations of free men seems justifiable. Thus in Colossians the service of Christ is not only the more 'religious' acts mentioned in the epistles treated earlier, but has been extended to cover all aspects of life, as long as the Christian remembers to honour his Lord in them.

Finally, the ministry of the Christian community is related to Christ in that it is from him, the head, that the nourishment comes for the growth of the Church, his body, mediated through the loving and harmonious interactions between believers. This relationship is further developed in Paul's epistle to the Ephesians, the study of which we must now take up.

CHAPTER FOURTEEN

EPHESIANS

Major problems confront anyone who wishes to exegete the epistle to the Ephesians against its historical background. Although many manuscripts contain the words 'at Ephesus' (*en Epheso*) in the opening greeting, some of the oldest of them (including p[46]) omit it. Furthermore, a close reading of the epistle indicates that it could not have been written to the Ephesian church, at least not by Paul. Comments made in the letter show that the author was unknown (except by second-hand report) to his readers and vice versa (cf. 1.15; 3.2; 4.21), yet Paul spent two years ministering in Ephesus (cf. Acts 19.10) and his relationship with the Ephesian elders was a close one (cf. Acts 20.17-38).

However, certain inferences concerning the addressees can be made from the contents of the epistle. We know they were predominantly Gentiles (2.11-12, 17-19; 3.1, 8, 13). If we assume that the exhortations given to the readers were to counter certain tendencies and to correct some unacceptable behaviour, or at least to preserve them from yielding to temptation in those directions, we can say that they were a group whose unity was threatened (4.1-6, 31-32), for whom immoral living was a real temptation (4.17-24; 5.3, 5-8), as was lying, stealing and evil talk (4.25, 28-29; 5.4). Further, the reminder that their salvation was by grace alone (2.8), a fact which takes away any basis for boasting (2.9), and the references to their condition prior to conversion—Gentiles estranged from God (2.11-12; 5.8)—suggests that the readers of this epistle had become proud and complacent, and some were possibly even looking down upon their Jewish Christian brethren (cf. Rom. 11.13-32 which shows that such a tendency was indeed found among the early Gentile Christian communities).

Pauline Authorship?

Up to this point we have assumed that Paul is the author of the epistle. The letter purports to come from him (1.1; 3.1). However, the Pauline authorship, though highly attested in early Christian tradition, has been called into question in recent times. The debate continues unresolved with the onus of proof resting with those who feel they can no longer accept what the letter itself purports to be.[1] Scholars who feel the epistle is non-Pauline date it after the apostle's death, anywhere between the time of that death and as late as AD 170. Those who accept the Pauline authorship date it before c.AD 63 when Paul was martyred and, depending on their view concerning the place of writing, suggest either c.AD 61-3 from Rome, or two or three years earlier from Caesarea.[2]

The Purpose of Ephesians

Many suggestions have been made concerning the purpose of Ephesians: (1) it was written (by Onesimus) to be an introductory letter to the first collection of Paul's epistles.[3] (2) Ephesians (and Colossians) were written to counter the competition of Johannine writings in Asia Minor.[4] (3) There was a threat to the unity of the Church (a breakdown in relations between Jewish and Gentile Christians) so that the aim of the letter was to meet this crisis.[5] (4) It was a response to the threat of Gnosticism in one way or another.[6] (5) It is an attempt by a later disciple to sum up and commend Pauline theology to a later generation.[7]

A Working Hypothesis

Seeing that the authorship, destination, date and place of writing, and purpose of the epistle are all debatable, we need to approach Ephesians in a frame of mind that is more than usually tentative. For the purposes of this study the following is adopted as a working hypothesis: at least the substance of the letter is Pauline, and it addresses a situation somewhere in Asia Minor where the Church was feeling the pressure of (incipient) gnostic teaching. It was, at the same time, threatened from within; threatened by spiritual complacency on the one hand, and by disintegrating forces which could divide it into Jewish and gentile factions on the other. In line with our working hypothesis, and to avoid circumlocutive references to 'the views of the author concerning Paul's apostleship' and the like, the author will be referred to simply as Paul.

Most of the ministerial themes which we have seen in the epistles discussed already are to be found again in Ephesians. However, there are also some quite significant developments, especially in regard to the activity and involvement of the exalted Christ in Christian ministry.

APOSTLESHIP

Corresponding sections in earlier chapters bore the heading 'Paul's Apostleship', but the shorter title of this section is chosen deliberately, for in this epistle reference is made, not only to Paul's apostolate but also to apostleship in general.

An Ambassador in Chains

Paul introduces himself in 1.1 as 'an apostle of Christ Jesus by the will of God' (words identical with those found in Col. 1.1). This introductory formula expresses the authority of the apostle, while mentioning again the double-sided character of his calling—called by Christ, but underlying that, chosen by the will of God. Paul refers to himself as a minister of the gospel (3.7, cf. Col. 1.23), and as an ambassador of the gospel in chains (6.20). 'Ambassador' is a politico-legal term which implies 'full power to represent a potentate or a government.'[8] Paul used the same concept in 2 Corinthians 5.20, only there he called himself an ambassador for *Christ*, whereas here he is an ambassador of the *gospel*. The intention is the same, for Paul is the ambassador of Christ by virtue of the fact that he is entrusted with the gospel of Christ. In both cases the representative character of his ministry is clearly implied.

Ephesians 3.1-13

The passage 3.1-13 contains an extended description (defence?) of Paul's apostolic ministry. It begins with the words: 'For this reason I, Paul, a prisoner for Christ Jesus on behalf of you Gentiles . . .' (1). The following verses (2-13) are parenthetical, and what he began to say in verse 1 is taken up again in verse 14: 'For this reason I bow my knees before the Father . . .'.

The parenthetical section includes several elements relevant to our present enquiry, but before these are discussed a brief comment upon the significance of the parenthetical section as a whole is called for.

Paul's defensive stance. The very existence of the parenthetical section suggests that Paul felt it necessary to defend his apostleship before his readers. He assumes that they have heard of the stewardship of God's grace which was given him (2), yet feels obliged to describe it at length. He repeatedly stresses that this grace and responsibility were given to *him*: 'the mystery was made known to *me*' (3); 'you can perceive *my* insight into the mystery of Christ' (4); 'of this gospel *I* was made a minister according to the gift of God's grace which was given to *me*' (7) 'to *me* . . . this grace was given, to preach to the Gentiles' (8). This repeated emphasis, together with the allusions to his apostolic sufferings[9] on behalf of his readers which introduce and conclude the parenthetical section, suggests that Paul's apostleship needed some defence before the readers of this epistle.

A steward of God's grace. In verse 2 Paul speaks of the stewardship (*oikonomia*)[10] of God's grace that was given to him. This concept is explained in the verses which follow: he has been entrusted with knowledge of 'the mystery of Christ',[11] the gospel, which he must proclaim to the Gentiles, so that through the Church called out by that proclamation, the manifold wisdom of God may be made known, not only to men, but to the principalities and powers in heavenly places as well (3-10).

The stress here falls upon the dynamic/functional aspect of Paul's stewardship. Thus the grace given to him is not so much the grace of apostolic office, as it is empowering grace for the faithful execution of his stewardship: 'Of this gospel I was made a minister according to the gift of grace which was given me by the working of his power . . . grace was given to preach to the Gentiles the unsearchable riches of Christ' (7-8). We see here Paul's strong sense of the dynamic involvement of God in his ministry. However, this is complemented by an awareness that he has been called by the will of God and in accordance with his plan for the ages. Ephesians, then, like the epistles studied earlier, presents a picture of Paul's apostleship which includes both dynamic and authoritative elements. In addition it provides an explicit statement of something only implied by the Corinthian letters, i.e., that Paul's stewardship of the gospel is an integral part of God's great plan for the ages (cf. discussion of 2 Cor. 5.18-20, in ch. 10 above).

Apostleship in General

The statements concerning apostleship in general are found in 2.20; 3.5 and 4.11-13. In 3.5 Paul says that the mystery of Christ, previously hidden from men, 'has now been revealed to his holy[12] apostles and prophets[13] by the Spirit', and in 4.11-13, having said that Christ has ascended on high and given gifts to men, he adds: 'And his gifts were that some should be apostles, some prophets, some evangelists . . . for the building up of the body of Christ.' Thus far we may say that, according to the Pauline view, apostles are those who receive God's revelation (for proclamation), and are Christ's gifts to the Church.

The foundation of the apostles. A further characterisation of apostleship is found in 2.20 where, having assured his readers that they have become members of the household of God, Paul alters the metaphor and says they are 'built upon the foundations of the apostles and prophets, Christ Jesus himself being the cornerstone (*akrogōniaios*).' Here apostles, with prophets, are likened to the foundation[14] of a temple in process of construction, Christians are likened to stones set upon that foundation, and Christ is portrayed as the *akrogōniaios*. Before we ask in what sense the apostles are said to be the foundation of the Church, and what this implies as far as their relationship to God's activity in Christ is concerned, we need to consider some special problems which the passage presents.

The question arises of why the apostles and prophets are here described as the foundation of the structure when in 1 Corinthians 3.11 Paul states that 'no other foundation can any one lay than that which is laid, which is Jesus Christ.' This is surely a case of the same metaphor being used, but in two different ways. In 1 Corinthians 3 Paul himself is not included in the building at all; he is the masterbuilder who lays the foundation.

Cornerstone or keystone? A second problem which needs some explanation is the meaning of *akrogōniaios*. Traditionally it has been translated 'cornerstone' to denote the main piece in the foundation. More recently J. Jeremias has maintained that it should be translated 'keystone', thus meaning the last stone placed in position at the top of the building.[15] This suggestion has been criticised on several counts. First, *akrogōniaios* is used in the Septuagint in Isaiah 28.16 where its meaning is clearly 'cornerstone', and not 'keystone', and we have New Testament attestation for the messianic interpretation of Isaiah 28.16 (Rom. 9.33; 1 Pet. 2.6). Second, Ephesians 2 refers to a building under construction of which Christ is the *akrogōniaios* in which/whom the whole is growing into a holy temple in the Lord. This could not be so if *akrogōniaios* meant keystone, since the keystone can be added only when the building has reached completion. Third, 'the unintelligibility of the idea of a building rising up to some aerially suspended topstone would have been as considerable for the ancients as the notion of a body growing up to a head.'[16] It would seem then, that the traditional interpretation of *akrogōniaios* is still to be preferred, viz. Christ is the cornerstone in the temple of God; the apostles and the prophets are the foundation.

We can now return to our question: in what sense can the apostles be called the foundation of the Church? The answer is that they can only be so called because through their *preaching* the erection of the Church/temple of God was commenced. In the words of H. Schlier: 'There is no other way to Christ than through the apostles and prophets, they preached him and in their preaching they themselves became and remain the foundation.'[17] Thus we may say that the temple/foundation/cornerstone figure expresses in yet another way the very close relationship between apostolic ministry and God's activity in Christ. God is the builder (he builds a temple in which Gentiles and Jews are set alongside one another), Christ is the cornerstone (his blood made peace between Jew and Gentile by removing the hostility between them), and the apostles are the foundation (they make known the mystery—Jews and Gentiles may become partakers together in the promise—and by so doing they enable both to be incorporated into the temple that God is building).

CHRIST IN APOSTOLIC PROCLAMATION
AND AS THE GIVER OF THE SPIRIT

In this section of our study we deal with two passages which are vital for our enquiry. It will be argued that the first, 2.17, speaks of a preaching activity of the exalted Christ through his apostles, and that the second, 4.7-11, teaches that Christ, after his ascension descended again in he Spirit to bestow gifts of ministry upon his people.

Ephesians 2.17

In 2.14-16 Paul outlines the reconciliation which Christ achieved. He broke down the dividing wall of hostility between Jew and Gentile so that he might reconcile both to God in one body through the cross. Having *made* peace, Paul goes on to say in 2.17: 'He [Christ] came and *preached* peace to you who were far off and peace to those who were near.' The question facing us is how we should understand Paul's reference to a coming of Christ for a preaching ministry. The question has been answered in many ways.

Some suggested interpretations. Chrysostom took the coming to mean Jesus' coming in the flesh, and the preaching to refer to the proclamation of the earthly Jesus who ministered not only to Jews but to some who were 'far off', such as the Syrophoeni-cian woman, the Samaritan leper, the Samaritan woman, and the centurion.[18] Another suggestion is that Christ's dying on the cross itself is a proclamation of peace. In this case the coming of Christ is none other than his coming from God: the incarnation or the earthly reality of Jesus.[19] A third interpretation sees in the verse a reference to Christ's coming from death, from his descent into hell, after his resurrection to make a personal proclamation of peace to his disciples who were gathered in the upper room.[20] A fourth interpretation, noting what is said in 1 Peter 3.18-20 and 1 Timothy 3.16, suggests that Ephesians 2.17 refers to the coming of Jesus by his ascension to proclaim victory to the principalities and powers, with whom the root of hostility lay.[21] Again it has been argued that the coming and the proclamation must refer to the whole salvation-work of Christ so that either/or questions (the work of the historical Jesus or the exalted Christ) are out of order.[22]

Other interpreters suggest it refers to the coming of Christ through the Spirit, which is by some linked with the preaching ministry of the apostles.[23]

A likely solution. In seeking to interpret Ephesians 2.17 we have to bear in mind two facts. First, the verb *euēggelisato* ('preached') is an aorist and, therefore, suggests a once only historic preaching occurrence. Second, those who were addressed by the preaching were a very definite group: the readers of the epistle to the Ephesians (*humin*: 'to you'). With reference to the second point, it needs to be remembered that the greater part of 2.17 is a citation from Isaiah 57.19. However, the author is not content to leave it at that and simply say: 'He came and preached peace to those who were far off and to those who were near.' He inserts the word 'you' (*humin*): 'He came and preached peace to *you* (*humin*) who were far off and to those who were near.' Clearly then the preaching of Christ is understood as preaching to the readers of Ephesians, men and women who lived in Asia Minor. If the *humin* ('you') grounds the preaching in Asia Minor, the aorist *euēggelisato* ('preached') must be taken to indicate the historic occasion on which the gospel was first proclaimed to the recipients of the letter.

Summing up, we may say Ephesians 2.17 indicates that Paul believed Christ continued his ministry of proclaiming peace through the preaching of his apostle. If, as seems certain, Ephesians was intended for a group of Christians who had never seen Paul in the flesh, then we must be prepared to extend this preaching activity of the risen Christ to include not only the witness of Paul, but also of his associates, and probably other faithful witnesses as well. In the light of other New Testament references we might wish to add that this preaching activity of Christ was effected through the agency of the Spirit, but this is not mentioned in Ephesians 2.17.

Ephesians 4.7-11

If it is correct to say that the purpose of Ephesians, in part at least, is to combat disintegrating forces within the congregation, then the passage 4.1-16 would have to be regarded as Paul's plea for unity. Our present passage, 4.7-11, forms part of that plea. Here Paul stresses the unity they have already in one body, and asserts that the diversity of gifts (of which different individuals are the recipients) is given to promote the up-building, not of those individuals primarily, but of the whole body of believers. The passage is relevant to our study at several levels, but here we are interested in what it reveals of Christ's relationship to the Spirit, and in turn, to the spiritual gifts exercised in the Church. However, the passage is not without its difficulties.

The problem of verse 7. The text runs: 'But grace was given (*edothē*) to each of us according to the measure of Christ's gift'. The problem immediately confronting us is to determine what is meant by the grace given to each one, and how it is according to the measure of the gift of Christ. Does the use of the aorist *edothē* recall the believer's baptism, that historic event at which grace was communicated to him personally by the Redeemer so that he was incorporated into the Church?[24] Or should we take Christ's gift to mean the gift of the Messiah, and the whole phrase, 'according to the measure of Christ's gift', to mean something similar to Romans 8.32: 'He who spared not his own son but gave him up for us all, will he not also give us all things with him'. If so, Ephesians 4.7 would say simply that grace was given to each of us with a generosity which holds nothing back. The grace given could then be identified with the various gifts given freely to the Church.[25] A third view is that Christ's gift is to be taken as the gift of the Spirit poured out by the risen Christ.[26]

The problem of Paul's use of Psalm 68.18. Verses 8-10, the citation from Psalm 68.18 ('When he ascended on high he led a host of captives, and he gave gifts to men') and the commentary which follows ('In saying, "He ascended", what does it mean but that he had also descended into the lower parts of the earth? He who descended is he who also ascended far above all heavens, that he might fill all things') also presents us with some difficult exegetical problems. First, the citation from Psalm 68.18 does not agree with either the Massoretic text or the Septuagint. Both these texts must be rendered 'he *received* gifts from men', and not 'he *gave* gifts to men'. Does this mean that the author has unintentionally misquoted from the Psalm,[27] or has he altered the wording deliberately to suit his present purpose,[28] or was he influenced by rabbinic exegesis of Psalm 68.18?[29] Second, to what do 'descended' and 'ascended' in verse 10 refer? It is generally agreed that 'ascended' refers to Christ's ascension or glorification, but there is a division of opinion concerning the meaning of 'descended'. Does it mean Christ's descent to the earth in his incarnation,[30] or a descent into the nether regions, the abode of the dead,[31] or could it refer to a descent of Christ through the Spirit *after* his ascension?[32]

Caird's Interpretation. One thing see⁻ns clear and it is that any solution to these various problems should be comprehensive; one that can resolve the individual exegetical difficulties while, at the same time, offering an acceptable interpretation of the passage as a whole. Caird has suggested such a comprehensive solution:

> The argument of the present passage, then, may be paraphrased as follows: To every member of the Church Christ has made his own particular gift of grace. These are the gifts referred to in Psalm 68, which declares that Christ ascended to heaven leading the captive powers of evil in his triumphal train, and then gave gifts to men. We can assume that his ascent was followed by a descent back to earth, and that the life-giving Spirit who descended is identical with the incarnate Lord who ascended. It is he who has given to the church all the varied gifts needed for the building up of its corporate life.[33]

In support of this thesis, Caird puts forward three types of evidence: textual, grammatical, and liturgical.

The textual and grammatical evidence. Dealing with the textual evidence, he maintains that the word *prōton* (first) appearing after *katebē* (descended) (9) in some manuscripts[34] is a later interpretative gloss. This gloss has unduly influenced interpretations of *katebē* (descended) so that the majority of exegetes make it refer to a descent of Christ *prior to* his ascension, i.e., to his incarnation or his descent to the abode of the dead. But if *prōton* (first) is removed *katebē* (descended) can just as easily refer to a descent *after* the ascension, i.e., to Christ's descent in the person of the Spirit.

Turning to the grammatical evidence, Caird says that *ta katōtera tēs gēs* should be interpreted as 'the lower regions, that is the earth', thereby construing the genitive case of *tēs gēs* as a genitive of apposition and not a partitive genitive. This interpretation has been followed by the translators of the NEB.

The liturgical evidence. Caird notes that Psalm 68 and Exodus 19 were set readings in the Jewish synagogue for Pentecost during the inter-testamental period, and by association Psalm 68 had come to be understood in rabbinic exegesis as a reference to Moses' ascent of Mount Sinai to receive the Law and his descent to deliver it as God's gift to his people. Caird cites the Targum:

> Thou hast ascended to heaven, that is Moses, the prophet; thou has taken captivity captive, thou hast learnt the words of the Torah; thou hast given it as gifts to men, and also with the rebellious, if they turn in repentance, the Shekinah of the glory of the Lord God dwells.

Noting that the text of Ephesians differs from the Massoretic text and the Septuagint in just the same way as the Targum on Psalm 68, Caird suggests that the Targum (though of late origin) preserves an early Jewish tradition available to the author of Ephesians. What the author has done is to take a piece of rabbinic exegesis which interprets Psalm 68 in relation to Moses' descent from Sinai bringing the Torah for Israel, and adapt it in such a way that Moses is replaced by Christ and the Torah by the Spirit. So what was once a Jewish pentecostal psalm has now become a Christian pentecostal psalm.[35]

The advantages and implications of this interpretation. Caird's thesis represents a comprehensive treatment of the passage and provides a satisfying solution to the particular exegetical problems which it presents. It seems to be the best overall treatment of the passage made to date. By adopting his thesis we can offer solutions to the problems posed by the passage. First, the 'grace' given to each one is the manifestation of the Spirit which each receives 'according to the measure of Christ's gift.' Second, Paul has not misquoted or altered Psalm 68.18, rather he has adapted a Jewish pentecostal interpretation of the psalm to make a Christian pentecostal interpretation. Third, the descent of Christ is a reference to neither his incarnation nor his descent to the nether regions, but to his descent after the ascension, and in the person of the Spirit, to distribute ministerial gifts to his people. This is not at variance with verse 11 where the gifts are said to be apostles, prophets, etc., for a minister who exercises a gift cannot be separated from the gift he exercises. The gifts of ministry are always 'personally packaged'.

If it is right to interpret Ephesians 4.7-11 along these lines, we may say that this passage explicitly relates Christ to Christian ministry as the one who bestows the gifts of ministry upon members of the Church, by which gifts alone they are equipped properly to carry out their individual ministries for the common good of the Church.

HEAD/BODY METAPHOR: CHRIST AND THE CHURCH

The figure of the body is used in several places in Ephesians to depict the Christian community. It underlies the exhortation in 4.25: 'Let every one speak the truth with his neighbour, for we are members one of another.' It is used again in 5.21-33 where a comparison is made between Christ and his body, the Church, on the one hand, and husbands and their wives on the other. It is found in two other passages which contribute very significantly to our understanding of the Christian Church and its ministry in relation to Christ. We will discuss them separately below.

Ephesians 1.23

This verse comes at the end of a passage (1.20-23) in which Paul speaks of the exalted Christ and his Church. Christ has been raised to a place of authority over all spirit-forces, but more significantly, he has been made head over the Church, his body. The Church is described as 'his body, the fullness of him who fills all in all (*to sōma autou to plērōma tou ta panta en pasin plēroumenou*)' (23). Unfortunately the meaning of this verse is also extremely difficult to determine with any degree of certainty. This difficulty is reflected in the ways in which modern translations have variously rendered verses 22-23:

RSV   And he [God] has put all things under his feet and has made him head over all things for the church, which is his body, the fullness of him who fills all in all.

JB   He has put all things under his feet, and made him, as the ruler of everything, the head of the Church; which is his body, the fullness of him who fills the whole creation.

NEB He has put everything in subjection beneath his feet, and appointed him as supreme head to the church, which is his body and as such holds within it the fullness of him who himself receives the entire fullness of God.

The sources of the confusion. The difficulty arises because the three key expressions (*to plērōma, ta panta en pasin, plēroumenou*) are all susceptible to more than one translation. *To plērōma* can be either active ('that which fills') or passive (that which is filled). *Ta panta en pasin* can be taken in either an adverbial sense (in every way) or an objective sense (all in all). *Plēroumenou* can be either passive (is being fulfilled), middle/reflexive (fills for himself), or middle/active (fills). With various possible translations for each of the three key expressions, verse 23 can be interpreted in many different ways.[36] Among the possible interpretations the following can be mentioned.

Some suggested interpretations. Lightfoot suggests an interpretation which takes *plēroumenou* as passive, *plērōma* as a passive noun, and *ta panta en pasin* with its adverbial force. Accordingly, J. A. T. Robinson, a later exponent of Lightfoot's view, translates: 'the church, which is his body, the fullness of him who all in all is being filled,' i.e., 'the Church, as the body of Christ, is constantly receiving from Christ the complete fullness which Christ receives from the Father.'[37]

J. A. Robinson, following the majority of the ancient versions, and Origen, Chrysostom and Calvin, takes *plēroumenou* as passive, *plērōma* as an active noun, and *ta panta en pasin* as adverbial. Thus he says, 'the Church is that without which the Christ is not complete,' and suggests the translation: 'the Church, the fullness of Him who all in all is being fulfilled.'[38]

S. Hanson takes *plēroumenou* in its middle/reflexive sense (he fills for himself) and *ta panta en pasin* in its objective sense.[39] He offers no translation, but his position implies something like: 'the Church, which is his body, the fullness of him who (for himself) fills every thing (in the Church).'

The RSV takes *plēroumenou* in its middle/active sense (he fills), *plērōma* as active, and *ta panta en pasin* in its objective sense, thus yielding the translation: 'the church, which is his body, the fullness of him who fills all in all.'

Finally, *plēroumenou* can be taken as middle/active (he fills), *plērōma* as an active noun in apposition to *autou* (Christ) not *sōma* (the Church), and *ta panta en pasin* as adverbial, thus yielding the translation: 'the Church, which is his body, the fullness of him (God) who fills all in all.'[40]

A possible solution. Grammatically all of these interpretations are possible. In light of the division among commentators it would be presumptuous to be dogmatic about any one of them. However, it can be noted that elsewhere in the epistle it is always God/Christ/the Spirit who do the filling, and where believers are concerned, they are invariably the recipients (cf. 3.19; 4.10; 5.18). Therefore it seems best to take *plērōma* as a passive noun, *plēroumenou* as middle/active or middle/reflexive and *ta panta en pasin* as objective. Thus the Church could be said to be the body of Christ in that it is filled in a special way by him who fills all things (cf. 4.10). In filling the Church he provides it with power for growth as we shall see in the discussion of the second passage.

Ephesians 4.11-16

These verses form the concluding section of the extended passage 4.1-16 which, as we have noted, possibly constitutes Paul's appeal for unity in face of disintegrating forces at work among his readers.

Verses 11-16 speak of the special ministers whom Christ gave/appointed (*edōken*) to/for the Church. The purpose of their appointment is the 'building up of the body of Christ' (12), to bring Christians to 'mature manhood' so that they be no longer 'tossed to and fro and carried about with every wind of doctrine by the cunning of men by their craftiness in deceitful wiles' (13-14). Instead they are to 'grow up in every way into him who is the head, into Christ, from whom the whole body . . . makes bodily growth' (15-16). The figure of the body is introduced at two points: first, in verse 12, simply as a metaphor for the Church, and second, in verses 15-16, where the growth which the body derives from the head is emphasised. In the latter, the head/body metaphor is applied to the process of growth in a special way: growth is mediated from the head to the body 'by every joint (*haphēs*) with which it is supplied, when each part is working properly' (16).

The meaning of the joints (haphai) *in verse 16.* It is important to be able to define clearly what Paul means by the mediation of power for growth from Christ the head via the joints (*haphai*) to the Church his body. In the treatment of the parallel passage in Colossians 2.19 (see ch. 12 above) it was argued that the joints (*haphai*) denoted the loving/harmonious interrelations/interactions between individual members of the Church. Can the joints (*haphai*) here in Ephesians 4.16 be interpreted in the same way?

Masson's interpretation. Theodoret said: 'As to the joints in the body, that refers to the apostles and prophets and teachers of the Church.'[41] Masson, who regards the determination of the meaning of *haphai* as a *crux interpretum*, develops Theodoret's view, and says that 'it is only by these [the special ministers of verse 11] that grace has been given to each believer according to the measure of the gift of Christ (v. 7). It is only by these that believers become mature in the Christian life, nourished by the Word and sacrament. . . . They live by the grace received from Christ by means of the ministers.'[42] Masson observed at the time of writing his commentary that most commentators did not even raise the question of the identity of the *haphai*, and for the most part this is still the case. However, two modern interpreters have addressed the problem, but they arrive at quite different conclusions from those of Masson.

Two alternative interpretations. Hanson says the nourishment/gifts which come from the head, Christ, are passed on by individual Christians to the rest of the body.[43] Barth, commenting upon Ephesians 4.16, supports the view adopted above in relation to Colossians 2.19, i.e., that the *haphai* refer to neither the special ministers nor all members of the Church, but to that more nebulous matter: the interrelation between members: 'In the context of Eph 4.16 only one paraphrase appears appropriate: every contact serves for supply. While this interpretation appears to be nearest the Greek original, in our translation it has been replaced by the even freer version "He provides sustenance to it through every contact." '[44]

This last view is not as 'tidy' as those suggested by Hanson and Masson, but 'tidiness' cannot be allowed to be the criterion for correct exegesis. Masson's view in particular is not without its weaknesses. His interpretation gives the passage a full-blown 'catholic' flavour; the special ministers of the Church stand between Christ and his people and become the only channels of grace.[45] However, we must remember (if we intend to press the metaphor of the joints this far) that the greater number of joints in the human body occur where the various members of the body come into contact, not with the head, but with one another. Thus if Masson interprets the joints as special ministers through whom alone the body/Church receives nourishment from the head/Christ, he presses the analogy beyond acceptable limits. It must be pointed out that the preceding verse (15), which also emphasises the growth of the body, says that the accompaniment of growth (if not the means by which it occurs) is the love among members: 'speaking the truth in love, we are to grow up in every way into him . . .' The same factor is emphasised in 16b, where the growth of the body is said to take place in (the environment of) love.

Summing up, it may be said that 4.16 does not imply that Christ's participation in the Church's ministry of upbuilding is effected only through special ministers. Rather, like Colossians 2.19, it teaches that '*in their mutual dependence and communication* all church members are chosen tools for communicating nourishment, vitality, unity, solidity to the body.'[46]

THE MINISTRY OF THE CHRISTIAN COMMUNITY

In preceding sections of this chapter the ministry of the Christian community has already been touched upon indirectly. We have seen that Christ, descending in the person of the Spirit, bestows gifts of ministry for the upbuilding of the Church. We have seen, too, that Christ himself is actively involved in this ministry of upbuilding for he it is who, as head of the body, makes available the power for growth through the mutual dependency and communication between members of the Church. In addition it can be noted that the Church is still regarded as a charismatic community. Its members are exhorted: 'Be filled with the Spirit, addressing one another in psalms and hymns and spiritual songs' (5.18-19)—another indication of the way in which Paul sees the growth of the community taking place, viz. by mutual dependency and communication. There is one other passage in Ephesians which also sheds some light on the ministry of the Christian community.

Ephesians 6.5-8

This passage contains similar instructions for slaves to those found in Colossians 3.22-4 which has already been discussed above (see ch. 13). As in the Colossian passage so here in Ephesians, too, the faithful service of a slave to his master is regarded as service to Christ. And if this is applied to slaves whose lives could be ordered by the whims of cruel masters, then it is right to assume that it applies also to other Christians who carry out faithfully the responsibilities of their various states in life.

Then, in Ephesians also, the service of Christ is not only the privilege of the special ministers of the Church, but is a privilege shared by all believers: the faithful carrying out of the responsibilities of their state in life is service acceptable to Christ.

CONCLUSIONS

Our study of Ephesians seems to justify the following conclusions concerning Christian ministry.

First, the exalted Christ continues to be seen as actively involved in apostolic ministry. He comes preaching peace to fragmented mankind as the mystery of the gospel is proclaimed by the apostles, and probably by unknown Christian witnesses as well. Further, having ascended to heaven, Christ is believed to have descended again in the person of the Spirit to distribute gifts of ministry to his people. Thus, what has been hinted at in epistles studied earlier has become explicit here in Ephesians: Christ is related to the ministry of the Christian community as the one who, being present in the person of the Holy Spirit, bestows the gifts of ministry upon each of its members.

In the conclusions to our study of Colossians we noted the absence in that epistle of the usual Pauline emphasis on the Spirit. However, in the epistle to the Ephesians we encounter once again that stress on the Spirit which is so characteristic of Paul's teaching. In Colossians the word *pneuma* is found only twice, and of these uses only one refers to the Holy Spirit. In contrast, *pneuma* is found fourteen times in Ephesians; eleven of these clearly refer to the Holy Spirit, and one other possibly does so. In Ephesians (as with the other epistles we have studied with the exception of Colossians) the Spirit and Christ are closely associated. Christ it is who comes to his people again in the person of the Spirit.

Second, the apostleship of Paul still involves both representative authority and a divine dynamic, but in Ephesians the scope of his apostolic influence is extended to cosmic dimensions: he is given grace to preach the riches of Christ, not only so that men might know the mystery of God's plan, but also that the very principalities and powers in heavenly places might, through the Church, come to understand the manifold wisdom of God. Further, Paul's apostolate is integrally related to God's plan for the ages; it is God's will and plan to overcome the hostility between Jew and Gentile and out of the two create one new man in Christ. However, it is only through the apostolic preaching that God's plan becomes a living reality, and Paul, as apostle to the Gentiles, has a definite part to play.

Third, the apostolic ministry in general is portrayed as the gift of the exalted Christ to his Church. Through the proclamation of the gospel apostles become closely associated with Christ as the foundation of the Church. The Church is likened to a temple. Its builder is God (who incorporates into its structure both Jews and Gentiles), its cornerstone is Christ (who made peace between Jews and Gentiles by the blood of his cross), and its foundation is the apostles (who are the agents of the proclamation of peace by which Jews and Gentiles are actually incorporated into the temple of God). Thus, as we saw in our study of the Corinthian letters, the apostolate is an integral part of God's activity in Christ.

Fourth, the ministry of the Christian community, as far as its relationship to Christ is concerned, finds its clearest expression in this epistle. Its gifts for ministry are bestowed upon it by Christ who is himself the source of its power for growth, and this power for growth he makes available through the mutual dependency and intercommunication of its members. Further, this epistle repeats what we have already seen in Colossians: all Christians are truly serving Christ as they faithfully carry out the normal responsibilities of their state in life. In brief, men not only serve Christ by the exercise of special gifts which are given to them, but they serve him also in the faithful fulfilment of everyday obligations.

In conclusion we need to ask whether there has been any light shed upon the complex problem of the authorship of Ephesians by the limited study we have undertaken. Two observations can be made. First, the suggestion that the view of ministry reflected in Ephesians is more institutionalised than that found in earlier epistles lacks solid foundation. Neither the 'holy apostles and prophets' nor the 'joints' with which the body is supplied can be confidently claimed as evidence of a post-Pauline view of ministry. In fact, both are better explained in terms which place them very much in the sphere of characteristically Pauline thought. Second, the emphases on the close relationship between Christ and the Spirit, and on the gifts of ministry given to members of the Church are certainly emphases we have seen in the undisputed letters of Paul. In this respect the view of ministry espoused in Ephesians must be said to be genuinely Pauline.

In brief, although this evidence on its own does not allow us to assert that the letter could not have been written by a disciple of the apostle using Pauline material, it does support the view that the letter is in substance Pauline, if not from his own hand.

CHAPTER FIFTEEN

GENERAL CONCLUSIONS

The aim of this study has been to understand just how Christian ministry in the apostolic community was related to the historical Jesus on the one hand, and to the exalted Christ on the other. By so doing, it was hoped, some light would be thrown upon the nature of Christian ministry today. In the next (and final) chapter some of the implications of this study for today will be noted. Before that is done we need to summarise the results of our study of ministry in the apostolic community.

SUMMARY OF RESULTS

Our study has revealed that the major themes used by Jesus in the synoptic tradition are found also in the letters of Paul. Although these themes were applied by the apostle to meet various situations which arose in the early churches, nevertheless, their meaning and significance remain essentially the same. However, it has also been seen that Paul introduced new ministerial themes which have no counterpart in the synoptic record of the sayings of Jesus.

Ministerial Themes Common to Jesus and Paul

We note first those themes which are found both in the synoptic sayings of Jesus and the writings of the apostle Paul.

Apostleship. Jesus had a strong sense of being sent by God. This sending he understood, in part, after the fashion of the sending of the Old Testament prophets, yet it involved more than that. The prophets came to proclaim the word of the Lord, the promises of the kingdom. Jesus not only proclaimed the coming of the kingdom and its attendent blessings, he inaugurated it and pronounced its blessings upon men. Further, when Jesus sent the Twelve on the Galilean mission, he made their ministry an extension of his own. The same limitations applied (to the house of Israel) and the same task was to be undertaken (to proclaim the presence/nearness of the kingdom, and to demonstrate this through exorcisms and healings). They were Jesus' representatives; they represented both Jesus and the God who had sent him. The form of Jesus' commission sayings to the Twelve strongly suggests that he understood their relationship to him (at least for the duration of that mission, though he seems to have had a later time in mind as well) as that of šĕlūḥîm (envoys) to their principal. They represented him and bore his authority.

From Paul's letters it is clear that he also had a strong sense of divine calling, and that he too understood that calling, to a certain extent, to be after the fashion of the calling of the Old Testament prophets of God. In every epistle studied there was, to a greater or lesser degree, evidence of a realisation that his apostleship involved both a delegated authority and a responsibility to represent his lord. He called himself an ambassador of Christ, and felt himself charged with responsibility for the interests of Christ among men. The language which he used concerning the representative character of his apostolate suggests that he understood it in terms not unlike those used in relation to the Jewish šālîaḥ concept. In addition, his apostleship involved a proclamation and a demonstration of the power of God by signs and wonders (evidence of the presence, proleptically at least, of the kingdom of God). In all these areas the Pauline view of the apostolate differs little from what we have seen of Jesus' understanding of it in the synoptic gospels.

However, in a few areas, Paul's understanding of the apostolate goes beyond what we know of Jesus' conception of the same through the synoptic witness. Paul came to regard the apostolate as an *integral* part of God's activity in Christ for the salvation of men; God reconciled men to himself through Christ, the apostle besought men, on behalf of Christ, to be reconciled to God. Paul's ministry was an *indispensable* part of God's plan, for through it that which is lacking in the afflictions of the Christ was filled up. The indispensability of the apostolic ministry is further reflected in Paul's application of the metaphor of the temple to the Church. Apostles, together with Christ the cornerstone, form the very foundation of the Church. Further, apostles are the gifts of Christ to his Church, and the apostolic ministry has cosmic dimensions: through apostolic preaching a Church made up of Jews and Gentiles comes into being and through its existence the manifold wisdom of God is made known not only to men, but to the principalities and powers in heavenly places.

Servanthood. Jesus, who consistently portrayed his ministry as one of humble service, understood this in the light of the Deutero-Isaiah servant-prophecies. His service involved suffering and culminated in the giving of his life a ransom for many. He served God by serving men, and he laid down the same pattern of service for his disciples' ministry, warning them that they too would be called upon to suffer as he had done. That their ministry was also to be one of suffering servanthood, suggests that Jesus expected the servant-prophecies to find fulfilment in their ministries.

Paul frequently referred to himself as the servant of Christ/God, and implied that all Christians faithfully carrying out their duties in life were serving Christ too. He believed that suffering was an inevitable part of apostolic ministry. He referred to the scars of persecution that marred his body as the 'marks of Jesus', and was convinced that his apostolic sufferings filled up the lack in 'the afflictions of Christ'. All this, together with Paul's teaching that Christians are destined to suffer, is best understood in the light of the Deutero-Isaiah servant-prophecies.

Paul went beyond what we know of Jesus' teaching about suffering servanthood in one notable instance. In face of criticisms of his apostolate Paul appealed to his sufferings as evidence for its genuineness. Suffering, he said, is not a denial of his claim to be the servant of the exalted Christ, rather it is legitimatising evidence of the same. The only true servant of Christ is a suffering servant.

The role of the Spirit. Jesus had a clear consciousness of the power of the Spirit at work in him. He regarded the exorcisms and healings which he performed as evidence that the power and blessings of the New Age were present in the here and now. Jesus expected this same Spirit to help his disciples when they faced times of trial (a reference probably to the troublous times at and immediately following his death).

In response to criticisms of his apostolate, Paul claimed that he had not failed to perform the signs of an apostle and these were the evidence of the power of the Spirit at work in him. Further, he claimed that it was Christ himself who worked these signs and wonders through him, a claim which strongly suggests that Paul understood his apostolic ministry as a continuation of the ministry begun by Jesus in the days of his flesh.

Going beyond the teaching of Jesus on the Spirit, Paul linked the giving of the Spirit with the death of Jesus; he described Christ/God as the one who supplies the Spirit to, and works miracles among, members of the Christian community; and he taught explicitly that Christ himself, after his ascension, descended again in the person of the Spirit to bestow gifts of ministry upon his people. In these last respects Paul's teaching approximates the Spirit-theology of Luke-Acts.

Eschatological Validation. Apart from the major themes of apostleship, servanthood, and the role of the Spirit, the minor theme of eschatological validation of ministry which is found in Paul's letters also has its counterpart in the synoptic sayings of Jesus. In particular it appears in the parables which use as their starting point the accountability of servants to their masters.

Ministerial Themes Unique to Paul

We must now note those aspects of Paul's teaching regarding the relationship between Christian ministry and Christ for which there are no parallels in the synoptic sayings of the historical Jesus.

The active involvement of the exalted Christ. In almost all of the Pauline letters we have studied there may be seen a conviction that the exalted Christ himself is actively involved either in the ministry of the apostle or in the Christian community, or in both. Christ is presented as the one who establishes Christians in their faith, directs the paths of the apostle, and supplies the Spirit to, and works miracles within, the Christian community. He is the ultimate initiator of apostolic ministry: he 'authors' the 'living letters' while the apostles are his 'scribes' who carry out their work with the 'ink' of the Spirit. Christ is also the source of the Christian experience of the Spirit and the bestower of the gifts of ministry. His compassion finds expression in the apostle's yearning over his converts. Paul confidently expects the help of Christ's Spirit when he faces trials. Christ himself energises the apostle so he may fulfil the heavy demands of the apostolate. Finally, it is from Christ that the power for the growth of the Christian community comes.

The simultaneity of weakness and power. Paul's critics asserted that his unimpressive presence and frequent afflictions were incompatible with the claim he made to be the representative of the exalted Christ. In response Paul propounded his view concerning the simultaneity of weakness and power. His weakness was not a denial of his claim that the power of Christ was manifest through him, on the contrary, it was the necessary accompaniment of that power, for the power of Christ is made perfect through weakness.

The priestly ministry. It was possibly in response to Jewish Christian suspicions about the 'cleanness' of Paul's gentile converts that the apostle was prompted to think of his ministry in priestly and sacrificial terms. He saw himself as priest responsible for the offering (consisting) of the Gentiles, and particularly for the purity of that offering. He presided over the offering of the Gentiles, and by his preaching and teaching ministry ensured that they were an offering acceptable and well-pleasing to God. Contemplating an imminent death, and using the priestly/sacrificial imagery in a different way, Paul spoke of his own martyrdom as a libation to be offered with the sacrifice of the faith of the Gentiles. Here the real sacrifice is that made by believers. Each member of the Church is portrayed as a priest responsible for the offering of the works of his faith to God.

The body of Christ. The most notable Pauline innovation as far as ministerial themes are concerned is the use made by him of the figure of the body. In Romans and 1 Corinthians it is used to depict the unity of spiritually 'gifted' Christians. In Colossians and Ephesians, in modified form, it refers to Christ's headship over the Church, emphasising, not that he is Lord of the Church (though this is clearly implied), but that he is the source of its nourishment and power for growth.

Summary. When Paul wanted to express the relationship of Christian ministry to Christ and his ministry he used the same major ministerial themes as Jesus used with essentially the same meaning. In addition we may say that as Paul faced concrete situations in his work among the early churches, he made specific applications of these themes which go beyond what we know of Jesus' understanding of them through the witness of the Synoptics. In some instances Paul introduced new ministerial themes which have no counterpart in the sayings of Jesus, but these are not incompatible with the synoptic teaching of Jesus.

PAUL'S UNDERSTANDING OF MINISTRY: EVOLUTIONARY DEVELOPMENT OR SITUATIONAL RESPONSE?

The primary aim of this study was to examine and compare the teaching of Jesus and the writings of Paul concerning ministry. A secondary aim has been to see what development if any there is of this subject across the epistles of Paul. In the preliminary remarks to the study of Paul's epistles it was noted that they are occasional letters, letters addressed to particular situations on particular occasions. Therefore, what might at first appear to be development in Paul's ideas could well turn out to be only varied responses to different situations. Bearing this in mind, we need to ask whether Paul's understanding of ministry represents an evolutionary development of thought or varied situational responses? To answer this question we need to review some of the key ministerial themes used by the apostle.

Christ and the Spirit. Christ is closely related to the Spirit in all but one of the epistles studied. The exception is Colossians where this emphasis is notably absent, a fact which may possibly be explained by Paul's desire to correct an unhealthy spiritualism by emphasising the importance of Christ himself. It is interesting to note that this typically Pauline emphasis, though absent in Colossians, is emphasised again in Ephesians.

The suffering motif. Suffering is a theme which is found in all epistles except Ephesians. The way in which it is handled seems to depend entirely upon the situation the apostle is addressing. Where his apostleship is under attack he appeals to his sufferings as proof of the genuineness of his apostolate. Where his readers are suffering he explains that suffering is the lot and privilege of the people of God.

The metaphor of the body. The use of the figure of the body also seems to be governed largely by the situation to which the apostle responds. In 1 Corinthians where he combats individualism, party-spirit and pride of spiritual experience, Paul uses it to show that the true Christian experience of the Spirit creates unity; it is 'body-forming'. In Romans where Paul may well be combating disintegrating forces at work in the Roman church, the image of the body is used to stress that, though members of a church may be many and varied, they are still one body in Christ. In Colossae an early christological hymn seems to have been the cause of an inadequate appreciation of the pre-eminence of Christ. The head/body metaphor was used in this hymn to portray Christ as the Lord of the cosmos. Paul takes up the hymn, accepts what it asserts, but modifies it to include an important truth that it omits. Further, if Ephesians was written by Paul about the same time as Colossians, the similar use made of the head/body metaphor could be accounted for by postulating a similar situation. If it was written by a disciple using Colossians (and other Pauline letters), the similar use can be explained by literary dependence upon Colossians.

The priestly ministry. It was suggested that Paul's use of priestly and sacrificial terminology was first introduced in face of Jewish Christian suspicions concerning the 'cleanness' of Paul's gentile converts. In Romans he portrays himself as a priest responsible for the offering up of the Gentiles and for the purity of that offering. But in Philippians, when he was contemplating an imminent death, he pictures his martyrdom as a libation to be poured out in accompaniment with the offering of the Gentiles' faith.

Summing up, then, it seems that the variations in the way ministerial themes are used in the different epistles can be accounted for almost entirely by Paul's different responses to life-situations. There is little evidence for an evolutionary development of thought, rather we see here the working of the agile mind of an outstanding missionary answering the needs of the churches he founded and/or was responsible for, and coping with the vicissitudes of his own career.

This study has revealed a significant correspondence between the historical Jesus and the apostle Paul as far as their understanding of ministry is concerned. This correspondence was seen in their conception of apostleship as being sent from and responsible to, God; of the apostolic ministry as a fulfilment of the role of the Servant of Deutero-Isaiah; and of ministry as empowered by the Spirit. Although in each case these themes were developed by Paul in response to specific situations encountered in the course of his ministry, nevertheless the essential elements remain the same.

There is, therefore, a distinct continuity between the historical Jesus and the apostle Paul, and this continuity can be accounted for in two ways. First, Paul's thought is probably *dependent* upon the historical Jesus. This dependency may be traced through the tradition handed on by those who knew the Lord in the flesh. Second, Paul's understanding of ministry was formed by his personal encounter and experiences with the exalted Christ. There is, of course, a continuity between the historical Jesus and the exalted Christ. We should expect, therefore, that there would be a correspondence between the teachings of the historical Jesus and the impressions received by the apostle Paul in his encounter and experiences with the exalted Christ.

There is more to the continuity between the ministry of the historical Jesus and the apostle Paul than this correspondence of understanding alone. We have seen very clearly how Paul believed that the exalted Christ was actively involved in his apostolic mission. At one point there is a strong suggestion that what Christ effected through his apostle was nothing other than a continuation of the same ministry he had begun as the historical Jesus. We noted the words of Paul in Romans 15.18-19: 'I will not venture to speak of anything except what Christ has wrought through me to win obedience from the Gentiles, by word and deed, by the power of signs and wonders, by the power of the Holy Spirit'. The correspondence between this portrayal of Paul's ministry and that of the historical Jesus presented in the synoptic gospels is obvious. Paul appears to imply that what Jesus began to do in Palestine the exalted

Christ continues to do through the ministry of his apostle. (This, as we have also noted, is exactly the view put forward by Luke in Acts 1.1-2.)

In the light of these observations in the area of ministry at least, we ought to resist attempts to drive a wedge between Jesus and Paul.

CHAPTER SIXTEEN

IMPLICATIONS FOR MINISTRY TODAY

This study of Jesus, Paul and ministry has many implications for Christian ministry today.

The Involvement of the Living Christ

One of the striking things to have emerged from our study is Paul's strong conviction that the exalted Christ was actively involved in his apostolic mission. The successes of that mission Paul described as 'what Christ has wrought through me to win obedience from the Gentiles' (Rom. 15.18a). These successes were won 'by word and deed, by the power of signs and wonders, by the power of the Holy Spirit' (Rom. 15.18b-19), i.e., by the continuation through the ministry of Paul of those activities and that power so characteristic of the ministry of the historical Jesus. Further, Christ himself was believed to come preaching—it was his voice that was heard through the proclamation of the apostle or his colleagues (Eph. 2.17). Again, Paul thought of Christ as the one who was the author of 'living letters' written in the hearts of men and women. This he achieved through the 'scribal' ministry of the apostles to whom was entrusted the precious 'ink' of the Spirit (2 Cor. 3.1-3). It was also, Paul believed, none other than Christ himself who inspired him with the energy he needed to meet the demands of a preaching and teaching ministry aimed to present men and women mature in Christ (Col. 1.28-29). Finally, Christ is presented as the one who bestows upon all believers the ministerial gifts; gifts which are then 'personally packaged' as Christ's gifts to his Church. So in this way, as the 'gifted' believers function properly, the Church grows as a body drawing its power for growth from Christ the head (Eph. 4.7-16).

As has been noted previously, no matter into what special category we may wish to place the apostle Paul, he was, theologically speaking, a man of our era. Unlike the Twelve, for instance, his call, commissioning and empowering for ministry all fall within the post-Pentecost era of the Spirit and of the world-wide mission. There is, therefore, every reason to believe that the sort of involvement on the part of our Lord evident in the ministry of Paul can and ought to be found in our ministries today. Of course, our different situations will affect the way in which this involvement is manifested. Nevertheless, our ministries can and should be the continuation by the exalted Christ of the ministry he began as the historical Jesus. As we seek to promote the interests of Christ by intelligent participation in what we believe he is doing in the Church and in the world, our Christian service will be saved from the irrelevant and the mundane.

A Spiritual Dynamic

In our study we have encountered repeated references to the operation of a powerful spiritual dynamic in the ministries of both Jesus and Paul. Jesus believed that his exorcisms were accomplished by the Spirit of God (Matt. 12.28), and so deadly serious was he about the operation of the Spirit in his mission that he regarded wilful refusal to recognise this and ascription of that power to Beelzebul as an unforgivable sin (Matt. 12.31-32). Paul spoke of the power of the Spirit at work through his own preaching ministry (1 Thess. 1.5) and in the signs which accompanied it (Rom. 15.18-19; 2 Cor. 12.12). When he was criticised because of his unimpressive presence and when dogged by persecution, suffering and weakness he was led to see that the power of Christ rested upon him all the more at such times (2 Cor. 10.10; 11.23-30; 12.7-10). It may have been this realisation that led the apostle to bring together both a longing to know the power of Christ's resurrection and a longing to share the fellowship of his sufferings (Phil. 3.10).

However, this spiritual dynamic was not confined to the ministries of Jesus and Paul. The Pauline epistles reflect the fact that the early churches were charismatic communities. In them, the Spirit was active both in bestowing ministerial gifts upon each member (1 Cor. 12.4-11) and in performing mighty works among them (Gal. 3.5; 1 Thess. 5.19-20).

The early Christian communities as well as the apostle Paul

belong to the same era as we do today. There is, then, every reason to expect that the same spiritual dynamic will be experienced in our ministries and within our Christian communities today. We may look for the same life and attitude changing power of the Spirit at work in our Christian communities. Further, if there were mighty works and other manifestations of the Spirit accompanying the ministry of Paul and occurring in the early Christian fellowships, there is no reason to exclude the possibility of their occurrence from time to time among us today. We will need, of course, to be as careful to 'test the spirits' and to see that all things are done 'decently and in order' as the early Christians were urged to be.

The Gospel and Ministerial Authority

The apostle Paul spoke of himself as an ambassador of the gospel and he understood his ambassadorship to be integrally related to God's reconciling activity in Christ. On the one hand it was God who reconciled men to himself through the death of Christ, and on the other it was the apostle who, on behalf of Christ, urged men to be reconciled to God (2 Cor. 5.19-20). Paul clearly saw himself as a representative of Christ and this gave him a sense of authority (1 Cor. 5.3-5; 14.37; 1 Thess. 4.2-8; 2 Thess. 3.6). He did not lord it over his converts because his authority was not something which inhered in him personally, but was derived from the gospel entrusted to him by the exalted Christ. As he was faithful in the proclamation of that gospel a spiritual dynamic operated so that what he proclaimed in human words became the word of God working powerfully in the hearts of his hearers (1 Thess. 2.13). This meant that when men and women responded to Paul's ministry their new-found faith did not rest upon Paul's wisdom or authority, but upon the power of God they experienced through his preaching of the gospel (1 Cor. 2.1-5). However, the gospel basis of Paul's authority is seen not only in his proclamation of the *kerygma*, but in his ethical teaching as well. Paul consistently based his ethical instructions upon the implications of the gospel. This is clearly illustrated by 1 Corinthians. Here, dealing with problems of party-spirit, immorality, litigation, eating meat offered to idols and attending feasts in idol temples, Paul does not once appeal to any personal authority to settle the matters. Consistently he seeks to bring the implications of the gospel itself to bear upon the problems. Apostolic authority is derived from the gospel entrusted by Christ to his servants.

He who called Paul to be an ambassador of the gospel still calls men and women today to be ministers of that gospel. Like Paul, their authority is to be derived from the gospel. Its proclamation can still have that ring of authority because it is accompanied by the same spiritual dynamic. Though proclaimed in our faltering words it is still heard as the word of God. Similarly, in so far as our exhortations are seen to be the ethical outworkings of the gospel they will be received as authoritative too.

Our various ecclesiastical organizations seek to recognise the divine call which comes to some to be pastors, teachers and evangelists, and to set them apart with authority to function within their respective churches. However, this ecclesiastical authority must never be allowed to become a substitute for the true authority of the Christian minister which is derived from the gospel entrusted to him and the spiritual dynamic which accompanies its preaching and application.

The Priestly Ministry

We have seen how Paul lays priestly and sacrificial terminology under tribute to describe both his own apostolic ministry and the service of Christian people in general. Paul saw himself as a priest presiding over the offering (consisting) of the Gentiles and charged with the responsibility of ensuring its purity. The Gentiles by nature were 'unclean', but by preaching the gospel to unbelievers and teaching those who believed Paul became the agent by whom the Holy Spirit sanctified the Gentiles so that they became an offering holy and acceptable to God (Rom. 15.15-16). But it is not only the apostolate that can be described as a priestly ministry. Paul used priestly and sacrificial imagery to depict every Christian's service to God. All believers act as priests in so far as they are responsible to present themselves as living sacrifices to God. This offering they make as their response to the manifold mercies of God made known to them in the gospel (Rom. 12.1).

It is surely significant that Paul chose to apply priestly terminology, not to the ministry of the sacraments, but to the ministry of the gospel and to men's response to that. Today we too function as priests when we respond to the gospel by offering our lives as living sacrifices acceptable to God. And according to Romans 12.1-2 to become living sacrifices holy and acceptable to God involves the transformation of our lives so they are less and less conformed to the values of the world in its alienation from God, and more and more conformed to the values of the kingdom of God. We also act as priests today when through our ministry of the gospel other men's and women's lives are transformed so that they too become living sacrifices acceptable to God.

The Servant Role

We have seen that Jesus spoke of his disciples as his servants and also hinted that they were to be fellow-servants with him in whom the Deutero-Isaianic servant-prophecies would find a (partial) fulfilment. Jesus adopted a servant style in his own ministry and told his disciples to follow his example. And in following, they, like him, would be vulnerable to persecution and suffering. Paul spoke often of himself as a servant of Christ and taught his converts that the faithful carrying out of the various responsibilities of life was in fact true service to the Lord Christ (Col. 3.22-4; Eph. 6.5-8). He taught them that they were privileged, not only to believe in Christ, but also to suffer for his name's sake. This was their lot and destiny (Phil. 1.29; 1 Thess. 3.1-4).

As we seek to follow the servant pattern laid down by our Lord it is well to remember that Christ served God by serving men (Mark 10.45). Paul told the Corinthians that he was their servant for Jesus' sake (2 Cor. 4.5). There can be no true service of God without that finding expression in the service we render to men. However, it must be remembered that while both Jesus and Paul were among men as those who served, neither of them ever regarded those they served as their masters. Both held themselves accountable only to God. Paul wrote: 'But with me it is a very small thing that I should be judged by you or by any human court. I do not even judge myself. . . . It is the Lord who judges me' (1 Cor. 4.3-4). So the servant role will involve us in a willingness to render humble service to men, yet in doing that we need not come into the bondage of men-pleasing, for though we serve men we own no master but our Lord.

The teaching of both Jesus and Paul reminds us that there is a darker side to the service of Christ. There is always the possibility of suffering for his name's sake. Throughout the history of the Church this has been a recurring phenomenon, and one which parts of the Church of Christ are experiencing today. We should not be taken by surprise if some of us, like the apostle Paul, are called to 'complete what is lacking in Christ's afflictions for the sake of his body, that is, the church' (Col. 1.24). Our consolation is that in such circumstances the power of Christ will rest upon us.

Eschatological Accountability

If it is true that, as servants of Christ, we have no master but him, then it is equally true that it is to him that we are accountable. In some of his parables Jesus taught that men are accountable for the way in which they use the gifts and opportunities entrusted to them (cf., e.g., Matt. 24.45-51; Luke 19.12-27). In our study of Paul's epistles we have seen that the apostle anticipated a final evaluation of his ministry at the Last Day. It was for that reason he accounted all human evaluation as such a small thing (1 Cor. 4.3-4). But we have also seen that Paul not only held himself ready to give an account of his ministry; he also taught that every man's work comes under scrutiny at the Last Day (1 Cor. 3.10-15).

It is an awareness of this eschatological accountability that we need to recover again today. It is not enough to find self-satisfaction in our service, nor even to satisfy our peers. Each of us must give an account of himself to God. It is this realisation which will reinject into our Christian ministries that needed sense of seriousness. Further, such an awareness will mean there will be less looking to the past, to ecclesiastical recognition, and more looking to the future, to hear that final divine word of validation: 'Well done, good and faithful servant . . . enter into the joy of your master' (Matt. 25.21).

Summary

In conclusion it can be said that every Christian is called by Christ and privileged to share with him in what he is doing in the Church and in the world. For the exalted Christ is continuing what he began as the historical Jesus, and this he does by active involvement in the ministry of his servants today. For this sharing the Lord bestows upon his servants various gifts for ministry so that they may each play their part in his great plan. It is the recognition of this essential nature of ministry which gives purpose to our Christian service, and it is in light of this that we can set our specific personal and group goals.

Therefore, my beloved brethren, be steadfast, immovable, always abounding in the work of the Lord, knowing that in the Lord your labour is not in vain.

(1 Cor. 15.58)

NOTES

CHAPTER ONE

1. Cf., e.g., the results of studies reported in H. R. Niebuhr, *The Purpose of the Church and its Ministry* (Harper & Row, New York, 1956); R. S. Paul, *Ministry* (Eerdmans, Grand Rapids, 1965); S. Hiltner, *Ferment in the Ministry* (Abingdon, Nashville, 1969); *Ordained Ministry Today—A Discussion of its Nature and Role: The Report of a Working Party of the Ministry Committee of the Advisory Council for the Church's Ministry* (Church Information Office, Westminster, U.K., 1969); C. R. Feilding, *Education for Ministry* (American Association of Theological Schools, Dayton, Ohio, 1966); N. W. H. Blaikie, *The Plight of the Australian Clergy* (University of Queensland, St Lucia, 1979).

2. For proponents of this view see, e.g., C. Gore, *The Church and the Ministry* (Longmans, Green & Co., London, 1919); K. E. Kirk, ed., *The Apostolic Ministry* (Hodder & Stoughton, London, 1946); E. L. Mascall, *Corpus Christi: Essays on the Church and the Eucharist* (Longmans, London, 1953); A. G. Hebert, *Apostle and Bishop: A Study of the Gospel, the Ministry and the Church-Community* (Faber & Faber, London, 1963). Critics of the view include A. C. Headlam, *The Doctrine of the Church and Christian Reunion* (John Murray, London, 1921); G. W. H. Lampe, *Some Aspects of the New Testament Ministry* (Hodder & Stoughton, London, 1948); J. K. S. Reid, *The Biblical Doctrine of the Ministry* (*SJT* Occasional Paper 4, 1955); A. Ehrhardt, *The Apostolic Ministry* (*SJT* Occasional Paper 7, 1958); J. A. T. Robinson, 'Kingdom, Church and Ministry', *The Historic Episcopate*, ed., K. M. Carey (Dacre, London, 1954), pp. 11-12.

3. Cf., e.g., J. A. T. Robinson, *The Body: A Study in Pauline Theology* (SBT 5; SCM, London, 1952) who puts forward a 'realistic' interpretation of the image of the body, and E. Best, *One Body in Christ: A Study in the Relationship of the Church to Christ in the Epistles of the Apostle Paul* (SPCK, London, 1955) who argues that it should be regarded as a metaphorical expression only.

4. F. D. Brunner, *A Theology of the Holy Spirit: The Pentecostal Experience and the New Testament Witness* (Eerdmans, Grand Rapids, 1970) provides a sympathetic account of the origins and experiences of the neo-pentecostals, together with his own assessment of the movement in the light of the New Testament witness.

CHAPTER TWO

1. J. Jeremias, *New Testament Theology 1: The Proclamation of Jesus* (SCM, London, 1971), p. 37.

2. For some recent discussions of the criteria and their limitations, see M. D. Hooker, 'On Using the Wrong Tool', *Theology* 75 (1972), pp. 570-81; D. G. A. Calvert, 'An Examination of the Criteria for Distinguishing the Authentic Words of Jesus', *NTS* 18 (1971-2), pp. 209-19; D. R. Catchpole, 'Tradition History', *New Testament Interpretation*, ed., I. H. Marshall (Paternoster, Exeter, 1977), pp. 172-8.

CHAPTER THREE

1. Luke 11.49: 'Therefore also the Wisdom of God said, "I will send them prophets and apostles (*apostolous*), some of whom they will kill and persecute"'. It is difficult to know how to treat the introductory formula, 'the Wisdom of God said'. Is it equivalent to 'God in his wisdom said' (so J. M. Creed, *The Gospel according to St Luke* [Macmillan, London, 1960], p. 167), does it refer to a lost writing (so R. Bultmann, *The History of the Synoptic Tradition* [Harper & Row, New York, 1976], p. 114), or is it best understood as an oracle from the exalted Jesus (so E. E. Ellis, *The Gospel of Luke* [NCB; Oliphants, London, 1974], pp. 171-4)? If the text does preserve a saying of the historical Jesus, we need to remember that the original saying would have been most likely in Aramaic and that *apostolous* stands in the text only as a translation equivalent.

2. So V. Taylor, *The Gospel according to St Mark* (Macmillan, London, 1952), p. 184.

3. So, e.g., H. Conzelmann, *The Theology of Luke* (Faber, London, 1960), p. 41.

4. Bultmann, *Synoptic Tradition*, p. 38.

5. Ibid., p. 155. Cf. F. Hahn, *Mission in the New Testament*, (SBT 47, SCM, London, 1965), pp. 54-9.

6. Cf. J. Jeremias, *Jesus' Promise to the Nations* (SCM, London, 1967), p. 27; P. Bonnard, *L'Évangile selon Saint Matthieu* (Delachaux & Niestlé, Neuchâtel, 1970), p. 232.

7. Jeremias, *Jesus' Promise*, p. 26, n. 2.

8. Bultmann, *Synoptic Tradition*, pp. 155-6.

9. Jeremias, *Jesus' Promise*, p. 27.

10. 'The Parable of the Wicked Husbandmen: A Test of Synoptic Relationships', *NTS* 21 (1974-5), pp. 446-51.

11. Ibid., p. 451.

12. The following scholars are listed by Taylor, *St Mark*, p. 472, as supporters of the view that the parable/allegory is a construction of the early Church: Bultmann, Klostermann, Branscombe, Loisy, and Montefiore. M. Black, 'The Parables as Allegory', *BJRL* 42 (1959), pp. 273-87, defends the allegorical elements in some of Jesus' parables: 'The Jülicher canon is a much too pedantic and mechanical rule of thumb to apply to the living oracles and the living words of Jesus . . .' (p. 283).

13. E. Lohmeyer, *Das Evangelium des Markus* (Vandenhoeck & Ruprecht, Göttingen, 1951), p. 249.

14. C. H. Dodd, *The Parables of the Kingdom* (Nisbet, London, 1935), p. 130.

15. So J. Jeremias, *The Parables of Jesus* (Scribner, New York, 1963), p. 72.

Cf. C. D. Crossan, 'The Parable of the Wicked Husbandmen', *JBL* 90 (1971), pp. 461-2, where it is maintained that the application of the criterion of dissimilarity shows that both 'in function and form' the story is distinctively Jesus-tradition.

16. *The Parables of the Triple Tradition* (Fortress, Philadelphia, 1975), p. 187.

17. C. F. D. Moule, *The Gospel according to Mark* (Cambridge University, Cambridge, 1965), p. 93.

18. So Creed, *St Luke*, p. 66.

19. For the discussion of these passages, see J. D. G. Dunn, *Jesus and the Spirit* (Westminster, Philadelphia, 1975), pp. 53-62. Cf. treatment of Luke 4.16-30 in G. R. Beasley-Murray, 'Jesus and the Spirit', *Mélanges Bibliques en hommage au R. P. Bedá Rigaux*, eds., A. Descamps, A. Halleux (Duculot, Gembloux, 1970), p. 473.

20. Bultmann, *Synoptic Tradition*, pp. 142-3.

21. E. Schweizer, *The Good News according to Matthew* (John Knox, Atlanta, 1975), p. 253; W. Grundmann, *Das Evangelium nach Lukas* (Evangelische Verlagsanstalt, Berlin, 1961), p. 211.

22. *Jesus et l'Enfant. 'Enfants', 'Petits' et 'Simples' dans la Tradition synoptique* (Gabalda, Paris, 1969). Cf. 'L'enfant dans l'évangile', *VSpir* 122 (1970), pp. 407-21.

23. Cf. H. Anderson, *The Gospel of Mark* (NCB; Oliphants, London, 1976), pp. 234-5; Bonnard, *Saint Matthieu*, p. 268; R. Leaney, 'Jesus and the Symbol of the Child (Luke 9:46-48)', *ExpTim* 66 (1954), pp. 91-2.

24. Cf. H. Schürmann, *Das Lukasevangelium*, Erster Teil (Herder, Freiburg, 1969), p. 576; Bultmann, *Synoptic Tradition*, pp. 142-3.

25. F. Schleiermacher, *Ueber die Schriften des Lukas: ein kritischer Versuch*, Erster Theil (Reimer, Berlin, 1817), p. 88; W. Seufert, *Der Ursprung und die Bedeutung des Apostolats in der christilichen Kirche der ersten Zwei Jahrhunderte* (1887), cited H. Mosbech, 'Apostolos in the New Testament', *ST* 2 (1949), p. 178; Bultmann, *Synoptic Tradition*, pp. 343-6. See also E. M. Kredel, 'Der Apostelbegriff in der neueren Exegese', *ZKT* 78 (1956), pp. 169-93; 257-305, and the summaries in E. Hennecke–W. Schneemelcher, eds., *New Testament Apocrypha* 2 (Westminster, Philadelphia, 1965), pp. 25-31.

26. Cf. C. K. Barrett, *A Commentary on the First Epistle to the Corinthians* (Harper & Row, New York, 1968), p. 341; G. Schille, *Die urchristliche Kollegialmission* (Zwingli, Zürich, 1967), pp. 147-9; Jeremias, *New Testament Theology* 1, pp. 233-4; J. Roloff, *Apostolat—Verkündigung—Kirche* (Gütersloh, Gerd Mohn, 1965), pp. 158-61; K. H. Rengstorf, 'δώδεκα', *TDNT* 2 (1964), pp. 325-8; B. Rigaux, 'Die "Zwölf" in Geschichte und Kerygma', *Der historische Jesus und der kerygmatische Christus*, eds., H. Ristow, K. Matthiae (Evangelische Verlagsanstalt, Berlin, 1961), pp. 468-84; Anderson, *Mark*, pp. 136-7.

27. 'Jesu Schwertwort, Lukas xxii.35-38: Überlieferungsgeschichtliche Studie', *NTS* 20 (1973-4), pp. 190-203.

28. Cf., e.g., Bonnard, *Saint Matthieu*, p. 158; E. Klostermann, *Das Matthäusevangelium* (Mohr, Tübingen, 1971), p. 93; Schweizer, *Matthew*, p. 252.

29. *New Testament Theology* 1, pp. 238-9.

196

30. Cf. Tanch תולדות (32b), cited Str-B 1, p. 574, where Israel is likened to sheep and gentile nations to wolves.

31. *Synoptic Tradition*, p. 158.

32. 'The Name and Office of an Apostle', *St Paul's Epistle to the Galatians* (Macmillan, London, 1921), pp. 93-4.

33. *The Expansion of Christianity in the First Three Centuries* (Williams & Norgate, London, 1904), p. 412.

34. 'ἀπόστολς', *TDNT* 1 (1964), pp. 398-447, espc. pp. 413-20.

35. 'The Ministry in the Early Church', *The Apostolic Ministry*, ed., K. E. Kirk (Hodder & Stoughton, London, 1946), pp. 183-303.

36. Cf., e.g., W. Schmithals, *The Office of Apostle in the Early Church* (Abingdon, Nashville, 1969).

37. Cited from I. Epstein, ed., *The Babylonian Talmud* 3/6 (Soncino, London, 1936), p. 40. The dating is that of C. G. Montefiore and H. Loewe, *A Rabbinic Anthology* (Schocken, New York, 1974), p. 706, cf. p. 697.

38. 'The Development of the Apostolate in Judaism and its Transformation in Christianity', *HUCA* 2 (1925), pp. 100-101, 106.

39. 'ἀπόστολς', p. 414.

40. Cf. J. A. Kirk, 'Apostleship since Rengstorf: Towards a Synthesis', *NTS* 21 (1974-5), p. 260.

CHAPTER FOUR

1. *The Suffering Servant in Deutero-Isaiah* (Oxford University, Oxford, 1948), p. 218. Cf. V. Taylor, *Jesus and His Sacrifice* (Macmillan, London, 1948); H. W. Wolff, *Jesaja 53 im Urchristentum* (Evangelische Verlagsanstalt, Berlin, n.d., Vorwort, 1949); W. Manson, *The Servant Messiah* (Cambridge University, Cambridge, 1953); R. H. Fuller, *The Mission and Achievement of Jesus: An examination of the Presuppositions of New Testament Theology* (SCM, London, 1954); J. L. Price, 'The Servant Motif in the Synoptic Gospels', *Int* 12 (1958), pp. 28-38; R. T. France, 'The Servant of the Lord in the Teaching of Jesus', *Tyndale Bulletin* 19 (1968), pp. 26-52.

2. Cf. C. F. D. Moule, 'From Defendent to Judge—and Deliverer: An Enquiry into the Use and Limitations of the Theme of Vindication in the New Testament', *Bulletin of the Studiorum Novi Testamenti Societas* 3 (1952), pp. 40-53; M. D. Hooker, *Jesus and the Servant* (SPCK, London, 1959); C. K. Barrett, 'The Background of Mark 10:45', *New Testament Essays: Studies in Memory of T. W. Manson*, ed., A. J. B. Higgins (Manchester University, Manchester, 1959), pp. 1-18. H. E. Tödt, *The Son of Man in the Synoptic Tradition* Westminster, Philadelphia, 1965).

3. R. Bultmann, *Theology of the New Testament* 1 (SCM, London, 1952), p. 31.

4. F. J. Foakes-Jackson and K. Lake, eds., *The Beginning of Christianity* 1 (Macmillan, London, 1920), pp. 383-4.

5. O. Cullmann, *The Christology of the New Testament* (Westminster, Philadelphia, 1959), p. 65.

6. C. K. Barrett, *Jesus and the Gospel Tradition* (SPCK, London, 1967), p. 40.

7. Bultmann, *Synoptic Tradition*, p. 124

8. Ibid., p. 125 and n. 1.

9. *New Testament Theology* 1, p. 280.

10. Ibid., p. 295.

11. For a summary of the textual evidence, see B. M. Metzger, *A Textual Commentary on the Greek New Testament* (United Bible Societies, London, 1971), pp. 173-7.

12. *Jesus and the Servant*, pp. 81-2. For a fuller discussion of *pollōn*, see treatment of Mark 10.45 below.

13. *New Testament Theology* 1, p. 293. A. J. B. Higgins, *Jesus and the Son of Man* (Lutterworth, London, 1964), pp. 38-9, argues that if there is dependence between Mark 10.45 and Luke 22.27 it is the latter that is secondary: 'If Mark 10.45 were based on Luke 22.27 it would be a sheer archaizing fabrication of a saying about the Son of Man out of an I-word from the *Greek*-speaking church' (p. 38). The semitic flavour of Mark 10.45 is further illustrated by a comparison with 1 Tim. 2.5-6:

Mark 10.45   *ho huios tou anthrōpou   elthen . . . dounai*

1 Tim. 2.5, 6   *anthrōpos Christos Iēsous ho dous   tēn psuchēn autou lutron   anti pollōn heauton   antilutron huper pollōn*

Each word and phrase of 1 Tim. 2.5, 6 is a more hellenised form of the equivalent word or phrase in Mark 10.45. This supports the view that Mark 10.45 circulated independently; it was not assimilated to the Greek world as was 1 Tim. 2.5, 6 and as was Luke 22.24-7 to a lesser extent. So Jeremias, *New Testament Theology* 1, pp. 293-4. Cf. Higgins, *Jesus and the Son of Man*, p. 44; W. J. Moulder, 'The Old Testament Background and Interpretation of Mark x.45', *NTS* 24 (1977), p. 120.

14. H. Rashdall, *The Idea of the Atonement in Christian Theology* (Macmillan, London, 1919), p. 51; Bultmann, *Synoptic Tradition*, p. 144; Tödt, *The Son of Man*, pp. 206-7; R. H. Fuller, *The Foundations of New Testament Christology* (Lutterworth, London, 1965), p. 118.

15. Cf. J. Jeremias, 'παις θεου', *TDNT* 5 (1967), p. 212; Taylor, *Jesus and His Sacrifice*, pp. 101-2; C. E. B. Cranfield, *The Gospel according to Saint Mark* (Cambridge University, Cambridge, 1966), p. 342; Fuller, *Mission and Achievement*, pp. 57-8; Price, 'Servant Motif', p. 36.

16. Hooker, *Jesus and the Servant*, pp. 74-7; Barrett, 'Background of Mark 10:45', pp. 2-7. Cf. F. Buchsel, 'διδωμι', *TDNT* 2 (1964), p. 166; Moule, 'From Defendent to Judge', pp. 45-6.

17. Cf. Moulder, 'Mark x.45', p. 121; France, 'The Servant of the Lord', p. 34; E. Lohse, *Märtyrer und Gottesknecht* (Vandenhoeck & Ruprecht, Göttingen, 1955), pp. 120-21.

18. Cf. C. Westermann, *Isaiah 40-66: A Commentary* (SCM, London, 1969), p. 263. It is noted that substitution in various forms had obtained both in Israel and among her neighbours. The new element in Isaiah 53 is that the suffering which atoned was that endured by an ordinary and insignificant individual. Westermann adds, 'the healing gained for others (v.5) by his stripes includes as well the forgiveness of their sins and the removal of their punishment, that is to say, the suffering. Luther's rendering once more

expresses this well—"the punishment lies on him, in order that we might have peace (*šālōm*)"'.

19. Berakh 58b Bar. This and other examples from the rabbinic literature are cited in Str-B 1, pp. 577-8.

20. G. Bornkamm, *Jesus of Nazareth* (Harper & Row, New York, 1975), pp. 144-5.

21. *Matthew*, p. 244.

22. *Synoptic Tradition*, p. 76, cf. p. 69.

23. See examples cited in Str-B 1, pp. 917-18. The Qumran literature shows that status was also very important to members of the sect of the Scrolls (1QS 2.19-23; 6.8-9; CD 14.3-8).

24. In this connection it is worthy of note that Paul and Barnabas apply the servant-prophecies to their ministry in this way in the Acts of the Apostles (13.47. Cf. Isa. 49.6). It is interesting to see also that Paul could say in Col. 1.24: 'Now I rejoice in my sufferings for your sake, and in my flesh I complete what is lacking in Christ's afflictions for the sake of his body, that is the church'. This we take to mean those sufferings which Paul endured while proclaiming the gospel among the Gentiles—which ministry is a part of that committed to the servant of the Lord (Isa. 49.6). See discussion of Col. 1.24 in ch. 13 below.

25. Cf. Jesus' enigmatic words to the sons of Zebedee: 'The cup that I drink you will drink, and with the baptism with which I am baptised you will be baptised' (Mark 10.39). If these words are not simply a statement that, like Jesus, these two disciples would end their lives in martyrdom, they could be taken as a reflection of a belief on Jesus' part that his disciples would also share the sufferings spoken of in the servant-prophecies of Deutero-Isaiah.

CHAPTER FIVE

1. Cf. E. Schweizer, *Church Order in the New Testament* (SCM, London, 1961), p. 23 (2b): 'Of the Holy Spirit, Baptism and Church Assemblies Jesus never spoke', and 'πνεῦμα', *TDNT* 6 (1968), p. 402: 'There are surprisingly few statements about the Spirit in Mt. and Mk. With certainty only one of these (Mk. 13:11 and par.) may be traced back in substance to Jesus Himself.' Cf. C. K. Barrett, *The Holy Spirit and the Gospel Tradition* (SPCK, London, 1966), p. 2, where it is asserted that the few references to the Spirit made by Jesus in the synoptic gospels are of doubtful authenticity.

2. P. 158, cf. p. 120.

3. Cf., e.g., the emphatic statements to this effect made by H. van Campenhausen, *Ecclesiastical Authority and Spiritual Power in the Church of the First Three Centuries* (A. & C. Black, London, 1969), p. 6; E. Käsemann, *Essays on New Testament Themes* (SCM, London, 1964), p. 39; Dunn, *Jesus and the Spirit*, p. 39; Beasley-Murray, 'Jesus and the Spirit', p. 468.

4. Bultmann says the saying can 'claim the highest degree of authenticity which we can make for any saying of Jesus: it is full of that feeling of eschatological power which must have characterised the activity of Jesus' (*Synoptic Tradition*, p. 162). Cf. Klostermann, *Matthäus-evangelium*, pp. 108-9;

Käsemann, *Essays*, p. 39; N. Perrin, *Rediscovering the Teaching of Jesus* (SCM, London, 1967) pp. 64-5; J. M. Robinson, *A New Quest for the Historical Jesus* (SCM, London, 1959), p. 121.

5. Klostermann, *Matthäusevangelium*, p. 109. A. Schlatter, *Das Evangelium Lukas* (Calwer, Stuttgart, 1960), p. 511, also sees Luke's 'by the finger of God' as an allusion to Exod. 8.19 ('This is the Finger of God') and seems to imply that the expression in Luke is the result of the evangelist's reflection upon the passage in Exodus.

6. 'Jesus and the Spirit', p. 469, n. 1.

7. *Jesus and the Spirit*, pp. 45-6.

8. C. S. Rodd, 'Spirit or Finger', *ExpTim* 72 (1961), pp. 157-8.

9. H. Windisch, *War Jesus Pneumatiker?* p. 229, cited by Barrett, *Holy Spirit*, p. 63. In this connection it is interesting to note W. C. van Unnik's comment: 'It is striking that in John 8:48ff. and 10:20f. Jesus is also accused of having a demon. There was something peculiar about him. His opponents see here a demonic power; his followers the Spirit of God and that was Jesus' own idea' ('Jesus the Christ', *NTS* 8 [1961-2], p. 116).

10. 'Jesus and the Spirit', p. 469.

11. The meaning of *ephthasen* (*RSV* 'has come') is debated—whether it denotes action in the recent past or imminent future. But Barrett is surely right when he says: 'They may be signs that the Kingdom has come, or proleptic manifestations of it; or, perhaps, not exactly either of these things; but certainly it is meant that the exorcisms are taking place in virtue of the divine Kingdom' (*Holy Spirit*, p. 62).

12. So C. H. Dodd, *According to the Scriptures* (Nisbet, London, 1952), p. 110.

13. It has been argued that the saying about the unforgivable sin arose at a time when the Palestinian church was suffering persecution and abuse because of some more overt manifestations of the Spirit, possibly prophetic utterances or healings/exorcisms. Dunn argues persuasively against this view: (1) If 'Son of Man' had become a popular title for Jesus in the early Palestinian community, it is unlikely that it would be used on the 'wrong' side of such an antithesis. (2) The early Christian prophets (whose utterances in the Spirit were supposedly being despised) would not want to place their inspiration on a higher level than that of the Son of Man, albeit the earthly Son of Man. (3) The primitive community was used to 'testing' the word of its prophets, and it is unlikely that such a saying, if uttered by one of its prophets, would have been accepted by the community and become a prized part of the Jesus-tradition. For a full discussion and documentation, see Dunn, *Jesus and the Spirit*, p. 53.

14. Ibid.

15. So, e.g., Barrett, *Holy Spirit*, pp. 130-31; Jeremias, *New Testament Theology* 1, p. 79; Dunn, *Jesus and the Spirit*, p. 86; Schweizer, 'πνεῦμα', p. 402. But cf. Bultmann, *Synoptic Tradition*, p. 122, where the words of Mark 13.11 are classified as '*vaticania* from the Church's mission and persecution'. Cf. also W. Marxsen, *Mark the Evangelist* (Abingdon, Nashville, 1969), p. 175, where the latter part of Mark 13.11 is regarded as an interpretative addition, possibly by Mark, possibly already in Mark's source. The distinct possibility

that Mark's *en ekeinē tē hōra* and Luke's *en autē tē hōra* are different renditions of a common Aramaic original (so Taylor, *St Mark*, p. 508, cf. M. Black, *An Aramaic Approach to the Gospels and Acts* [Oxford University, Oxford, 1946], pp. 78-81) suggests at least a Palestinian life-setting for the saying.

16. *Holy Spirit*, pp. 131-2.

17. *St Mark*, p. 508.

18. E. Schweizer, *The Good News according to Mark* (John Knox, Richmond, 1970), p. 271.

19. That for Luke Jesus' ministry/death could be thought of as effecting a second exodus—a counterpart of the exodus of Israel from Egypt—is suggested by his account of the transfiguration. Luke reports that the matter spoken of by *Moses*, Elijah and *Jesus* was his 'departure (*exodon*), which he (Jesus) was to accomplish at Jerusalem' (9.21). This report is found only in Luke and the word *exodos* is used only here in the gospels.

20. Str-B 1, p. 459, cites such a comparison made by R. Tanchuma (c.AD 380) which is, of course, well beyond New Testament times. However, even in the Old Testament such comparisons are drawn (cf., e.g., Isa. 49.15).

21. See Str-B 3, pp. 282-3 for the rabbinic applications of Isa. 52.7 to the messianic age.

22. See Schweizer, 'πνεῦμα', p. 384 for documentation of the existence of this belief in first century Judaism.

23. Barrett, as we have noted, suggests this is because Jesus himself wanted to keep his messiahship veiled; too open a claim to be the bearer of the Spirit would militate against this. Schweizer, on the other hand, says it may have been because Jesus regarded himself only as messiah *designatus*, or because his disciples could not understand teaching about the Spirit until after Jesus' work was completed, or even because Jesus did not expect an out-pouring of the Spirit ('πνεῦμα', p. 403). If the fewness of Jesus' Spirit-sayings was matched by a reticence on the part of the evangelists to associate the Spirit with his ministry, we could say they were seeking to ensure that Jesus was not reduced to the stature of the first in a long line of pneumatic men. However, this is not the case, and in the final analysis we must admit that we just do not know why the Synoptics preserve so few Spirit-sayings of Jesus.

24. It is true, of course, that Jesus did command the Twelve to exorcise the demon-possessed (something which he himself did 'by the Spirit of God'), but the indications are that the Twelve's authority to exorcise was dependent upon the authority attaching to the name of Jesus rather than derived from their own relationship to the Spirit at that time (Luke 10.17; Mark 9.38/Luke 9.49).

CHAPTER SIX

1. Paul also associates his commissioning with the appearance/revelation of the risen Christ to him; that on the Damascus road (Gal. 1.15-17, cf. Acts 26.12-18).

2. *Holy Spirit*, p. 132.

3. The Matthean commission saying presents us with many problems. It alone contains the command to baptise in the triune name, yet the practice of the early Church was to baptise in the name of Jesus. It contains an explicit command that the Twelve (less Judas) make disciples of the nations, yet Acts portrays a Jewish Church reluctant to do so. Cf. discussion in C. F. Evans, *Resurrection and the New Testament* (SCM, London, 1970), p. 88. Further, Eusebius habitually quotes this commission saying in another form: 'Go ye into all the world and make disciples of all the Gentiles in my name.' The Eusebian saying lacks both the command to baptise and the trinitarian reference. This has led some scholars to regard the present form of Matt. 28.19-20 as a later rendition of the Eusebian text (see discussion in Foakes-Jackson and Lake, *Beginnings* 1, pp. 335-7; Barrett, *Holy Spirit*, pp. 102-3), but this is doubtful. If Matthew originally had the shorter version we would expect some trace of it at least to survive in the MSS or versions, but such a trace is completely lacking. Various attempts have been made to overcome the difficulties presented by Matt. 28.18-20. However, because of the limited scope of our enquiry at this point, it is not necessary to go any further into this discussion.

4. The evidence for this almost universal opinion is summarised by Metzger, *Textual Commentary*, pp. 122-6. This view has been questioned in recent times by W. R. Farmer, *The Last Twelve Verses of Mark* (Cambridge University, Cambridge, 1974). In his concluding statement Farmer claims no final result, but says the question should be still considered open (p. 109).

5. In Matthew the risen Jesus appears to the Eleven in Galilee, and the fourth gospel, too, reports an appearance in Galilee, by the Sea of Tiberias, but Luke reports appearances in and around Jerusalem only. The appearances in Jerusalem, then Galilee, and then Jerusalem again do not necessarily mean that the tradition is confused at this point. As C. F. D. Moule has suggested, the post-resurrection appearances could well have been so widely dispersed geographically because of the disciples' own locations at the various times. Their locations, in turn, could have been dictated by the pilgrim festivals; they were originally in Jerusalem for the Passover, returned afterwards to their homes in Galilee, only to journey once more to Jerusalem for the feast of Pentecost ('The Post-Resurrection Appearances in the Light of Festival Pilgrimages', *NTS* 4 [1957-8], pp. 58-61).

6. A. Richardson, *An Introduction to the Theology of the New Testament* (SCM, London, 1958), p. 118, says 'Luke's itemizing of the original threefold unity of resurrection, ascension and out-pouring of the Spirit is based upon current rabbinic patterns.' Rabbinic Judaism regarded the feast of Pentecost as a commemoration of the giving of the Law at Sinai which was supposed to have taken place fifty days after the exodus from Egypt. So, it is said, Luke, in keeping with his theological viewpoint, has separated the resurrection (the new exodus) and Pentecost (the writing of the Law upon men's hearts) by a similar period of fifty days. This historicised theology was never meant to be taken as history. I. H. Marshall, *Luke: Historian and Theologian* (Paternoster, Exeter, 1970), pp. 51-2, disagrees with this approach to Luke's writings. He maintains that they are historical (but not, of course, in the sense that modern critical method is used). If Luke's own declared intention is accepted, we

must allow for a more historical than historicising approach (Luke 1.1-4). In similar vein, Creed, writing about the passage Luke 23.50-24.53, says: 'the τάξις has been imposed by the historian upon his materials, and the links are the least original part of the story', but, he adds, 'he would not have understood the scruples or methods of a modern critic . . . it was his task to give literary form and consistency to the traditions of the life and work of Jesus Christ and to set them in broad historical perspective' (*St Luke*, pp. 289, 291).

7. J. D. G. Dunn, *Baptism in the Holy Spirit* (SCM, London, 1970), pp. 42-3.

CHAPTER SEVEN

1. As a sample of the more important works, the following can be listed: Lightfoot, 'The Name and Office of an Apostle'; O. Cullmann, 'Le caractère eschatologique du devoir missionaire et de la conscience apostolique de S. Paul: Étude sur le κατέχον (-ων) de 2 Thess. 2:6-7', *RHPR* 16 (1936), pp. 210-45; A. Fridrichsen, *The Apostle and His Message* (Almqvist & Wiksells, Uppsala, 1947); H. von Campenhausen, 'Der urchristliche Apostelbegriff', *ST* 1 (1947), pp. 96-130; Mosbech, 'Apostolos in the New Testament'; J. Munck, 'Paul, the Apostles and the Twelve', *ST* 3 (1950), pp. 96-110; E. Lohse, 'Ursprung und Prägung des christlichen Apostolates', *TZ* 9 (1953), pp. 259-75; L. Cerfaux, 'Pour l'histoire de titre Apostolos dans le Nouveau Testament', *RSR* 48 (1960), pp. 78-92; Rengstorf, 'απόστολος'; G. Klien, *Die Zwölf Apostel: Ursprung und Gehalt einer Idee* (Vandenhoeck & Ruprecht, Göttingen, 1961); Roloff, *Apostolat*; T. Holtz, 'Zum Selbstverständnis des Apostels Paulus', *TLZ* 91 (1966), pp. 321-30; Schille, *Kollegialmission*; Schmithals, *Office of Apostle*; K. Kertelge, 'Das Apostelamt des Paulus, sein Ursprung und seine Bedeutung', *BZ* 14 (1970), pp. 161-81; R. Schnackenburg, 'Apostel vor und neben Paulus', *Schriften zum Neuen Testament* (Kösel, München, 1971), pp. 338-58; Kirk, 'Apostleship since Rengstorf'; J. H. Schütz, *Paul and the Anatomy of Apostolic Authority* (Cambridge University, Cambridge, 1975).

2. Any chronological arrangement of Paul's letters can only be tentative, because it depends upon prior decisions concerning the destination, occasion and dating of the various epistles. The arrangement adopted is that found in W. G. Kümmel, *Introduction to the New Testament*, revd. (Abingdon, Nashville, 1975), except that Galatians is placed at the head of the list. For a defence of the feasibility, at least, of this early date for Galatians, see F. F. Bruce, 'Galatian Problems 4: The Date of the Epistle', *BJRL* 54 (1971), pp. 250-67.

CHAPTER EIGHT

1. *Galatians*, p. 29.

2. J. B. Tyson, 'Paul's Opponents in Galatia', *NovT* 10 (1968), pp. 241-54.

3. J. Munck, *Paul and the Salvation of Mankind* (SCM, London, 1959), pp. 87-134.

4. R. Jewett, 'The Agitators and the Galatian Congregation', *NTS* 17 (1970), pp. 198-212. Jewett says that the Galatians received the advice of these Jewish Christians from Judea, not out of any respect for the Law, but because they saw in it a means of mystical connection with the 'seed of Abraham'.

5. W. Schmithals, *Paul and the Gnostics* (Abingdon, Nashville, 1972), pp. 13-64. Cf. W. Nikolaus, 'Einführung in den Galaterbrief des Paulus', *Die Zeichen der Zeit* 27 (1973), pp. 201-7. For a negative response to Schmithals' view, see R.McL. Wilson, 'Gnostics—in Galatia?' *SE* 4.2 (1968), pp. 358-67. Cf. also F. Pereira, 'The Galatian Controversy in the Light of the Targums', *Indian Journal of Theology* 20 (1971), pp. 13-29, where it is said that a study of parallels in the Targums shows that Paul is at acking contemporary Jewish attitudes when he insists on justification by faith.

6. For a recent discussion of the autobiographical data in Galatians, see F. F. Bruce, 'Galatian Problems 1: Autobiographical Data', *BJRL* 51 (1968), pp. 292-309.

7. It is possible that the Galatians' attitude to the rite of circumcision was in the end quite different from that of the Judaizers who introduced it to them. As already noted, it has been suggested that they saw in circumcision a rite which could link them with the 'mythical seed of Abraham', and thereby enabling them to gain membership in a new race. If this was the case, did it lead to false conclusions about liberty for members of the new race, conclusions which led to the libertinism which Paul had to combat (cf. 5.13-6.5) as well as the legalism? Cf. discussion in R. P. Martin, *New Testament Foundations: A Guide for Christian Students* 2 (Eerdmans, Grand Rapids, 1978), pp. 152-6.

8. Cf. Bruce, 'Galatian Problems 4: The Date of the Epistle', cited above, in which the feasibility of this early date for Galatians is argued.

9. R. Bring, *Commentary on Galatians* (Muhlenberg, Philadelphia, 1961), p. 44.

10. Adv. Marc. i.20, v.3 and esp. iv.2, cited by Lightfoot (*Galatians*, p. 103). H. Schlier, *Die Brief an die Galater* (Vandenhoeck & Ruprecht, Göttingen, 1965), pp. 68-9, supports Tertullian's view.

11. So, e.g., Lightfoot, *Galatians*, pp. 103-4; E. Burton, *A Critical and Exegetical Commentary on the Epistle to the Galatians* (ICC, T. & T. Clarke, Edinburgh, 1921), pp. 72-5; P. Bonnard, *L'Épitre de Saint Paul aux Galates* (Delachaux & Niestlé, Neuchâtel, 1972), pp. 37-8; F. Mussner, *Der Galaterbrief* (Herder, Freiburg, 1974), pp. 104-5; Bring, *Galatians*, p. 63; Schütz, *Apostolic Authority*, pp. 139-40.

12. Mussner, *Galaterbrief*, p. 105.

13. An expression which should be interpreted to mean not that Paul had a special distinct gospel of his own which he preached to the Gentiles, and Peter had another for the Jews (so Fridrichsen, *The Apostle and his Message*, pp. 8-16), but rather that Paul had been entrusted with the one essential gospel for proclamation among the uncircumcised as Peter had for proclamation among the circumcised. Otherwise the basis of Paul's rebuke to Peter in Antioch (Gal. 2.11-21) loses its point—Peter would only have been acting according to *his* gospel, and could not be blamed for not being 'straightforward about the truth of *the* gospel' (2.14).

14. *Paulus und Jesus: Eine theologische Grundlegung* (Kösel, München, 1968), p. 227. Trans. mine.

15. *Galatians*, p. 225.

16. W. M. Ramsay, *A Historical Commentary on St Paul's Epistle to the Galatians* (reprint: Baker, Grand Rapids, 1965), p. 472. U. Borse, 'Die Wundmale und der Todesbescheid', *BZ* 14 (1970), pp. 88-111, suggests that Paul was referring to a definite experience, the wounds from which were still fresh. He identifies the experience with that reported in 2 Cor. 1.8-10.

17. See Josephus, *Jewish Wars* 1, 10.2. Cf. W. Klassen, 'Galatians 6.17', *ExpTim* 81 (1969-70), p. 378.

18. Bring, *Galatians*, p. 109.

CHAPTER NINE

1. Schmithals argues against the early dating of the Thessalonian letters on the ground that Paul is combatting gnostic-Christian opponents again (*Paul and the Gnostics*, pp. 202-12), but his case is not convincing. Cf., e.g., Kümmel's reply to Schmithals' argument (and other arguments) for a later date for the epistles (*Introduction*, pp. 258-60, 263-4).

2. This was the view of the Greek fathers.

3. So, e.g., F. C. Baur, *Paul the Apostle of Jesus Christ: His Life and Work, His Epistles and His Doctrine* vol. 2, ed., E. Zeller (Williams & Norgate, London, 1875), pp. 319-20.

4. So, as we have already seen, Schmithals, *Paul and the Gnostics*, pp. 202-12.

5. So W. Lütgert, 'Die Vollkommenen im Philipperbrief und die Enthusiasten in Thessalonich', BFCT 13/6 (1909), pp. 547-654, and more recently, R. Jewett, *Paul's Anthropological Terms: A Study of their Use in Conflict Settings* (Brill, Leiden, 1971), p. 17; 'Enthusiastic Radicalism and the Thessalonian Correspondence', SBL Proc 108/1 (1972), pp. 181-232.

6. So J. E. Frame, *A Critical and Exegetical Commentary on the Epistles of St Paul to the Thessalonians* (ICC, T. & T. Clarke, Edinburgh, 1912), p. 10.

7. So E. Dobschütz, *Kritisch-exegetischer Kommentar über das Neue Testament: Die Thessalonicher-Briefe* (Vandenhoeck & Ruprecht, Göttingen, 1910), pp. 106-7.

8. So C. Masson, *Les Deux Épîtres de Saint Paul aux Thessaloniciens* (Delachaux & Niestlé, Neuchâtel, 1957), p. 32.

9. *Saint Paul: Les Épîtres aux Thessaloniciens* (Gabalda, Paris, 1956), p. 158. Trans. mine.

10. Taking *hoti* as causal. It could be epexegetical, in which case 1, 1.5 would give, not the reason for Paul's knowledge of the Thessalonians' election, rather it would refer to 'the historical occasion and manner of their election'. So E. Best, *A Commentary on the First and Second Epistles to the Thessalonians* (A. & C. Black, London, 1972), p. 73, following Lightfoot.

11. A very different view is suggested by W. Grundmann, 'δύναμαι/ δύναμις', *TDNT* 2 (1964), p. 311, who takes *en dunamei* as a reference to miracles performed by Paul in Thessalonica. Certainly, comparison with Rom. 15.18-19 ('For I will not venture to speak of anything except what

Christ has wrought through me to win obedience from the Gentiles, by word and deed, by the power of signs and wonders, by the power of the Holy Spirit . . .') and 2 Cor. 12.12 ('The signs of a true apostle were performed among you in all patience with signs and wonders and mighty works') lends support to Grundmann's view. On the other hand, Rom. 1.16 ('For I am not ashamed of the gospel: it is the power of God for salvation . . .'), 1 Cor. 1.18 ('For the word of the cross . . . is the power of God'), and 1 Cor. 2.4 ('my speech and my message were not in plausible words of wisdom, but in demonstration of the Spirit and power . . .') show that Paul frequently used *dunamis* in connection with the power of the preached gospel. In the Thessalonian epistles where the reception of the apostolic message not as mere human word, but as the word of God is emphasised, it is better to take *en dunamei* as a reference to the sense of spiritual power attaching to the preached gospel so that it came to be accepted as the word of God. Cf. Masson, *Thessaloniciens*, p. 20, n. 3.

12. The copula 'is' has been supplied. It could be argued that the copula 'will be' would be more appropriate in the eschatological context. However, 'are' (*este*) is used in the following verse in the same context so the first alternative, 'is' is to be preferred. In any case, with the parousia regarded as an imminent event, either would be appropriate.

13. The terms 'joy' and 'crown' are used by Paul again in Phil. 4.1 to describe the Philippian believers, but without overt eschatological connotation. However, the two ideas are found together in 1QS 4.7 where there are eschatological overtones. The expression 'crown of boasting' appears to have been drawn from the Old Testament (cf. Prov. 16.31; Ezek. 16.12; 23.42) rather than from the hellenistic world. Cf. Best, *Thessalonians*, p. 128; Masson, *Thessaloniciens*, p. 37, n. 2.

14. The afflictions in verse three are taken to be those experienced by both Paul and his readers. It could conceivably mean only those endured by Paul and his colleagues—understanding the 'we' references in the narrower sense, but in the light of 1, 1.6; 2.14 and 2, 1.4-7 it is better to take them in the wider sense: Paul, his colleagues and his readers.

15. *mē* with the pres. imper. (*sbennute*) and not the aor. subj., indicates that this is a command to cease doing something already being done.

16. So, e.g., Best, *Thessalonians*, p. 238; Rigaux, *Thessaloniciens*, p. 591; Masson, *Thessaloniciens*, pp. 75-6; W. C. van Unnik, 'Den Geist löschet nicht aus (I Thessalonicher v. 19)', *NovT* 10 (1968), pp. 256-7. But cf. L. L. Morris, *The First and Second Epistles to the Thessalonians* (Eerdmans, Grand Rapids, 1959), p. 175, where it is pointed out that manifestations of the Spirit in the New Testament are both ethical and ecstatic, and that quenching the Spirit could be brought about by 'loafing, immorality, and other sins about which Paul has had occasion to warn his friends.' Against Morris' view, we may note van Unnik's statement that the Spirit in 1, 5.19 must be related to charismatic activity, for while it is conceivable that men may repress charismatics or kill prophets, they cannot silence the Spirit. He finds support for his view in parallels in Plutarch's writings where mention is made of the 'unquenchable spirit' and to 'quenching enthusiasm', and van Unnik says, Plutarch means the same thing by 'enthusiasm' as Paul does by 'Spirit' in 1, 5.19 ('Den Geist', pp. 256-7).

17. Prophets are mentioned alongside apostles in 1 Cor. 12.28 and Eph. 2.20; 3.5.

18. J. Jeremias, *Unknown Sayings of Jesus* (SPCK, London, 1964), pp. 80-83.

19. M. Dibelius, *An die Thessalonicher I.II* (Mohr, Tübingen, 1937), p. 25.

20. 1 Cor. 2.9 may be an exception. J. Héring, *The First Epistle of Saint Paul to the Corinthians* (Epworth, London, 1962), pp. 18-19, cites the statement of Origen that Paul was quoting from the Apocalypse of Elijah. There is no extant copy of this apocalypse, and attestation for Origen's statement is meagre, so there is only a remote possibility that 1 Cor. 2.9 represents a Pauline quotation from the Apocalypse of Elijah. In any case, it would not help us very much, for the quotation in 1 Cor. 2.9 is introduced with the unambiguous words *kathōs gegraptai*, clearly indicating a written source, whereas the words *en logō kuriou* in our passage are susceptible to various interpretations.

21. Rigaux, *Thessaloniciens*, p. 539.

22. E.g., Masson, *Thessaloniciens*, p. 63; H. Schlier, *Der Apostel und seine Gemeinde: Auslegung des Ersten Briefes an die Thessalonicher* (Herder, Freiburg, 1972), p. 78; B. Henneken, *Verkündigung und Prophetie im Ersten Thessalonicherbrief: Ein Beitrag zur Theologie des Wortes Gottes* (Kath. Bibelwerk, Stuttgart, 1969), p. 98; Best, *Thessalonians*, p. 193.

CHAPTER TEN

1. On the whole most modern commentators agree with Barrett's historical reconstruction to this point. Cf., e.g., Kümmel, *Introduction*, pp. 286-7; H. Conzelmann, *1 Corinthians* (Fortress, Philadelphia, 1975), p. 4; J. Héring, *The Second Epistle of Saint Paul to the Corinthians* (Epworth, London, 1967), pp. xiii-xiv; W. Schmithals, *Gnosticism in Corinth: An Investigation of the Letters to the Corinthians* (Abingdon, Nashville, 1971), pp. 101-10 (but with a few significant variations); K. Schelkle, *The Second Epistle to the Corinthians* (Herder, New York, 1969), pp. x-xii; F. F. Bruce, *1 and 2 Corinthians* (Oliphants, London, 1971), pp. 164-6; T. W. Manson, 'Paul in Ephesus (3): The Corinthian Correspondence', *BJRL* 26 (1941-2), pp. 101-2.

2. C. K. Barrett, *A Commentary on the Second Epistle to the Corinthians* (Harper & Row, New York, 1973), pp. 5-10. The unusual feature of Barrett's reconstruction is his suggestion that 2 Corinthians 10-13 is a letter subsequent to 2 Corinthians 1-9. Kümmel (*Introduction*, pp. 287-93), on the other hand, defends the unity of 2 Corinthians, explaining the change in tone which occurs at 10.1 by postulating a brief lapse in time between the dictating of chs. 1-9 and the addition of the concluding chs. 10-13. Other commentators, as we have already noted, identify chs. 10-13 as the painful letter, so, e.g., Héring, *2 Corinthians*, pp. xi-xiv. Cf. discussion of the 2 Corinthians 10-13 problem in Bruce, *Corinthians*, pp. 166-70.

3. Bruce, *Corinthians*, pp. 20-21.

4. Cf. R. McL. Wilson, 'How Gnostic were the Corinthians?' *NTS* 19

(1972), pp. 65-74; Conzelmann, *1 Corinthians*, pp. 14-16; Bruce, *Corinthians*, p. 21.

5. For a full but concise description of the characteristics of these opponents discernible in 2 Corinthians, see G. Friedrich, 'Die Gegner des Paulus im 2. Korintherbrief', *Abraham unser Vater*, eds., O. Betz, M. Hengel, P. Schmidt (Köln, Leiden, 1963), pp. 181-91.

6. Baur, *Paul: His Life and Work* 1, pp. 258-307. Cf. Manson, 'Corinthian Correspondence', p. 118.

7. E. Käsemann, 'Die Legitimität des Apostel: Eine Untersuchung zu II Korinther 10-13, *ZNW* 41 (1942), pp. 33-71.

8. D. H. Lietzmann–W. G. Kümmel, *An die Korinther* I.II (Mohr, Tübingen, 1969), p. 211.

9. Schmithals, *Gnosticism in Corinth*, pp. 113-16, 293-301. But cf. S. Arai, 'Die Gegner des Paulus im I. Korintherbrief und das Problem der Gnosis', *NTS* 19 (1972-3), pp. 430-37, who maintains that Paul's opponents in 1 Corinthians were open to gnostic influences and could have become gnostics, but had not yet done so.

10. Friedrich, 'Gegner', pp. 181-215. Cf. G. Bornkamm, 'Die Vorgeschichte des sogennanten Zweiten Korintherbriefs', *Sitzungsberichte der Heidelberger Akadamie der Wissenschaften, Phil.—hist. Klasse 1961*, no. 2 (Universitätsverlag, Heidelberg, 1961); D. Georgi, *Die Gegner des Paulus im 2 Korintherbrief* (Neukirchener, Neukirchen-Vluyn, 1964).

11. C. K. Barrett, 'Paul's Opponents in II Corinthians', *NTS* 17 (1971), pp. 233-54, see espc. pp. 251, 253. Cf. 'ΨΕΥΔΑΠΟΣΤΟΛΟΙ (2 Cor. 11.13)', *Mélanges Bibliques en Hommage au R. P. Béda Rigaux*, eds., A. Deschamps, A. de Halleux (Duculot, Gemblaux, 1970), pp. 377-96; 'Cephas and Corinth', *Abraham unser Vater*, eds., O. Betz, M. Hengel, P. Schmidt (Köln, Leiden, 1963), pp. 1-12. Good summaries of recent studies of the problem are to be found in Georgi, *Gegner*, pp. 7-16; Friedrich, 'Gegner', pp. 192-96.

12. For documentation see G. Bornkamm, 'πρεσβεύω', *TDNT* 6 (1968), p. 681.

13. For the figurative use of *presbeuō* and *presbeutēs* in the religious sphere, see Bornkamm, 'πρεσβεύω', pp. 681-2.

14. The differences are noted by Rengstorf, 'απόστολος', pp. 413-20, and Schmithals, *Office of Apostle*, pp. 98-110.

15. Cf. H. Kasting, *Die Anfänge der urchristlichen Mission* (Kaiser: München, 1969), pp. 74-5.

16. Whether the statement in 14.37 also covers the prohibition on women speaking in church services (34-5) which appears to contradict the implications of 11.5, is debatable. Verses 34-6 are regarded by some as a later non-Pauline interpolation (so recently, e.g., Conzelmann, *1 Corinthians*, p. 246), but others suspend judgement (e.g., Barrett, *1 Corinthians*, pp. 330-33).

17. The RSV translation here represents one construction, but many others are possible. Conzelmann lists six possible constructions (*1 Corinthians*, p. 97). Even if we settle on one or other of these, the problem of meaning is still formidible. Is the offender to be excommunicated (see, e.g., von Campenhausen, *Ecclesiastical Authority*, p. 134; 147, n. 1; Héring, *1 Corinthians*, p. 40) or delivered to death, as Acts 5 reports was the case with Ananias and

208

Sapphira (thus Lietzmann–Kümmel, *Korinther*, p. 23; Conzelmann, *1 Corinthians*, p. 97; Schmithals, *Office of Apostle*, p. 42)? Further, what does Paul mean by 'absent in the body . . . present in the Spirit'? Is it merely a Greek epistolary formula (so G. Karlsonn, 'Formehaftes in Paulusbriefen?' *Er Jb* 54 1956, pp. 138-41, cited by Conzelmann, *1 Corinthians*, p. 97, n. 33) or is it to be connected somehow with the charismatic power with which Paul was endued (so R. W. Funk, 'The Apostolic *Parousia*: Form and Significance', *Christian History and Interpretation*, eds., W. R. Farmer, C. F. D. Moule, R. R. Niebuhr (Cambridge University, Cambridge, 1967), pp. 264-5)?

18. *1 Corinthians*, p. 97.

19. It has been generally regarded as an allusion to the Roman triumphal procession. Thus Christ is pictured as the triumphant general returning from battle and the apostles as soldiers who follow their general and share his glory. The 'aroma', then, is regarded as the fragrance of perfumes sprinkled along the triumphal way—an aroma of life and joy to those who participate in the victory, but an aroma of death for the captives (so, e.g., Bruce, *Corinthians*, pp. 187-8; Héring, *2 Corinthians*, pp. 18-19). For a sampling of modern literature on the subject see BAG 'Θριαμβεύω'.

20. T. W. Manson, '2 Cor. 2.14-17: Suggestions towards an Exegesis', *Studia Paulina*, Fs. J. De Zwaan, eds., J. N. Sevenster, W. C. van Unnik (Bohn, Haarlem, 1953), pp. 155-62, accepts the majority view as far as the triumphal procession of Christ and the apostles is concerned, but prefers to interpret the aroma of life/death against the background of Jewish ideas about the Torah, which 'is thought of as something good in itself, which brings life to the right people, whether it be the Chosen Race, or the righteous, or the disinterested student; and death to all others, Gentiles, or unrighteous, or self-seeking students'.

L. Williamson, 'Led in Triumph', *Int* 22 (1968), pp. 317-32, says: 'Until further evidence is adduced, the faithful exegete must assume that the life-situation of *thriambeuō* is the triumphal entry of a military hero into the city of Rome', but maintains that the verb must be taken in its usual first century meaning: 'to lead as captive in a triumphal procession' (see espc. pp. 322-5). This would mean the passage does not teach Christian triumphalism, but Christian subordination to Christ who has taken them captive, and reminds Christians that, like Paul, they may be exposed to ridicule and shame.

R. B. Egan, 'Lexical Evidence on Two Pauline Passages', *NovT* 19 (1977), pp. 34-62, argues against the Roman triumphal procession background for both 2 Cor. 2.14 and Col. 2.15—the only two places in the New Testament where the verb *thriambeuō* is found. In both cases he says *thriambeuō* should be rendered as 'manifest, show forth, make known, display', suggesting as a translation of 2, 2.14: 'But thanks be to God who is always making us known in Christ and revealing through us the odor of his knowledge in every place' (p. 50).

Barrett, *2 Corinthians*, p. 98, despite the lack of supporting lexical evidence, says Paul pictures himself as one of the victorious general's soldiers sharing in the glory of the triumphal procession. However, he says the aroma is an allusion to the odour of sacrifice, and so translates 2, 2.15: 'For we are the sweet savour of sacrifice that rises from Christ to God' (p. 99). This leads

Barrett to see here an allusion to Paul's identification with Jesus, crucified and risen: 'The life of suffering and of devotion to God that Paul lives is (in secondary continuation of the life of Jesus) a manifestation of the nature and purpose of God. Where Paul's mission advances, the smoke of Christ's sacrifice ascends; it reaches, and is well-pleasing to, God, and at the same time it communicates the truth to men' (p. 100).

21. The same principle lies behind Paul's teaching in 1 Corinthians 1-2. There he says he deliberately chose not to present his message with a show of oratorical power/wisdom (1, 2.2). When he preached to the Corinthians it was from a position of weakness (1, 2.3), but his proclamation was 'in demonstration of the Spirit and power'. As Conzelmann observes, there is and must be a unity between the preaching and the preacher (*1 Corinthians*, pp. 53-4). If the content of the preaching is Christ crucified in weakness, but raised by the power of God, then it is only fitting that the preacher and his preaching should be weak (foolish in the eyes of the wise), but yet be a demonstration of the power of the Spirit of God.

22. *este epistolē Christou diakonētheisa huph' humōn* literally translated means 'you are an epistle of Christ ministered/serviced by us'. Paul's ministry and service in this respect was not the delivering of a completed letter (so RSV), rather through his missionary preaching in the power of the Spirit, he is the agent (scribe) by whom Christ produces his 'letter'. Cf. Bruce, *Corinthians*, p. 189.

23. Cf. J. Denny, *The Second Epistle to the Corinthians* (Armstrong, New York, 1900), p. 161; Barrett, *2 Corinthians*, p. 139.

24. *2 Corinthians*, pp. 61-2.

25. To these references some (e.g., Schweizer, 'πνεῦμα', p. 434; Barrett, *2 Corinthians*, pp. 122-3; Lietzmann, *Korinther*, p. 113—but not Kümmel, p. 200) would add 2, 3.17-18: 'Now the Lord is the Spirit . . . this comes from the Lord who is the Spirit.' However, both J. D. G. Dunn, '2 Corinthians III.17—"The Lord is the Spirit"', *JTS* 21 (1970), pp. 307-20, and C. F. D. Moule, '2 Cor. 3:18b, καθάπερ ἀπὸ κυρίου πνεύματος', *Neues Testament und Geschichte*, Fs. O. Cullmann, eds., H. Baltensweiler, B. Reicke (Mohr, Tübingen, 1972), pp. 231-7, have argued convincingly that 'the Lord' here refers not to Christ as commonly supposed, but rather to Yahweh. This conclusion is based on analysis of Paul's argument in 2 Corinthians 3, especially his 'midrash' on Exodus 34. For the relevant literature see articles by Dunn (p. 307) and Schweizer (pp. 433-4) cited above.

D. Greenwood, 'The Lord is the Spirit: Some Considerations of 2 Cor 3:17', *CBQ* 34 (1972), pp. 467-72, who acknowledges the basic cogency of Dunn's argument, suggests that Paul was not thinking *solely* of Yahweh when he wrote 2, 3.17. He says he 'prefers to think of him as writing κύριος in 17a with the notion of *Yahweh in Christ* at the back of his mind' (p. 470). He cites 2, 5.19 as a parallel expression, and mentions some texts where similar functions are ascribed to Yahweh and Christ. But Greenwood's argument lacks cogency because he lets general considerations take precedence over the exegesis of the text in its context.

In other places in the Corinthian letters the Spirit is identified as the Spirit of God (1, 2.14; 7.40) or from God (1, 2.12). In Romans the Spirit is spoken of as both 'the Spirit of God' and 'the Spirit of Christ' and these expressions are clearly understood as interchangeable with one another and with 'the Spirit' and even with 'Christ' (8.9-10). Cf. E. E. Ellis, 'Christ and the Spirit in 1 Corinthians', *Christ and the Spirit in the New Testament*, Fs. C. F. D. Moule, eds., B. Lindars, S. Smalley (Cambridge University, Cambridge, 1973), pp. 272-3.

26. Cf., e.g., Héring, *1 Corinthians*, p. 149.

27. '1 Corinthians 15:45—Last Adam, life-giving spirit', *Christ and the Spirit in the New Testament*, Fs. C. F. D. Moule, eds., B. Lindars, S. Smalley (Cambridge University, Cambridge, 1973), pp. 127-41.

28. *peri de tōn pneumatikōn* may be translated either as 'now concerning spiritual gifts' or 'now concerning spiritual men/men of the Spirit'. In 1, 14.37 *pneumatikos* is used with the meaning 'spiritual men' and at 1, 14.1 it is used again, but clearly with the sense 'spiritual gifts'. Seeing that 1 Corinthians 12 emphasises gifts (*charismata*) it is better to take *pneumatikōn* in 1, 12.1 as a reference to spiritual gifts. So, e.g., Conzelmann, *1 Corinthians*, p. 204; Héring, *1 Corinthians*, p. 106; Lietzmann–Kümmel, *Korinther*, p. 60. Schmithals, *Gnosticism in Corinth*, pp. 171-2, favours 'pneumatic persons'.

29. This is not the first time that Paul has used the image of the body in this epistle (cf. 1, 6.15-20; 10.14-22; 11.24-9), but it is the only unambiguous reference to the Church as such in the epistle. E. Schweizer and F. Baumgartel, 'σῶμα, σωματικός, σύσσωμος', *TDNT* 7 (1971), pp. 1024-94, provide a full discussion of the use of *sōma* in both biblical and extra-biblical contexts, as well as a helpful section on Paul's use of the expression 'body of Christ' (pp. 1067-81).

30. So, e.g., H. Schlier, *Christus und die Kirche im Epheserbrief* (Mohr, Tübingen, 1970), pp. 40-41; Best, *One Body in Christ*, pp. 95-105, 195.

31. Cf., e.g., Lietzmann–Kümmel, *Korinther*, pp. 62, 187; Conzelmann, *1 Corinthians*, pp. 211-12; Robinson, *The Body*, p. 51; E. Käsemann, *Perspectives on Paul* (Fortress, Philadelphia, 1971), p. 104; *Leib und Leib Christi*, BHT 9 (1933), pp. 161f., 170f.

32. The observation of E. Schweizer, *The Church as the Body of Christ* (John Knox, Richmond, 1964), p. 63, is germane here: 'Therefore the Corinthians are fundamentally and primarily the body of Christ, and only in a secondary way individual members (verse 27). The main reality is the oneness of Christ's body. The individuality of the members is only a secondary characteristic of the one body. We shall never understand the nature of the human body if we begin thinking about the single members severed from the body and try to conceive of the body as a mere sum of hundreds of those members. We shall never understand Paul's concept of the church if we begin our theological thinking with the individual Christian and consider the church as something like a social gathering or an association of individuals sharing some common interest.'

33. Dunn, *Jesus and the Spirit*, p. 264. Cf. Schweizer, *Church Order*, p. 99 (7i): 'The Church becomes a Church by the repeated action of the Spirit'. Cf. also von Campenhausen, *Ecclesiastical Authority*, p. 57: 'The life of the Church is to be found only in the continual interplay of a variety of spiritual capacities, which complement one another, and which precisely in this way reveal the fullness and harmony of the Spirit of Christ.'

34. The association of 'the Day' with 'fire' and the testing of men's works, almost certainly indicates that by 'the Day' is meant the Last Day—the coming of the Lord.

CHAPTER ELEVEN

1. T. W. Manson, 'St Paul's Letter to the Romans—and Others', *The Romans Debate*, ed. K. P. Donfried (Augsburg, Minneapolis, 1977), pp. 1-16.
2. G. Bornkamm, 'The Letter to the Romans as Paul's Last Will and Testament', *Romans Debate*, pp. 17-31.
3. G. Klein, 'Paul's Purpose in Writing the Epistle to the Romans', *Romans Debate*, pp. 32-49.
4. J. Jervell, 'The Letter to Jerusalem', *Romans Debate*, pp. 61-74.
5. P. S. Minear, *The Obedience of Faith: The Purpose of Paul in the Epistle to the Romans* (SCM, London, 1971).
6. W. Wiefel, 'The Jewish Community in Ancient Rome and the Origins of Roman Christianity', *Romans Debate*, pp. 100-119.
7. For a full discussion, see Kümmel, *Introduction*, pp. 314-20. Cf. also a recent article by J. I. H. McDonald in support of the view that ch. 16 was a separate letter: 'Was Romans xvi a Separate Letter?' *NTS* 16 (1969-70), pp. 369-72.
8. *Introduction*, p. 320. Cf. K. P. Donfried, 'A Short Note on Romans 16', *Romans Debate*, pp. 50-60.
   Schmithals, *Paul and the Gnostics*, pp. 219-38, analyses 16.17-20 and concludes that the opponents against whom Paul warns his readers are Gnostics. As there is no hint of anti-gnostic polemic in chs. 1-15, he regards his conclusion as supporting evidence that ch. 16 was originally addressed to Ephesus, and only subsequently came to be added as a final chapter to Romans. But cf. discussion of arguments for and against an Ephesian destination for ch. 16 in Kümmel, *Introduction*, pp. 318-20.
9. H. Schlier, *Der Römerbrief* (Herder, Freiburg, 1977), p. 20.
10. The natural antecedent for 'his' is 'Jesus Christ', and this is in line with the fact that Paul's apostolate is said here to be received from Christ. Thus O. Michel's view that the 'name' here means God's name (*Der Brief an die Römer* [Vandenhoeck & Ruprecht, Göttingen, 1966], p. 42) is unlikely.
11. 'Spirit' here is to be taken as Paul's spirit rather than the Holy Spirit. Cf. E. Käsemann, *An die Römer* (Mohr, Tübingen, 1974), p. 15.
12. C. K. Barrett, *A Commentary on the Epistle to the Romans* (A. & C. Black, London, 1967), p. 25, seems to imply that Paul intended to impart some specific (but to us unknown) spiritual gift to the Romans. M. Black, *Romans* (NCB; MMS, London, 1973), p. 41, and C. E. B. Cranfield, *A Critical and Exegetical Commentary on the Epistle to the Romans* 1 (T. & T. Clarke, Edinburgh, 1975), p. 79, regard it as a general benefaction, but Käsemann, *An die Römer*, p. 16, and A. Viard, *Saint Paul: Épître aux Romains* (Gabalda, Paris, 1975), p. 43, take the gift to mean the gospel. Käsemann draws attention to the fact that only here does Paul use the expression *charisma pneumatikon* and suggests that Paul deliberately avoided the use of *pneumatika* (used in 1 Corinthians 12). In

the light of Rom. 15.27 where *pneumatikos* is used in a more general sense of the gospel and its attendent blessings, he concludes that *charisma pneumatikon* in 1.11 should be interpreted as the gospel (*An die Römer*, p. 16). Viard supports this view by suggesting that Paul looked upon his forthcoming trip to Rome as he did upon his return visits to the churches he founded on his first missionary journey—he comes to confirm and strengthen the new believers in their understanding of the gospel (*Romains*, p. 37).

13. Rom. 1.11-15 is important for Klein's thesis that Paul regarded the Roman church as a church without apostolic foundation. He points out that Paul, who in 15.20 claims to avoid building on another man's foundation by not preaching where Christ has already been named, here in 1.11-15 says he wants to come to Rome to impart a spiritual blessing, to reap some harvest among them, and to preach the gospel to them. Obviously, then, he believed the church was not one of another man's founding and he wanted to ensure that this group of spontaneous formation was founded upon the true apostolic gospel. See 'Paul's Purpose in Romans', p. 48.

14. *hierourgeō* has the basic meaning 'to perform holy or sacrificial ministry'. It is used by both Josephus and Philo always with the meaning 'to offer sacrifice'. In 4 Macc. 7.8 ('Such should be those [worthy priests] whose office is to serve the Law [*tous hierourgountas ton nomon*] and defend it with their own blood and honourable sweat in the face of sufferings to the death' [*APOT* 2 (1913), p. 674]) the word is used to describe sacrificial service for the sake of the Torah. Paul's usage in Rom. 15.16 is closer to the base meaning of the word—he sees himself as a priest responsible for the offering up of the Gentiles. The emphasis, however, is not on the act of offering, but upon its preparation. Cf. G. Schrenk, 'ἱερουργέω', *TDNT* 3 (1965), pp. 251-2.

15. If the church in Rome had originated without apostolic foundation, Paul may well have suspected the purity of the kerygma embraced there. Seeing himself as a priest charged with responsibility for the purity of the offering of the Gentiles, he could well have written Romans (as Klein suggests) to provide them with a genuine apostolic kerygma, and to seek to ensure an acceptable offering out of Rome.

16. In Rom. 1.3-4 Christ is styled as God's Son 'who was descended from David according to the flesh and designated Son of God in power according to the Spirit of holiness by his resurrection from the dead.' In a recent study, J. D. G. Dunn ('Jesus—Flesh and Spirit: An Exposition of Romans. 1.3-4', *JTS* 24 [1973], pp. 40-68) seeks to show that this verse reflects the early Church's attempt to explain the continuity between the historical Jesus of the tradition and the exalted Christ whom the Church worshipped. This continuity was tentatively explained in terms of the Spirit. At the resurrection the historical Jesus, who was inspired by the Spirit, was transformed into the Lord of the Spirit: 'the Spirit which empowered Christ from Jordan onwards was now wholly identified with Christ as his Spirit, the Spirit of Christ.' Thus, in the Christian mission, Jesus Christ directs his disciples by his Spirit.

17. 'παῖς θεοῦ', p. 708. Cf. possible allusions to servant prophecies in 4.25 (Isa. 53.5); 5.18-19 (Isa. 53.11); 8.34 (Isa. 53.12).

18. Schlier, *Römerbrief*, p. 433, is right when he says that Paul's use of Isa. 52.15 here does not constitute a claim on his part to fulfil the role of the

suffering servant. Nevertheless, it does imply a claim that this part of the prophecy finds a fulfilment in his missionary preaching. Cf. Käsemann, *An die Römer*, p. 381.

19. Black, *Romans*, p. 176.

20. Paul's call for a 'living sacrifice' would have been a concept easily received by his readers, for in both the Jewish and hellenistic worlds of the first century there was a growing tendency to move from the literal concept of sacrifice. For documentation, see J. Behm, 'θύω', *TDNT* 3 (1965), pp. 186-9.

21. The Stoic Epictetus (Discourses I, xvi, 20f.) declared: 'If I were a nightingale I would do what is proper to a nightingale . . . ; but in fact I am a rational (*logikos*) creature, so I must praise God', and in the Hermetic writings (xiii.19, 21) a hymn of praise is called rational (*logikē*) sacrifice (cited by Barrett, *Romans*, p. 231. Cf. Michel, *Römerbrief*, p. 292). This would seem to suggest that the origin of the expression should be sought in the hellenistic world. On the other hand, it needs to be remembered (as is pointed out in Str-B 3, p. 296, cf. p. 26) that *logikē latreia* is comparable with עבודה שדיא בלב 'the service of God from the heart' advocated in the rabbinic writings (SDt. 11, 13 §41). Though many commentators see in the *logikēn latreian* of Rom. 12.1 a borrowing on Paul's part of Stoic terminology which came to him through the hellenistic synagogue (so, e.g., Michel, *Römerbrief*, pp. 292-3; Käsemann, *An die Römer*, p. 316), the question must be left open because the expression/concept could equally well have been taken over from the Old Testament and/or rabbinic tradition (cf. Barrett, *Romans*, p. 322; Viard, *Romains*, p. 257).

22. *eiper* which the RSV translates 'provided' (indicating a condition) is better rendered 'seeing that' (a statement of fact). Cf. Cranfield, *Romans* 1, p. 407. Verse 17 brings out an idea of suffering as the pathway to glory similar to that found in the saying attributed by Luke to the risen Jesus: 'Was it not necessary that the Christ should suffer these things and enter into his glory?' (Luke 24.26)

23. In the rabbinic writings (see Str-B 3, pp. 258-60) Ps. 44.22 is applied to the death of martyrs, and also to the lives of the godly.

CHAPTER TWELVE

1. The authenticity of Philippians is regarded by most commentators as beyond doubt, though it has been questioned in recent times by A. Q. Morton and J. McLeman, *Paul, the Man and the Myth: A Study in the Authorship of Greek Prose* (Harper & Row, New York, 1966), pp. 93-4. However, the conclusions drawn from their statistical investigations have not (as they suspected) commended themselves to most scholars. Cf., e.g., the critique by J. H. Houlden, *Paul's Letters from Prison* (Penguin, Harmondsworth, 1970), pp. 40-41.

The complex problem of the place and date of the writing of Philippians has been the subject of a long investigation by scholars. The problem is compounded by the issue of the epistle's integrity and the place of Paul's

214

imprisonment at the time. As a result no consensus has been reached and in fact there is now a sort of impasse. Cf., e.g., discussion in Kümmel, *Introduction*, pp. 324-32; R. P. Martin, *Philippians* (NCB; Oliphants, London, 1976), pp. 36-57.

2. E.g., J. F. Collange, *L'Épître de Saint Paul aux Philippiens* (Delachaux & Niestlé, Paris, 1973), p. 23, suggests the epistle was made up of three separate letters: A = 4.10-20 (or 4.10-23); B = 1.1-3.1a + 4.2-7 (+4.21-3); C = 3.1b-4.1 + 4.8-9. Similarly, with some variations, J. A. Fitzmyer, 'The Letter to the Philippians', *The Jerome Biblical Commentary*, eds., R. E. Brown, J. A. Fitzmyer, R. E. Murphy (Prentice Hall, Englewood Cliffs, N.J., 1968), p. 248. J. Gnilka, *Der Philipperbrief* (Herder, Freiburg, 1968), p. 10, postulates two letters: A = 1.1-3.1a + 4.2-7, 10-23; B = 3.1b-4.1, 8f.; similarly, with minor variations, G. Friedrich, *Der Brief an die Philipper* (Vandenhoeck & Ruprecht, Göttingen, 1965), p. 95; Schmithals, *Paul and the Gnostics*, pp. 65-122.

3. Commentators who hold that the unity of the epistle is defensible include: E. Lohmeyer, *Die Briefe an die Philipper, und die Kolosser und an Philemon* (Vandenhoeck & Ruprecht, Göttingen, 1953), pp. 7-8; R. Jewett, 'The Epistolary Thanksgiving and the Integrity of Philippians', *NovT* 12 (1970), pp. 40-53; Kümmel, *Introduction*, pp. 332-5; Martin, *Philippians*, pp. 10-22; Houlden, *Paul's Letters from Prison*, pp. 40-41.

4. Cf. discussion in R. P. Martin, *Carmen Christi: Philippians ii.5-11 in Recent Interpretation and in the Setting of Early Christian Worship* (Cambridge University, Cambridge, 1967), pp. 42-62, 315; 'Appended note on Phil. 2.6-11', *Philippians*, pp. 109-16, espc. pp. 112-13.

5. Martin, *Philippians*, pp. 22-36, provides a concise well-documented discussion of the modern debate.

6. A. F. J. Klijn, 'Paul's Opponents in Philippians iii', *NovT* 7 (1964), pp. 278-84.

7. J. Müller-Bardorff, 'Zur Frage der literarischen Einheit des Philipperbriefes', *Wissenschaftliche Zeitschrift der Universität Jena, Gesellschafts und sprachewiss.* Reihe 7 (1957-8), pp. 591-604.

8. H. Koester, 'The Purpose of the Polemic of a Pauline Fragment (Philippians III)', *NTS* 8 (1961-2), pp. 317-32.

9. Schmithals, *Paul and the Gnostics*, pp. 65-122.

10. R. Jewett, 'Conflicting Movements in the Early Church as Reflected in Philippians', *NovT* 12 (1970), pp. 362-90.

11. The word *apostolos* is used only once in Philippians (2.25) and there it does not refer to Paul but to Epaphroditus, the messenger of the Philippian Christians who brought their gifts to Paul (4.18).

12. Cf. G. Sass, 'Zur Bedeutung von δοῦλος bei Paulus', *ZNW* 40 (1941), pp. 24-32; F. W. Beare, *A Commentary on the Epistle to the Philippians* (A. & C. Black, London, 1969), p. 51; Collange, *Philippiens*, p. 38; Martin, *Philippians*, p. 60.

13. What does Paul mean when he says 'they all look after their own interests'? Collange sees in it a sweeping exaggeration by which Paul means to reinforce the worth and authority of Timothy (*Philippiens*, p. 104). Martin suggests it is a sorrowful, but matter-of-fact statement which applies to both

Christian communities, the one in the city of his imprisonment, the other in Philippi (*Philippians*, p. 118). Jewett relates it to Paul's adversaries in 1.15-17 who preach Christ out of partisanship to make Paul's imprisonment more bitter to him ('Conflicting Movements', p. 390). Beare notes that Paul's statement cannot apply to all in the Christian community in the city of his captivity, for in 1.14 Paul speaks in approving terms of the majority of the brethren who have been made confident in the Lord because of his imprisonment, and are now bold to speak the word of God without fear (*Philippians*, p. 97). Likewise, there can hardly be in this statement an implied criticism of the Philippian community, for despite some problems which Paul had to deal with they were still shining 'as lights in the world' (2.15). P. Bonnard must be close to Paul's intention when he says that of all those fellow-workers available to Paul at that time only Timothy was worthy of his trust for such a mission (*L'Épître de Saint Paul aux Philippiens* [Delachaux & Niestlé, Paris, 1950], p. 55). Cf. Gnilka, *Philipperbrief*, p. 159.

14. See, e.g., Beare, *Philippians*, p. 62; Friedrich, *An die Philipper*, p. 103; Collange, *Philippiens*, p. 58; Gnilka, *Philipperbrief*, pp. 66-7.

15. In the expression *epichorēgias tou pneumatos Iēsou Christou* the genitive is regarded as subjective, i.e., the Spirit of Jesus Christ is the source/dispenser of the aid which Paul expects. So, e.g., Beare, *Philippians*, p. 62; Gnilka *Philipperbrief*, p. 67.

16. B. M. Ahern, 'The Fellowship of his Sufferings (Phil 3, 10): A Study of St Paul's Doctrine on Christian Suffering', *CBQ* 22 (1960), p. 28, notes that the word order of 3.10 closely parallels the events of Paul's conversion as reported in Acts. The first element of his conversion was a confrontation by the risen Christ, the second, the disclosure of Christ's plan for him: 'I will show him how much he must suffer for the sake of my name' (Acts 9.16).

J. A. Fitzmyer, '"To Know Him and the Power of His Resurrection" (Phil 3.10)', *Mélanges Bibliques*, fs. R. P. Béda Rigaux, eds., A. Descamps, R. P. A. de Halleux (Duculot, Gembloux, 1970), p. 420, argues that the view which interprets 'the power of the resurrection' to mean the influence of the risen Christ upon the Christian is inadequate, for it includes also a reference to the power of the Father upon Christ himself. The power that Paul seeks to know is, therefore, that which 'emanates from the Father, raises Jesus from the dead at his resurrection, endows him with a new vitality, and finally proceeds from him as the life-giving, vitalizing force of the "new creation" and of the new life that Christians in unison with Christ experience and live.'

17. So Lohmeyer, *An die Philipper*, pp. 138-9.

18. Bonnard, *Philippiens*, p. 66. Ahern's view, if I understand him correctly, is the same as Bonnard's. He identifies the *pathēmata autou* as a lifelong '*state of death*, through the power of the Spirit, to the flesh, and to sin', yet in a somewhat puzzling way he identifies that, in turn, with the daily dying to which Paul refers in Rom. 8.36; Col. 3.5 etc. ('The Fellowship of His Sufferings', p. 31).

19. Beare, *Philippians*, p. 123.

20. H. Seesemann, *Der Begriff KOINΩNIA im Neuen Testament* (Töpelmann, Giessen, 1933), p. 85.

21. F. Hauck, 'κοινωνία', *TNDT* 3 (1965), p. 806.

216

22. Cf. Collange, *Philippiens*, p. 116; Martin, *Philippians*, pp. 134-5; Dunn, *Jesus and the Spirit*, p. 334. In our study of the Corinthian letters we saw that the same basic argument was used against the false apostles. It is not only the miraculous 'signs of an apostle'—the spiritual power—which characterises the true servant of Christ, but also the sufferings, persecutions, and hardships he bears for the sake of Christ.

23. Modern commentators note the overt eschatological context of 2.16 and 4.1. Cf., e.g., Gnilka, *Philipperbrief*, p. 153; Beare, *Philippians*, p. 93; Collange, *Philippiens*, p. 124; Martin, *Philippians*, pp. 106, 151; Bonnard, *Philippiens*, p. 73.

24. So, e.g., Martin, *Philippians*, p. 85; Collange, *Philippiens*, p. 70. If we are correct in seeing here an implied polemic against false teachers whom Paul answers in ch. 3, this would constitute supporting evidence for the integrity of the letter—another common idea binding the various parts of the letter together.

25. It is not certain what the force of *epechein* is here, whether it should be rendered 'holding fast' (RSV) or 'holding forth' (AV). The word is found only here in the generally undisputed Pauline epistles, and its varied uses elsewhere in the New Testament give us little help in deciding.

CHAPTER THIRTEEN

1. For a discussion of the Colossian 'heresy' see Kümmel, *Introduction*, p. 338-40; C. F. D. Moule, *The Epistle to Colossians and to Philemon* (Cambridge University, Cambridge, 1968), pp. 29-34; F. O. Francis and W. A. Meeks, eds., *Conflict at Colossae: A Problem in the Interpretation of Early Christianity Illustrated by Selected Modern Studies* (University of Montana/SBL, Missoula, 1973); R. P. Martin, *Colossians and Philemon* (NCB; Oliphants, London, 1974), pp. 9-19. E. Schweizer, 'Christianity of the Circumcised: The Background of Matthew and Colossians', *Jews, Greeks and Christians: Religious Cultures in Late Antiquity*, fs. W. D. Davies, eds., R. Hamerton-Kelly, R. Scroggs (Brill, Leiden, 1976), pp. 245-60, has recently suggested that this false teaching was a 'kind of Pythagorean philosophy, embellished with rites borrowed from both Hellenistic mystery religions and Judaism', and adds 'the whole movement might have grown out of a Jewish Christianity that adapted itself more and more to its Hellenistic environment' (p. 255). Cf. also the excursus, 'die kolossische Philosophie (2, 8)', in his commentary, *Der Brief an die Kolosser* (Benziger, Zürich, 1976), pp. 100-104. A dissenting voice has been raised by M. D. Hooker, 'Were there false teachers in Colossae?' *Christ and the Spirit in the New Testament*, fs. C. F. D. Moule, eds., B. Lindars, S. S. Smalley (Cambridge University, Cambridge, 1973), pp. 315-31. She says 'to suppose that belief in such forces [other powers besides Christ] can only be the result of explicit "false teaching" in the Colossian Christian community is to underestimate the pressures of a pagan environment, and to forget the background of these converts' (p. 323). The rather 'calm' approach of the apostle to the subject matter of Colossians (as compared, say, with Galatians) on first reflection seems to support Hooker's view, but on the other hand, it needs to

be remembered that Paul's involvement in the Colossian situation was secondhand, and this in itself would make for a more dispassionate response to any false teaching there.

2. For a discussion of the authenticity problem, see, e.g., Kümmel, *Introduction*, pp. 340-46; Schweizer, *An die Kolosser*, pp. 20-27; Martin, *Colossians and Philemon*, pp. 32-40.

3. Cf. B. Reicke, 'The Historical Setting of Colossians', *RevExp* 70 (1973), pp. 429-38.

4. U. Wickert, 'Der Philemonbrief—Privatbrief oder Apostolisches Schreiben', *ZNW* 52 (1961), pp. 230-38. Cf. P. Stuhlmacher, *Der Brief an Philemon* (Benziger, Zürich, 1975), pp. 24-6.

5. So E. Lohse, *Colossians and Philemon* (Fortress, Philadelphia, 1971), p. 199; G. Friedrich, *Philemon* (Vandenhoeck & Ruprecht, Göttingen, 1965), p. 193; Stuhlmacher, *An Philemon*, pp. 37-8.

6. Cf. Wickert, 'Privatbrief oder Apostolisches Schreiben', p. 235; Moule, *Colossians and Philemon*, p. 144; Martin, *Colossians and Philemon*, p. 163.

7. Schmithals, *Office of an Apostle*, p. 50.

8. See Lohse, *Colossians and Philemon*, p. 69. Cf. L. S. Thornton, *The Common Life in the Body of Christ* (A. & C. Black, London, 1963), pp. 34-7, 305; Robinson, *The Body*, p. 70.

9. Lohse, *Colossians and Philemon*, p. 69.

10. R. Yates, 'A Note on Colossians 1:24', *EvQ* 42 (1970), p. 90.

11. See Lohse, *Colossians and Philemon*, p. 70, for a concise description of the Jewish apocalyptic teaching on the woes of the Messiah. Cf. discussion in ch. 10 above.

12. Lohse, *Colossians and Philemon*, p. 70.

13. Schmithals, *Office of an Apostle*, p. 50.

14. Cf. Moule, *Colossians and Philemon*, p. 76; F. F. Bruce, *Commentary on the Epistle to the Colossians* (Eerdmans, Grand Rapids, 1957), pp. 215-16; Yates, 'A Note on Colossians 1:24', pp. 91-2.

15. See discussion in ch. 10 above. So also now R. J. Bauckham, 'Colossians 1.24 again', *EvQ* 47 (1975), pp. 169-70. L. Cerfaux, *Christ in the Theology of St Paul* (Herder, New York, 1959), pp. 414-15, n. 13, adopts a similar view, but extends it (in an unwarranted way) to say that Paul saw 'his sufferings accepted as a ransom in order that [the Gentiles] may obtain salvation.'

16. So, e.g., Lohse, *Colossians and Philemon*, p. 41; H. Conzelmann, *Der Brief and die Kolosser* (Vandenhoeck & Ruprecht, Göttingen, 1965), pp. 135-40; Martin, *Colossians and Philemon*, pp. 61-6; Schweizer, *An die Kolosser*, p. 50. But see Moule, *Colossians and Philemon*, pp. 60-62, for a cautionary statement.

17. For full discussion with bibliography, see Schweizer, *An die Kolosser*, pp. 44-74; Lohse, *Colossians and Philemon*, pp. 41-8. Cf. R. P. Martin, 'Reconciliation and Forgiveness in Colossians', *Reconciliation and Hope: New Testament Essays on Atonement and Eschatology*, fs. L. L. Morris, ed., R. Banks (Eerdmans, Grand Rapids, 1974), pp. 108-13; P. Benoit, 'L'Hymne christologique de Col. ı, 15-20: Jugement critique sur l'état des recherches', *Christianity, Judaism and Other Greco-Roman Cults* 1, fs. M. Smith, ed., J. Neusner (Brill, Leiden, 1975), pp. 226-63.

218

18. 'Reconciliation and Forgiveness in Colossians', pp. 109-10.

19. We are assuming that *tēs ekklēsias* is a genitive of apposition and not a simple genitive of possession, for, as C. Masson notes: 'Paul never says that the Church has a body, rather that it is a body' (*L'Epître de Saint Paul aux Colossiens* [Delachaux & Niestlé, Paris, 1953], p. 102, n. 1). Trans. mine.

20. 'For a long time the world had been understood as a living and divine body, or even more precisely as the body of God, even as the body whose head God is. God and the world were one in this Greek thinking. This view was thought to be confirmed by Paul's preaching about the body of Christ. The only change would be the substitution of Christ for the rather nebulous Greek deity with the revered old name of "Zeus" or the more modern names like "destiny" or "ether". Then Christ would be understood as this power which holds together and vivifies the whole cosmos' (Schweizer, *Church as the Body*, pp. 65-6).

21. Verses 12-14 and 20b seem to make it clear that, for Paul, this communion with the head was made possible only 'by the blood of the cross' and is experienced by those who have been 'delivered from the dominion of darkness and transferred into the kingdom of his beloved Son, in whom we have redemption, the forgiveness of our sins.' In other words, there is a very definite moral dimension to the relationship.

22. Lightfoot lists evidence for the use of both *haphai* and *sundesmoi* in contemporary physiology which, he says, indicates that 'contact and attachment are the primary ideas in ἁφαί and σύνδεσ μοι respectively.' Speaking of the *haphai*, he says: 'When applied to the human body they would be "joints", provided that we use the word accurately of the relations between contiguous limbs, and not loosely (as it is often used) of the parts of the limbs themselves in the neighbourhood of the contact.' Commenting on *sundesmos* he says it 'has a general and a special sense. In its general and comprehensive meaning it denotes any of the connecting bands which strap the body together, such as muscles or tendons or ligaments properly so called; in its special and restricted use it is a "ligament" in the technical sense', and adds, 'in our text indeed σύνδεσμος must be taken in its comprehensive sense' (*Saint Paul's Epistles to the Colossians and Philemon* [Macmillan, London, 1892], pp. 196-9).

23. In support of this interpretation, it is worth recalling Lightfoot's description of the physiological meaning of *haphai* cited earlier: 'When applied to the human body *they would be "joints" provided that we use the word accurately of the relations between contiguous limbs, and not loosely (as it is often used) of the parts of the limbs themselves* in the neighbourhood of the contact.' Ital. mine.

An alternative method of seeking to determine what Paul meant by the *haphai* and *sundesmoi* in Col. 2.19 would be to ask what agents are mentioned in this epistle as contributors to the growth of the Church. To this we would have to reply that Paul himself is one (2.1-2), as are Epaphras (1.7; 4.12-13) and Archippus (4.17), but so also is each member of the Christian community (3.16). Thus such an approach to the problem would lead us to conclude that the *haphai* and *sundesmoi* represent both the special ministers and the 'rank and file' members of the Church, all of whom together are those through whom Christ, the head, mediates nourishment for growth to the Church, his body.

24. This reserve with regard to the Spirit is possibly due, as E. Schweizer suggests, to Paul's desire to counter a misguided pneumatism in Colossae: 'A doctrine of the Spirit was much more difficult to defend against misunderstandings than a doctrine of Christ simply because the teaching of the total conduct of Jesus is a clear example of what kind of life he expects from his disciples' ('Christ in the Letter to the Colossians', *RevExp* 70 [1973], pp. 462-3).

CHAPTER FOURTEEN

1. For recent discussions of the various views, see Kümmel, *Introduction*, pp. 357-63; M. Barth, *Ephesians* 1 (AB: Doubleday, New York, 1974), pp. 36-41; C. L. Mitton, *Ephesians* (NCB; Oliphants, London, 1976), pp. 2-11.

2. Cf. Barth, *Ephesians* 1, pp. 50-52. The problem of authorship is further compounded by the close similarities between, and significant differences from, Colossians. For further discussion of the problem see E. Percy, *Die Probleme der Kolosser und Epheserbriefe* (Carl Bloms, Lund, 1946), pp. 360-433.

3. E. Goodspeed, *The Key to Ephesians* (University of Chicago, Chicago, 1956), pp. xii-xvii.

4. C. von Weizächer, *The Apostolic Age of the Christian Church* 2 (Putnam, New York, 1895), pp. 240-45.

5. H. Chadwick, 'Die Absicht des Epheserbriefes', *ZNW* 51 (1960), pp. 145-53.

6. Cf., e.g., M. Albertz, *Die Botschaft des Neuen Testaments* 1, 2 (Evangelische Verlag, Zürich, 1952), p. 168; H. Schlier, *Der Brief an die Epheser* (Patmos, Düsseldorf, 1963), p. 19; E. Käsemann, 'Epheserbrief', *RGG* 2 (1958), p. 518; P. Pokorný, *Der Epheserbrief und die Gnosis* (Evangelische Verlagsanstalt, Berlin, 1965); R. P. Martin, 'Epistle in Search of a Life-Setting', *ExpTim* 79 (1967-8), pp. 296-302.

7. Cf. F. W. Beare, 'The Epistle to the Ephesians', IB 10 (1953), pp. 602-5; Mitton, *Ephesians*, pp. 25-32.

8. Barth, *Ephesians* 2, pp. 781-2.

9. We have already seen that when Paul makes reference to his personal sufferings it is (almost) always in order to support the legitimacy of his apostolate.

10. *Oikonomia* is found in the inscriptions and papyri where it relates primarily to household administration with the sense 'direction, administration, provision' (O. Michel, 'οἰκονομία', *TDNT* 5 [1968], p. 151). The word occurs in two other places in Ephesians (1.10; 3.9) and in both cases clearly refers to the 'plan' of God for the salvation of Jews and Gentiles. However, in 3.2 its meaning is neither direction/administration or plan, but more like stewardship—Paul had been entrusted with a message which he must share with the Gentiles.

11. The 'mystery' in Ephesians is the plan of God (long hidden from men's minds but now revealed) that the Gentiles should become fellow-heirs with the believing Jewish Christians. The wall which had so long separated them has been broken down (2.14). This new unity is graphically expressed by Paul

in 3.6 with a series of words beginning with the prefix *sun-*: *sugklēronoma* (fellow-heirs), *sussōma* (members of the same body), and *summetocha* (fellow-partakers).

12. The use of *hagios* with *apostolos* is unusual in the New Testament and has been adduced as evidence for a later date for the epistle: a time when the apostles had come to be more highly revered and regarded as a closed group. Cf., e.g., Mitton, *Ephesians*, p. 122; H. Merklein, *Das kirchliche Amt nach dem Epheserbrief* (Kösel, München, 1973), pp. 187-93. However, such a conclusion is by no means certain. *Hagios* is used to denote anyone set apart for God's service. In the New Testament Christians are called *hagioi* (cf. 1 Cor. 6.2; Col. 1.26; Eph. 3.18). The Qumran sectarians referred to themselves as saints (1QM 3.5; 6.6) and the expression 'holy presbyters' is found in Ign. Magn. 3.1. It is doubtful, therefore, whether a more modern understanding of the word 'holy' (indicating some special degree of sanctification or some special status) can be introduced here. Cf. Barth, *Ephesians* 1, p. 335.

13. In the light of the later reference to apostles and prophets as those given by Christ to the Church (4.11), the prophets here and in 2.20 are not to be taken as Old Testament prophets, but rather as New Testament prophets.

14. The expression *tō themeliō tōn apostolōn kai prophētōn* can be taken to mean either the foundation laid by the apostles and prophets, or the foundation consisting of them, depending on the way the genitive *tōn apostolōn kai prophētōn* is construed (possessive genitive in the first case, genitive of apposition in the second case). Grammatically either is possible. There is precedent for the former in 1 Cor. 3.10-11, but since the words following are 'Christ Jesus himself being the chief cornerstone', it is better to adopt the second alternative which preserves the parallelism—apostles and prophets *are* the foundation, Christ *is* the cornerstone. Most modern commentators adopt this view. So, e.g., Schlier, *Epheser*, p. 142; Barth, *Ephesians* 1, p. 314; C. Masson, *L'Épître de Saint Paul aux Éphésians* (Delachaux & Niestlé, Paris, 1953), p. 169. However, the translators of the NEB chose the first alternative.

15. 'λίθος', *TDNT* 4 (1967), p. 275. Jeremias cites several texts in support of his viewpoint, the most important of which is from the first-century apocryphal writing, *T.Sol.* 22.7-23.4. Here a story is told about the placing of the great cornerstone (*lithos akrogōniaios*) at the pinnacle of the temple. When this task was completed Solomon rejoiced and said: 'Now truly the scripture is fulfilled which says, "The stone which the builders rejected has become the head of the corner"' (C. C. McCown, *The Testament of Solomon* [J. C. Hinrich, Leipzig, 1922], pp. 66-70). Trans. mine.

16. R. J. McKelvey, 'Christ the Cornerstone', *NTS* 8 (1961-2), p. 358.

17. *An die Epheser*, p. 142. Trans. mine.

18. This view is adopted by Mitton, *Ephesians*, pp. 109-10.

19. H. Merklein, *Christus und die Kirche: Die theologische Grundstruktur des Epheserbriefs nach Eph 2, 11-18* (Katholisches Bibelwerk, Stuttgart, 1973), p. 59.

20. J. A. Bengel, *Gnomon of the New Testament* 4 (T. & T. Clark, Edinburgh, 1860), pp. 79-80.

21. Schlier, *An die Epheser*, pp. 137-9.

22. H. Conzelmann, *Der Brief an die Epheser* (Vandenhoeck & Ruprecht,

Göttingen, 1965), p. 69; G. Friedrich, 'ευαγγελίζομαι', *TDNT* 2 (1964), p. 718.

23. Cf. R. P. Martin, 'Ephesians', *The Broadman Bible Commentary* 11, ed., C. J. Allen (Broadman, Nashville, 1971), p. 147; J. Gnilka, *Der Epheserbrief* (Herder, Freiburg, 1971), pp. 145-6.

24. So Mason, *Éphésiens*, p. 189.

25. So Barth, *Ephesians* 2, pp. 429-30.

26. So, e.g., G. B. Caird, 'The Descent of Christ in Ephesians 4, 7-11', *SE* 2 (1964), pp. 535-45.

27. So Mitton, *Ephesians*, p. 145.

28. So J. Calvin, *The Epistles of Paul the Apostle to the Galatians, Ephesians, Philippians and Colossians*, eds., D. W. Torrance, T. F. Torrance, trans. T. H. L. Parker (Eerdmans, Grand Rapids, 1965), p. 174. Cf. Masson, *Éphésiens*, p. 189.

29. Cf. Caird, 'Descent of Christ', p. 541; J. C. Kirby, *Ephesians Baptism and Pentecost: An Enquiry into the Structure and Purpose of the Epistle to the Ephesians* (SPCK, London, 1968), p. 146; Barth, *Ephesians* 2, p. 475.

30. So, e.g., J. Cambier, 'La signification christologique d'Eph. ιv.7-10', *NTS* 9 (1962-3), p. 275; Mitton, *Ephesians*, p. 147; Merklein, *Kirchliche Amt*, pp. 68-9. In this case the *tēs gēs* in the phrase *ta katōtera tēs gēs* is taken as a genitive of apposition: 'the lower parts, that is the earth'.

31. So, e.g., Masson, *Éphésiens*, p. 190. Here the case of *tēs gēs* is regarded as a partitive genitive: 'the lower parts of the earth', and is regarded as a reference to Christ's descent to the abode of the dead.

32. Cf. Caird, 'Descent of Christ', p. 537.

33. 'Descent of Christ', p. 537.

34. *Prōton* is found in χᶜ B Cᶜ K P Ψ, but not in p⁴⁶ χ* A C* D G Iᵛⁱᵈ.

35. 'Descent of Christ', pp. 537-41. A similar treatment of the liturgical evidence was made several years later by Kirby, *Ephesians Baptism and Pentecost*, pp. 145-6.

36. For a recent discussion of the grammatical and linguistic problems associated with these words in Eph. 1.23 see R. Yates, 'A Re-examination of Ephesians 1:23', *ExpTim* 83/5 (1971), pp. 146-7.

37. Lightfoot, *Colossians and Philemon*, pp. 255-71. Robinson, *The Body*, pp. 66, 69.

38. *St Paul's Epistle to the Ephesians* (Macmillan, London, 1928), pp. 42-5. Yates, 'A Re-examination of Ephesians 1:23', pp. 149-51, adopts the same view.

39. *The Unity of the Church in the New Testament: Colossians and Ephesians* (Almqvist & Wiksells, Uppsala, 1946), p. 129.

40. Cf., e.g., C. F. D. Moule, 'A Note on Ephesians i.22, 23', *ExpTim* 60 (1948-9), p. 53. '"Fulness" and "Fill" in the New Testament', *SJT* 4 (1951), p. 81.

41. Cited by Lohse, *Colossians and Philemon*, p. 121, n. 65.

42. *Éphésiens*, p. 199. Trans. mine. Martin, 'Ephesians', pp. 198-9. also interprets *haphai* as special ministers within the Church; the apostles, prophets etc., of verse 11.

43. *Unity of the Church*, p. 136.

44. *Ephesians* 2, p. 449.

45. Even if the epistle be regarded as post-Pauline and of 'early catholic' character, that still would not account for the developed 'catholicism' of Masson's view.

46. Barth, *Ephesians* 2, p. 449. Ital. mine.

SELECT BIBLIOGRAPHY

GENERAL WORKS

Barrett, C. K., *The Holy Spirit and the Gospel Tradition* (SPCK, London, 1966)
—, *Jesus and the Gospel Tradition* (SPCK, London, 1967)
Best, E., *One Body in Christ: A Study in the Relationship of the Church to Christ in the Epistles of the Apostle Paul* (SPCK, London, 1955)
Black, M., *An Aramaic Approach to the Gospels and Acts* (Oxford University, Oxford, 1946)
—, 'The Parables as Allegory', *BJRL* 42 (1959), pp. 273-87
Blaikie, N. W. H., *The Plight of the Australian Clergy* (University of Queensland, St Lucia, 1979)
Bornkamm, G., *Jesus of Nazareth* (Harper & Row, New York, 1975)
Bultmann, R., *The History of the Synoptic Tradition* (Harper & Row, New York, 1976)
—, *Theology of the New Testament* 2 vols. (SCM, London, 1952 and 1955)
Calvert, D. G. A., 'An Examination of the Criteria for Distinguishing the Authentic Words of Jesus', *NTS* 18 (1971-2), pp. 209-19
Campenhausen, H. von, *Ecclesiastical Authority and Spiritual Power in the Church of the First Three Centuries* (A. & C. Black, London 1969)
Carlston, C. E., *The Parables of the Triple Tradition* (Fortress, Philadelphia, 1975)
Catchpole, D. R., 'Tradition History', *New Testament Interpretation*, ed., I. H. Marshall (Paternoster, Exeter, 1977), pp. 172-8
Conzelmann, H., *The Theology of Luke* (Faber, London, 1960)
Cullmann, O., *The Christology of the New Testament* (Westminster, Philadelphia, 1959)
Dodd, C. H., *According to the Scriptures* (Nisbet, London, 1952)
—, *The Parables of the Kingdom* (Nisbet, London, 1935)
Dunn, J. D. G., *Baptism in the Holy Spirit* (SCM, London, 1970)
—, *Jesus and the Spirit* (Westminster, Philadelphia, 1975)
Ehrhardt, A., *The Apostolic Ministry* (*SJT* Occasional Paper 7, 1958)
Feilding, C. R., *Education for Ministry* (American Association of Theological Schools, Dayton, Ohio, 1966)
Fuller, R. H., *The Foundations of New Testament Christology* (Lutterworth, London, 1965)
—, *The Mission and Achievement of Jesus: An Examination of the Presuppositions of New Testament Theology* (SCM, London, 1954)
Gore, C., *The Church and the Ministry* (Longmans, Green & Co., London, 1919)
Hahn, F., *Mission in the New Testament* (SBT, SCM, London, 1965)

Hanson, S., *The Unity of the Church in the New Testament: Colossians and Ephesians* (Almqvist & Wiksells, Uppsala, 1946)

Higgins, A. J. B., *Jesus and the Son of Man* (Lutterworth, London, 1964)

Hooker, M. D., *Jesus and the Servant* (SPCK, London, 1959)

—, 'On Using the Wrong Tool', *Theology* 75 (1972), pp. 570-81

Jeremias, J., *Jesus' Promise to the Nations* (SCM, London, 1967)

—, *New Testament Theology 1: The Proclamation of Jesus* (SCM, London, 1971)

—, *The Parables of Jesus* (Scribner, New York, 1963)

—, *Unknown Sayings of Jesus* (SPCK, London, 1964)

Jewett, R., *Paul's Anthropological Terms: A Study of their Use in Conflict Settings* (Brill, Leiden, 1971)

Käsemann, E., *Essays on New Testament Themes* (SCM, London, 1964)

—, *Leib und Leib Christi*, (BHT 9, 1933)

—, *Perspectives on Paul* (Fortress, Philadelphia, 1971)

Kasting, H., *Die Anfänge der urchristlichen Mission* (Kaiser, München, 1969)

Kirk, J. A., 'Apostleship since Rengstorf: Towards a Synthesis', *NTS* 21 (1974-75), pp. 249-64

Kirk, K. E., ed., *The Apostolic Ministry* (Hodder & Stoughton, London, 1946)

Lohse, E., *Märtyrer und Gottesknecht* (Vandenhoeck & Ruprecht, Göttingen, 1955)

Manson, T. W., *The Church's Ministry* (Hodder & Stoughton, London, 1948)

Manson, W., *The Servant Messiah* (Cambridge University, Cambridge, 1953)

Marshall, I. H., *Luke: Historian and Theologian* (Paternoster, Exeter, 1970)

Marxsen, W., *Mark the Evangelist* (Abingdon, Nashville, 1969)

Mascall, E. L., *Corpus Christi: Essays on the Church and the Eucharist* (Longmans, London, 1953)

Mosbech, H., 'Apostolos in the New Testament', *ST* 2 (1949), pp. 166-200

Munck, J., *Paul and the Salvation of Mankind* (SCM, London, 1959)

—, 'Paul, the Apostles and the Twelve', *ST* 3 (1950), pp. 96-100

Niebuhr, H. R., *The Purpose of the Church and its Ministry* (Harper & Row, New York, 1956)

North, C. R., *The Suffering Servant in Deutero-Isaiah* (Oxford University, Oxford, 1948)

Ordained Ministry Today—A Discussion of its Nature and Role: The Report of a Working Party of the Ministry Committee of the Advisory Council for the Church's Ministry (Church Information Office, Westminster, U.K., 1969)

Perrin, N., *Rediscovering the Teaching of Jesus* (SCM, London, 1967)

Quinn, J. D., 'Ministry in the New Testament', *Biblical Studies in Contemporary Thought*, ed., M. Ward (Trinity College Biblical Institute, Burlington, 1975), pp. 130-66

Robinson, J. A. T., *The Body: A Study in Pauline Theology* (SBT 5, SCM, London, 1952)

Schille, G., *Die urchristliche Kollegialmission* (Zwingli, Zürich, 1967)

Schmithals, W., *Gnosticism in Corinth: An Investigation of the Letters to the Corinthians* (Abingdon, Nashville, 1971)

—, *The Office of Apostle in the Early Church* (Abingdon, Nashville, 1969)

—, *Paul and the Gnostics* (Abingdon, Nashville, 1972)

Schütz, J. H., *Paul and the Anatomy of Apostolic Authority* (Cambridge University, Cambridge, 1975)

Schweizer, E., *The Church as the Body of Christ* (John Knox, Richmond, 1964)

—, *Church Order in the New Testament* (SCM, London, 1961)

Taylor, V., *Jesus and His Sacrifice* (Macmillan, London, 1948)

Thornton, L. S., *The Common Life in the Body of Christ* (A. & C. Black, London, 1963)

Vogelstein, H., 'The Development of the Apostolate in Judaism and its Transformation in Christianity', *HUCA* 2 (1925), pp. 92-123

Wolff, H. W., *Jesaja 53 im Urchristentum* (Evangelische Verlagsanstalt, Berlin, n.d., Vorwort, 1949)

EXEGETICAL STUDIES

Barrett, C. K., 'The Background of Mark 10:45', *New Testament Essays: Studies in Memory of T. W. Manson*, ed., A. J. B. Higgins (Manchester University, Manchester, 1959) pp. 1-18

Bartsch, H. W., 'Jesus Schwertwort, Lukas xxii.35-38: Überlieferungsgeschichtliche Studie', *NTS* 20 (1973-4), pp. 190-203

Bauckham, R. J., 'Colossians 1.24 again', *EvQ* 47 (1975), pp. 168-70

Beasley-Murray, G. R., 'Jesus and the Spirit', *Mélanges Bibliques en hommage au R. P. Béda Rigaux*, eds., A. Descamps, A Halleux (Duculot, Gembloux, 1970), pp. 463-78

Caird, G. B., 'The Descent of Christ in Ephesians 4.7-11', *SE* 2 (1964), pp. 535-45

Cambier, J., 'La signification christologique d'Eph. iv.7-10', *NTS* 9 (1962-3), pp. 262-75

Crossan, C. D., 'The Parable of the Wicked Husbandmen', *JBL* 90 (1971), pp. 451-65

Dunn, J. D. G., 'I Corinthians 15:45—Last Adam, life-giving spirit', *Christ and the Spirit in the New Testament*, eds., B. Lindars, S. Smalley (Cambridge University, Cambridge, 1973), pp. 127-41

—, '2 Corinthians iii.17—"The Lord is the Spirit"', *JTS* 21 (1970), pp. 307-20

Ellis, E. E., 'Christ and the Spirit in 1 Corinthians', *Christ and the Spirit in the New Testament*, eds., B. Lindars, S. Smalley (Cambridge University, Cambridge, 1973), pp. 269-77

France, R. T., 'The Servant of the Lord in the Teaching of Jesus', *Tyndale Bulletin* 19 (1968), pp. 26-52

Greenwood, D., 'The Lord is the Spirit: Some Considerations of 2 Cor 3:17', *CBQ* 34 (1972), pp. 467-72

Käsemann, E., 'Die Legitimität des Apostels: Eine Untersuchung zu ii Korinther 10-13', *ZNW* 41 (1942), pp. 33-71

Klassen, W., 'Galatians 6.17' *ExpTim* 81 (1969-70), p. 378

Leaney, R., 'Jesus and the Symbol of the Child (Luke 9: 46-48)', *ExpTim* 66 (1954), pp. 91-2

226

Légasse, S., *Jesus et l'Enfant.* '*Enfants*', '*Petits*' et '*Simples*' *dans la Tradition synoptique* (Gabalda, Paris, 1969)

McKelvey, R. J., 'Christ the Cornerstone', *NTS* 8 (1961-2), pp. 352-59

Manson, T. W., '2 Cor. 2.14-17: Suggestions towards an Exegesis', *Studia Paulina*, eds., J. N. Sevenster, W. C. van Unnik (Bohn, Haarlem, 1953), pp. 155-62

Martin, R. P., 'Reconciliation and Forgiveness in Colossians', *Reconciliation and Hope: New Testament Essays on Atonement and Eschatology*, ed., R. Banks (Eerdmans, Grand Rapids, 1974), pp. 104-24

Moulder, W. J., "The Old Testament Background and Interpretation of Mark x.45', *NTS* 24 (1977), pp. 120-27

Moule, C. F. D., '"Fulness" and "Fill" in the New Testament', *SJT* 4 (1951), pp. 79-86

—, 'A Note on Ephesians i.22, 23', *Exp Tim* 60 (1948-9), p. 53

—, 'The Post-Resurrection Appearances in the Light of Festival Pilgrimages', *NTS* 4 (1957-8), pp. 58-61

—, '2 Cor. 3:18b, καθάπερ ἀπὸ κυρίου πνεύματος, *Neues Testament und Geschichte*, eds., H. Baltensweiler, B. Reicke (Mohr, Tübingen, 1972), pp. 231-37

Price, J. L., 'The Servant Motif in the Synoptic Gospels', *Int* 12 (1958), pp. 28-38

Rengstorf, K., ἀπόστολος, *TDNT* 1 (1964), pp. 398-447

Robinson, J. A. T., 'The Parable of the Wicked Husbandmen: A Test of Synoptic Relationships', *NTS* 21 (1974-5), pp. 446-51

Rodd, C. S., 'Spirit or Finger', *Exp Tim* 72 (1961), pp. 157-8

Schweizer, E., 'Christ in the Letter to the Colossian', *RevExp* 70 (1973), pp. 451-67

—, πνεῦμα, *TDNT* 6 (1968), pp. 398-445

Unnik, W. C. van, 'Den Geist loschet nicht aus (I Thessalonicher v. 19)', *NovT* 10 (1968), pp. 253-69

Williamson, L., 'Led in Triumph', *Int* 22 (1968), pp. 317-32

Yates, R., 'A Note on Colossians 1:24', *EvQ* 42 (1970), pp. 88-92

—, 'A Re-examination of Ephesians 1:23', *ExpTim* 83/5 (1971), pp. 146-51

INDEX OF AUTHORS

Ahern, B. M., 215
Albertz, M., 219
Anderson, H., 195
Arai, S., 207

Barrett, C. K., 36, 43, 44, 50, 53, 59, 65, 102–3, 113, 150, 195, 196, 197, 198, 199, 200, 201, 206, 207, 208, 209, 211, 213
Barth, M., 172, 219, 220, 221, 222
Bartsch, H. W., 25
Bauckham, R. J., 217
Baumgartel, F., 210
Baur, F. C., 124, 204, 207
Beare, F. W., 214, 215, 216, 219
Beasley-Murray, G. R., 55, 56, 195, 198
Behm, J., 213
Bengel, J. A., 220
Benoit, P., 217
Best, E., 193, 204, 205, 206, 210
Black, M., 194, 200, 211, 213
Blaikie, N. W. H., 193
Blank, J., 82
Bonnard, P., 194, 195, 203, 215, 216
Bornkamm, G., 198, 207, 211
Borse, U., 204
Bring, R., 203
Bruce, F. F., 202, 203,

206, 207, 208, 209, 217
Brunner, F. D., 193
Buchsel, F., 197
Bultmann, R., 48, 194, 195, 196, 197, 198, 199
Burton, E., 203

Caird, G. B., 167–8, 221
Calvert, D. G. A., 194
Calvin, J., 170, 221
Cambier, J., 221
Campenhausen, H. von, 198, 202, 207, 210
Carlston, C. E., 18
Catchpole, D. R., 194
Cerfaux, L., 202, 217
Chadwick, H., 219
Chrysostom, 164, 170
Collange, J. F., 214, 215, 216
Conzelmann, H., 194, 206, 207, 208, 209, 210, 217, 220
Cranfield, C. E. B., 197, 211, 213
Creed, J. M., 194, 195, 202
Crossan, D. D., 195
Cullmann, O., 196, 202

Denny, J., 209
Dibelius, M., 206
Dix, G., 30
Dobschütz, E., 204

Dodd, C. H., 17, 194, 199
Donfried, K. P., 211
Dunn, J. D. G., 19, 20, 55, 67–8, 115, 195, 198, 199, 202, 209, 210, 212, 216

Egan, R. B., 208
Ehrhardt, A., 193
Ellis, E. E., 194, 210
Epstein, I., 196
Evans, C. F., 201

Farmer, W. R., 201
Feilding, C. R., 193
Fitzmyer, J. A., 214, 215
Foakes-Jackson, F. J., 196, 201
Frame, J. E., 204
France, R. T., 196, 197
Francis, F. O., 216
Fridrichsen, A., 202, 203
Friedrich, G., 207, 214, 215, 217, 221
Fuller, R. H., 196, 197
Funk, R. W., 208

Georgi, D., 207
Gnilka, J., 214, 215, 216, 221
Goodspeed, E., 219
Gore, C., 193
Greenwood, D., 209
Grundmann, W., 22, 195, 204

Hahn, F., 194
Hanson, S., 170, 172
Harnack, A., 29, 30
Hauck, F., 215
Headlam, A. C., 193
Hebert, A. G., 193
Hennecke, E., 195
Henneken, B., 206
Héring, J., 206, 207, 208, 210
Higgins, A. J. B., 197
Hiltner, S., 193
Holtz, T., 202
Hooker, M. D., 43, 44, 50, 194, 196, 197, 216
Houlden, J. H., 213, 214

Jeremias, J., 10–11, 27, 38, 42, 162, 193, 194, 195, 197, 199, 206, 220
Jervell, J., 211
Jewett, R., 203, 204, 214, 215
Jülicher, A., 17

Karlsonn, G., 208
Käsemann, E., 198, 199, 207, 210, 211, 213, 219
Kasting, H., 207
Kertelge, K., 202
Kirby, J. C., 221
Kirk, J. A., 196, 202
Kirk, K. E., 193
Klassen, W., 204
Klein, G., 202, 211, 212
Klijn, A. F. J., 214
Klostermann, E., 194, 195, 198, 199
Koester, H., 214
Kredel, E. M., 195
Kümmel, W. G., 202, 204, 206, 207, 208, 209, 210, 211, 214, 216, 217, 219

Lake, K., 196, 201
Lampe, G. W. H., 193
Leaney, R., 195
Légasse, S., 22
Lietzmann, D. H., 207, 208, 209, 210
Lightfoot, J. B., 29, 30, 76, 83, 170, 202, 203, 204, 218, 221
Loewe, H., 196
Lohmeyer, E., 194, 214, 215
Lohse, E., 197, 202, 217, 221
Lütgert, W., 204

McCown, C. C., 220
McDonald, J. I. H., 211
McKelvey, R. J., 220
McLeman, J., 213
Manson, T. W., 206, 207, 208, 211
Manson, W., 196
Marshall, I. H., 210
Martin, R. P., 153, 203, 214, 216, 217, 219, 221
Marxsen, W., 199
Mascall, E. L., 193
Masson, C., 172–3, 204, 205, 206, 217, 220, 221, 222
Meeks, W. A., 216
Merklein, H., 220, 221
Metzger, B. M., 197, 201
Michel, O., 211, 213, 219
Minear, P. S., 211
Mitton, C. L., 219, 220, 221
Montefiore, C. G., 196
Morris, L. L., 205
Morton, A. Q., 213
Mosbech, H., 195, 202
Moulder, W. J., 197
Moule, C. F. D., 18, 195, 196, 197, 201,

209, 216, 217, 221
Müller-Bardorff, J., 214
Munck, J., 202
Mussner, F., 203

Niebuhr, H. R., 193
Nikolaus, W., 203
North, C. R., 34

Origen, 170

Paul, R. S., 193
Percy, E., 219
Pereira, F., 203
Perrin, N., 199
Pokorný, P., 219
Price, J. L., 196

Ramsay, W. M., 83, 204
Rashdall, H., 197
Reicke, B., 217
Reid, J. K. S., 193
Rengstorf, K. H., 29, 30, 31, 195, 202, 207
Richardson, A., 201
Rigaux, B., 91–2, 195, 205, 206
Robinson, J. A., 170
Robinson, J. A. T., 16, 170, 193, 210, 217, 221
Robinson, J. M., 199
Rodd, C. S., 55, 199
Roloff, J., 195, 202

Sass, G., 214
Schelkle, K., 206
Schille, G., 195, 202
Schlatter, A., 199
Schleiermacher, F., 195
Schlier, H., 163, 203, 206, 210, 211, 212, 219, 220
Schmithals, W., 105, 196, 202, 203, 204, 206, 207, 208, 210, 211, 214, 217
Schnackenburg, R., 202

Schneemelcher,   W.,
    195
Schrenk, G., 212
Schürmann, H., 195
Schütz, J. H., 202, 203
Schweizer, E., 22, 47,
    60, 195, 198, 199,
    200, 209, 210, 216,
    217, 218, 219
Seesemann, H., 215
Seufert, W., 195
Stuhlmacher, P., 217

Taylor, V., 59, 194, 196,
    197, 200
Theodoret, 172
Thornton, L. S., 217
Tödt, H. E., 196, 197
Tyson, J. B., 202

Unnik, W. C. van, 199,
    205

Viard, A., 211, 212, 213

Vogelstein, H., 30–31

Weizächer, C. von, 219
Westermann, C., 197
Wickert, U., 217
Wiefel, W., 211
Williamson, L., 208
Wilson, R. McL., 203,
    206
Windisch, H., 56, 199
Wolff, H. W., 196
Yates, R., 217, 221

INDEX OF BIBLICAL AND OTHER ANCIENT WRITINGS

OLD TESTAMENT

EXODUS
4.11–12   60
8.19   55, 199
19   168
24   41
24.1–8   40
24.8   41
34   209

LEVITICUS
5.17–19   44
5.18   44
5.25   44
7.1   44

DEUTERONOMY
9.10   55

2 SAMUEL
10   29–30

2 CHRONICLES
17.7–9   31

PSALMS
2.7   53
22.6   38
44.22   130, 133, 213
68   168
68.18   166, 168

PROVERBS
16.31   205

ISAIAH
28.16   163
42.1–4   52, 57
42.1   53
49   80
49.1   79, 87, 91
49.5–6   82, 87
49.5   79
49.6   80, 198
49.15   200
52–53   82
52.7   200
52.15   128, 212
53   34, 35, 36, 40-41, 42, 43, 44, 45, 47, 49, 50, 133, 197
53.3   38
53.5   197, 212
53.10   44
53.11–12   43
53.11   212
53.12   24, 25, 36, 37, 41, 43, 44, 212
57.19   165
58.6   19
61   19, 20, 21
61.1   19–20, 21, 32, 52, 57–8, 63

JEREMIAH
1.5   79, 91
5.6   28
31   41
31.31–4   40

EZEKIEL
16.12   205
22.27   28
23.42   205

JOEL
2.28–9   62

HABAKKUK
1.8   28

APOCRYPHA AND PSEUDEPIGRAPHA

4 MACCABEES
7.8   212

1 ENOCH
49.3   53

TESTAMENTS OF THE 12 PATRIARCHS

T. Jud.
24.2f.   53

T. Levi
18.2–14   53

T. Sol
22.7–23.4   220

2 ESDRAS
5.18   28

PSALMS OF SOLOMON
17.42   53

DEAD SEA SCROLLS, JOSEPHUS
AND RABBINIC TEXTS

DEAD SEA SCROLLS		Zad. Fr.		JOSEPHUS		MENAHOT	
1QS		2.10	53	JEWISH WAR		93b	30
2.19–23	23, 198			1,10.2	204	NAZIR	
4.7	205			BABA MESI'A		12b	30
6.8–9	23, 198	*CD*		96a	30		
		14.3–8	23, 198	BERAKOT		QIDDUSIN	
				5.5	29, 30	41b	30
1QM				58b	198	SIPRE	DEUTER-
3.5	220	*4QFlor*		HAGIGA		ONOMY	
6.6	220	10–ı·	18	10b	30	11, 13 §41	213

NEW TESTAMENT

MATTHEW		12.15–21	56	24.45–51	191	9.2–10	37
1.20–23	52	12.15–20	36	25.21	191	9.11–13	37
3.17	34	12.17–21	52	26.12	35	9.12	35, 37–8, 45
4.1	52	12.18–21	34	26.28	38–40	9.13	37, 38
4.23	14	12.22–32	52	28.18–20	66–7, 69,	9.33–7	50
5.3–6	19, 20	12.22–30	54		201	9.35	49–50
7.11	56, 62–3	12.28	54–7, 59,	28.19–20	16, 26,	9.37	21, 22–3
7.15	28		60, 187		201	9.38	200
9.15	35	12.29	35	28.19	52	10.39	96, 198
10.1–42	61	12.31–2	187			10.42–5	42, 48–9
10.1–15	27	13.53–8	19	MARK		10.43–5	42
10.1	22	15.21–8	15, 16	1.1–11	52	10.45	41–5, 48,
10.5–6	15, 26	15.23–4	15	1.2	52		190, 196, 197
10.7–8	26–7	15.24	15–16, 26	1.35–8	14	12.1–12	16–18
10.5–15	25	17.12	37	1.38	14–15	12.38–40	23
10.16	27–9	18.1–5	50	2.20	35	13	61, 97
10.20	52, 58–62	18.5	21, 22–3	3.14–15	26	13.10	61
10.24–5	46–8	20.25–8	48	3.22–30	52	13.11	52, 58–60,
10.24	46	20.28	41–2	3.27–9	57		137, 199
10.28	97	21.33–46	16	3.27	35	13.12–13	96
10.40	21–2, 25,	23.1–12	23	6.1–6	19, 20	13.32	61
	27, 82, 86	23.7	49	6.7–13	25	14.8	35
11.2–6	19,	23.8–10	49	6.12–13	26	14.24	38–41
	20–21, 35	23.11	49	7.24–30	15, 16	16.9–20	67
11.4–6	58	23.25	38	8.34–7	96	16.14–18	67
11.25	56	23.29–37	18	9.1–13	37		
11.28–30	35	24.9	97	9.1	37		

LUKE		21.15	55, 58–61	6.1–4	69	8.35–6	133
1.1–4	202	22.19–20	39	8.4–25	26	8.36	130, 215
1.35	52	22.20	38–40	9.4	149	9–11	90
2.34	94	22.24–7	42, 197	9.6	79	9.33	163
3.16	67	22.25–7	48	9.10–19	79	11.13–32	158
4.1	52	22.27	41–2, 197	9.16	215	11.13	126
4.14	52	22.35–8	21, 24, 25,	10.1–48	15	12.1–2	190
4.16–30	19–21		35, 36	11.19–26	26	12.1	129, 141, 189,
4.18–21	19, 52	22.35	24–5	11.20–24	15		213
4.42–3	14	22.37	25, 34,	11.27–8	95	12.3–8	130
4.43	14–15		35–7, 45	13.1–3	95	12.4–5	130
5.35	35	23.24	35	13.46–7	151	12.4ff.	4
6.20–21	20	23.50–24.53	202	13.47	114, 198	12.11	129
6.20	19, 20	24–26	213	16	134	14.4	129
6.40	46–8	24.43	69	16.19–24	134, 141	14.18	129
7.18–23	20–21, 35	24.46–9	67–9	17–18	88	15.15–29	124
9–10	25	24.49	52, 68	17	90	15.15–21	126,
9	24			18	101		127–8
9.1–6	25, 27	JOHN		18.8	101	15.15–16	189
9.21	200	1.32–3	52	19.10	158	15.16	126, 127, 212
9.46–8	50	3.19	16	20.17–38	158	15.17	212
9.48	21, 22–3	8.42	16	21.10–11	95	15.18–19	127, 128,
9.49	200	8.48ff.	199	26.12–18	200		184,
10	24	10.20f.	199				186, 187, 204
10.1–16	25, 27	11.45–53	28	ROMANS		15.18	186
10.3	27–9	12.38	34	1.1–15	126	15.20–22	123
10.4	24	13.16	46	1.1	126, 129	15.20	124, 212
10.9	26	14.15–17	52, 58	1.3–4	212	15.21	128
10.16	21–2, 27	14.25–6	﹍	1.5	126	15.24	123
10.17	200	15.18–27	58	1.9	126	15.26	103
10.21	56	15.20	46	1.10–12	123	15.30–33	124
11.13	56, 62–3	15.26	52	1.11–15	127, 212	15.30–31	123
11.14–23	52, 54	16.1–11	58	1.11	127, 212	16.17–20	123, 211
11.20	54–6, 59, 60	16.2	97	1.13	127	16.17–18	129
11.22	35	16.7–15	52	1.14–15	127	16.25–7	125
11.47–51	18	16.28	16	1.15	124		
11.49	194	17.4	1	1.16	205	1 CORINTHIANS	
11.50–51	38	18.37	16	4.19	112	1–2	209
12.10	57	20.30–31	9	4.25	212	1.10–3.17	101
12.12	52, 58–60			5.18–19	212	1.10–12	103
12.49	68	ACTS		8.9–11	97–8	1.12	111
12.50	68	1.1–2	131, 184	8.9–10	209–10	1.17	106
13.33	38	1.1	70	8.16–17	129	1.18	205
14.16–30	57–8	1.2	52	8.17	130, 139	1.23	104
19.12–27	191	1.5	52, 67–9	8.22–3	130	1.26–8	101
20.9–19	16	1.8	52, 67–9	8.32	166	2.1–2	104
20.45–7	23	1.15–26	33, 69	8.34	212	2.1–5	188
21.10ff.	61	5	207	8.35–7	129	2.2	209

234

2.3	209	12–14	104, 116	3.1–3	111, 186	GALATIANS	
2.4	205	12	116, 117, 131,	3.2–3	114	1.1	78
2.7–10	97		132, 211	3.5	108	1.10	82
2.9	206	12.1	101, 210	3.6	111	1.11–2.10	78–82
2.12	209	12.4–11	116, 187	3.17	97, 209	1.11–17	78
2.14	209	12.4–6	114, 119	4.5	111, 190	1.12	79, 91
3.4	111	12.7	117	4.6	111	1.15–17	200
3.5–9	118	12.12	117	4.7–12	110, 112	1.15–16	79, 82,
3.5	111	12.14ff.	4	4.7	108, 149		87, 91
3.9	108, 118	12.15–16	116	4.10	112, 114	1.16	78, 80
3.10ff.	106	12.21	116	5.19–20	106, 107,	1.17	33
3.10–15	93,	12.27	130, 210		188	2.1–10	78
	118–19, 191	12.28–9	92	5.19	209	2.2	78, 80–81
3.10–11	220	12.28	206	5.20	107, 160	2.5	81
3.10	118	14	116	6.1	108	2.6	81
3.11–15	118	14.1	210	6.4–5	112	2.7	81
3.11	162	14.3	95	6.4	111	2.8	81
3.12	119	14.34–6	207	7.8	101	2.9	81
3.13	119	14.34–5	207	7.9	102	2.11–21	79, 203
3.14	119	14.37	108, 188,	8.1–9.15	102	2.14	203
3.15	119		207, 210	9.12	141	3.4–5	84, 94
4.1	111, 118	15.1–58	101	10–13	101, 102,	3.5	187
4.2	118	15.1–11	104		103, 105, 206	3.13–14	84–5
4.3–4	190, 191	15.5	24	10.1	102, 104, 206	4.4–6	85
4.3	118	15.8	106	10.7	104	4.14	81
4.5	118	15.9	106	10.10	104, 109, 187	5.13–6.5	203
4.19–21	102	15.10	108	10.12	104	5.13	82
5.1–13	101	15.45	114–15, 119	10.18	104	6.17	82, 83, 120,
5.3–5	108, 188	15.51–2	97, 98	11.4	104		204
5.9–13	108	15.51	97	11.7	104		
5.9	101	15.58	192	11.13	104	EPHESIANS	
5.11	101	16.5–7	102	11.15	104	1.1	159
6.1–11	101			11.22	104	1.10	219
6.2	220	2 CORINTHIANS		11.23–30	187	1.15	158
6.12–20	101	1–9	206	11.23	104, 110,	1.20–23	169
6.15–20	210	1.5	113, 139		111	1.22–3	4, 169–70
7.1	101	1.8–10	204	12.1–7	91	1.23	169–71
7.40	209	1.8–9	112	12.1–4	110	2.8	158
8.1	101	1.12–2.4	102	12.7–10	187	2.9	158
9.1	106	1.14	118	12.9–10	109	2.11–12	158
9.16–17	106	2.14–7.4	102	12.11–12	110	2.14–16	164
9.16	127	2.14–17	208	12.11	106	2.14	219
10.14–22	210	2.14–16	108	12.12	128, 131,	2.17–19	158
11.2–14.40	101	2.14–15	109		187, 205	2.17	164–5, 186
11.5	207	2.14	208	12.16	104	2.20	162–3, 206,
11.23	39	2.15	208	13.2–4	109		220
11.24–9	210	3	209	13.4	109	3.1–13	160–2
11.25	38–40	3.1	104	13.9–10	107–108	3.1	158, 159, 160

3.2–13	160	6.5–8	174, 190	1.12–14	144, 218	2.2	134, 141
3.2	158, 161, 219	6.20	147, 160	1.15–20	153–4,	2.3	89
3.3–10	161				217	2.5–6	89
3.3	91, 161	PHILIPPIANS		1.15–17	144	2.6	90
3.4	161	1.1	136	1.16	154	2.9–10	89
3.5	162, 206	1.8	137	1.18	4, 154	2.13–16	88
3.6	220	1.14	215	1.20	154, 218	2.13–14	92
3.7–8	161	1.15–18	135	1.23	146, 160	2.13	92, 188
3.7	160, 161	1.15–17	215	1.24	94, 139, 146,	2.14–16	90
3.8	158, 161	1.19	137	148–51,	154,	2.14	93, 205
3.9	219	1.28	135		191, 198	2.15–16	91
3.13	158	1.29–30	141	1.25–9	146	2.17–18	88
3.14	160	1.29	190	1.25	146	2.19–20	93
3.18	220	1.30	141	1.26	220	2.19	118
3.19	171	2.6–11	134	1.28–9	147, 186	3.1–5	88, 93
4.1–16	165, 171	2.14–16	140	2.1–2	218	3.1–4	190
4.1–6	158	2.15–16	142	2.1	144	3.2–3	94
4.3	155	2.15	215	2.5	156	3.3–4	94
4.4–16	4	2.16	140, 216	2.8	144	3.3	94
4.4	155	2.17	112, 140	2.10	154	3.6	88
4.7–16	186	2.19–23	136	2.15	208	3.11–13	96
4.7–11	164, 165–9,	2.19	134	2.16	144	4.1–12	88
	221	2.20–22	137	2.18–19	154–6	4.1	91
4.7	166, 172	2.21	135	2.18	144	4.2–8	188
4.8–10	166	2.25	214	2.19	154, 155, 172,	4.2–7	91
4.9	167	3	124		173, 218	4.2	91
4.10	167, 171	3.2–16	135	3.5	215	4.8	91
4.11–16	171–3	3.2	134, 135	3.14	155	4.9–5.11	88
4.11–13	162	3.4–6	136	3.15	154	4.11	95
4.11	92, 168, 172,	3.8–10	138	3.16	218	4.13–18	96
	220	3.10	138–9, 141,	3.22–5	151	4.13	96
4.12	171		187, 215	3.22–4	174, 190	4.14	96
4.13–14	171	3.11–16	138	3.22	151	4.15–17	95, 97
4.15–	171	3.12–16	139	3.23	152	4.15	91–2
4.15	173	3.17–19	135	3.24–5	152	4.15	96–8
4.16	155, 171–3	3.18	135	4.1	151	4.16–17	97, 98
4.17–24	158	4.1	140, 205, 216	4.3	144	5.12–13	88
4.21	158	4.9	137	4.10	144	5.14–18	88
4.25	158, 169	4.10	134	4.12–13	144, 218	5.19–22	94–5
4.28–9	158	4.15–16	142	4.17	218	5.19–20	88, 187
4.31–2	158	4.18	141, 214	4.18	144	5.19	205
5.3	158						
5.4	158	COLOSSIANS		1 THESSALONIANS		2 THESSALONIANS	
5.5–8	158	1.1	146, 160	1.2–10	88	1.4–7	93, 205
5.8	158	1.4	144	1.2–5	92	1.5–12	89
5.18–19	173	1.7–8	144	1.5	92, 187, 204	2.1–12	89
5.18	171	1.7	144, 218	1.6	93, 205	2.16–17	96
5.21–33	169	1.8	156	2.1–12	88, 89, 90	3.5	96

3.6	89, 91, 188	2.5–6	197	9	147	3.18–20	164
3.6–13	95	2.6	42	21	147		
3.7–9	89	3.16	164			REVELATION	
3.10	89					1.3	95
3.11	89			I PETER		10.11	95
3.16	96	PHILEMON		2.6	163	22.7	95
		8–9	146	2.22	34	22.10	95
I TIMOTHY		8	147	2.24–5	34	22.18–19	95

EARLY CHRISTIAN, GNOSTIC AND OTHER ANCIENT WRITINGS

EPICTETUS		IGNATIUS		TERTULLIAN		THOMAS, GOSPEL OF	
DISCOURSES						65	16
1, 16.20f.	213	Magn.		Adv. Marc.			
		3.1	220	1.20	203		
HERMETIC WRIT-				4.2	203		
INGS				5.3	203		
13.19, 21	213